Behind the Carbon Curtain

BEHIND THE CARBON CURTAIN

The Energy Industry, Political Censorship, and Free Speech

JEFFREY A. LOCKWOOD

FOREWORD BY BRIANNA JONES

University of New Mexico Press • Albuquerque

Library of Congress Cataloging-in-Publication Data
Names: Lockwood, Jeffrey Alan, 1960– author.
Title: Behind the carbon curtain : the energy industry,
   political censorship, and free speech / Jeffrey A. Lockwood,
   foreword by Brianna Jones.
Description: Albuquerque : University of New Mexico Press,
   [2017] | Includes bibliographical references and index.
Identifiers: LCCN 2016024728 (print) | LCCN 2016037660
   (ebook) | ISBN 9780826358073 (pbk. : alk. paper) |
   ISBN 9780826358080 (electronic)
Subjects: LCSH: Energy industries—Political aspects—
   Wyoming. | Business and Politics—Wyoming. | Arts—
   Censorship—Wyoming. | Intellectual Freedom—Wyoming.
   | Freedom of speech—Wyoming. | Wyoming—Politics and
   government.
Classification: LCC HD9502.U53 W856 2017 (print) |
   LCC HD9502.U53 (ebook) | DDC 333.8/209787—dc23
LC record available at https://lccn.loc.gov/2016024728

Cover: painting of the Jonah Field gas well by Travis Ivey
Designed by Lisa C. Tremaine
Composed in ITC Cushing Std and Veneer Three

To the people of Wyoming:
No severance tax can compensate for cutting off a people from their stories.

You load sixteen tons, what do you get
Another day older and deeper in debt
Saint Peter don't you call me 'cause I can't go
I owe my soul to the company store.

—"SIXTEEN TONS," WRITTEN BY MERLE TRAVIS AND
MOST FAMOUSLY SUNG BY TENNESSEE ERNIE FORD

An attack upon our ability to tell stories is not just censorship—it is a crime
against our nature as human beings.

—SALMAN RUSHDIE

CONTENTS

FOREWORD

My beautiful home state is torn by a long legacy of abundant resources, natural beauty, and the challenge in accessing either. Tourists from around the world travel to our nation's first national park by the millions, unwittingly loving Yellowstone to death. New methods and uses for natural commodities bring booms and busts to our vast state. And somewhere in there are the people of Wyoming, fighting for the past we cling to and the future we hold dear.

In *Behind the Carbon Curtain: The Energy Industry, Political Censorship, and Free Speech*, Jeffrey A. Lockwood tells the stories of Wyoming's recent past to set the stage for our near future. Now is an apt time to examine our shared history and individual stories to help us better plan for the next chapter in Wyoming's story. The same might be said of all communities across our country and around the world.

I recently learned about the tiny island of Nauru in the far-flung Pacific. Nauru was a beautiful island teeming with an abundant rainforest. The key to the lush landscape was soil so rich it turned out to be the purest phosphate found in the world at the time. The story of Nauru is an old one, a story of colonialism, industrialism, political corruption, and limited resources. You probably already know the conclusion. Once the phosphate and the money ran out, the people of Nauru were left, literally, with a desert island rather than a tropical paradise.

Nauru's story isn't over, but as I thought about the plight of the people of Nauru I couldn't help but think of how it paralleled the choices facing Wyoming today. The plot—extreme reliance on extractive industry for revenue coupled with volatile booms and busts, disregard for environmental protections to the detriment of the future, and leaders with a vision that history shows to be shortsighted—felt all too familiar.

Wyoming is not Nauru, though, as much as our economy can feel colonial. I don't know if there were dissenting voices that spoke out in Nauru, although I suspect there were, but I do know there were (and are) in Wyoming. The stories Lockwood shares here are important, not only for the results they achieved but also for the reactions they set off and the ways they were approached. In every case he points to a concerted effort to silence those voices and the medium they used—be it art, data, or the written or spoken word.

Silencing others is nothing new. There is a reason our founding fathers chose to protect us with a Bill of Rights whose very first article expressly prohibits Congress from making a law "abridging the freedom of speech." Silencing speech, as Lockwood vividly demonstrates, is censorship. Censorship today manifests itself with varying degrees of sophistication. As a democracy we cannot abide censorship, yet, as you will read, it creeps into our public debate and social life.

The Equality State Policy Center works to make sure all voices have the opportunity to participate in our messy, raucous marketplace of ideas. We believe robust, open, informed debate is critical to building and maintaining a free and open society and to building fair and equitable public policy.

That also means that the leaders we choose need to be elected fairly and openly. As you read this book, ponder the intersection between money and power. The two are rarely separate, particularly as more and more money pours into our elections and shapes our political discourse. These are tales from Wyoming, but there are potent implications for any place where wealth seeps into politics—which is to say, most every town, city, county, and state in our nation.

"Lord give us another boom, we promise not to squander this one," I once heard a Wyoming lawmaker quip. Lockwood tells the story of how policies, discourse, and censorship collude in Wyoming because economic power is so concentrated in a few industries. As Wyoming once again sinks into what is forecast to be an extensive downturn, the missed opportunity to diversify our revenue stream may finally force itself to the forefront. Or will it?

The world is changing, and Wyoming too will evolve. Our past is our prologue and we still have time to decide how the story will end. It's up to us; we need all citizens to have an equal seat at the table and an equal opportunity to raise their voices. Thankfully for Wyoming, we still have time to fully open our dialogue, end the censorship of dissenting opinions, and build the future we want—together.

BRIANNA JONES
Executive Director
Equality State Policy Center

PREFACE

I like a good story well told.

—MARK TWAIN

A book about censorship could be many things. For example, there is a robust history of scholarship on the influence of corporate funding on political processes and public discourse.[1] There is also a strong body of work on the nature of science in the corporate age[2] and on censorship by industry in general.[3] And there is growing interest in the influence of corporate funding and structures on public institutions.[4] These are all vital issues in our times, and tempting frameworks for analysis, and, to some extent (mostly by way of exemplification) this book reflects these perspectives. However, my central purpose is much simpler.

This book is about telling stories through a series of interrelated narratives. These are the accounts of real people who have suffered the oppression of censorship through the collusion of business and government. My purpose is to provide witness, to record events, to give voice, and in so doing to catalyze change. The philosopher Richard Kearney maintains that "telling stories is as basic to human beings as eating. More so, in fact, for while food makes us live, stories are what make our lives worth living."[5]

Through the real-life tales in this book, I hope that readers come to realize how their own experiences and those of their neighbors might be woven into a fabric of silencing dissent. Without hearing stories, we might each presume that our fear of speaking out, our reticence to protesting injustice, or our deciding to quietly avoid offending those who provide our paychecks is just a matter of our individual conditions. But a pattern is emerging, and we need to hear from others to understand that we are in this together. Although the events in this book take place in Wyoming, disturbingly similar tales are being told from Texas (where the energy companies curried the favor of the state to keep the Environmental Protection Agency from investigating the methane that appeared in the drinking water after fracking outside of Fort Worth)[6] to New York (where the energy industry tried both to discredit a faculty member at Cornell University who debunked the safety of natural gas and to misrepresent university officials as being in support of fracking) to Colorado (where a researcher was told by his administrator at the School of Mines that if the scientist wanted to keep his job, "the smart thing would be to never say anything about [fracking] again, even as a private citizen").[7]

This book is part of a growing conversation taking place in newspapers, magazines, websites, films, radio programs, and television shows that is beginning to knit together a dark tapestry of oppression. The stories I tell will not change society—at least not these alone. But maybe they will as part of a national narrative that includes the following: the families in Pennsylvania driven from their homes by leaking methane, whom energy companies compensate only in exchange for their silence; the citizens in West Virginia, who were sued for libel by a coal company for criticizing the industry in an environmental group's newsletter; and the untenured professor in the University of Oklahoma's ConocoPhillips School of Geology and Geophysics, who was intimidated into silence knowing that an oil tycoon and major donor demanded the dismissal of scientists studying the link between fracking and earthquakes. Accounts of censorship from across the United States are woven into the stories from Wyoming, making it apparent that free speech is under attack by the energy industry across the nation.

Social and political changes often begin with stories. Narratives are how we understand ourselves and find our place in the world. Shared stories stitch together communities, begin conversations, and move us to tears—and action. Scholars have long been writing, speaking, and teaching about institutional racism, but what seems to have catalyzed change in America and prompted police forces and justice departments to address structural racism are the stories of Michael Brown in Ferguson; Walter Scott in North Charleston; Eric Garner in New York; Tamir Rice in Cleveland; and Laquan McDonald in Chicago. No single story was sufficient. The protests in Ferguson would have likely faded from the national consciousness, dismissed as a local aberration, without the other accounts. And so this book is a chapter in an emerging narrative of how the energy industry (and in a more general sense, corporations) is silencing public discourse.

Stories are necessary, but they aren't sufficient. Critical thinking must take us beyond anecdotes, no matter how disturbing or compelling. We must connect the dots and make sense of the patterns through the devoted scholarship of the social sciences and humanities. I have great respect for academic theorizing; where would biology be without evolution or economics without Marxism? In fact, the reader will find in the introduction a primer on the conceptual framework that scholars have developed for understanding the nature and origins of censorship. Creating and refining conceptual frameworks to elucidate deep structures, causes, and explanations of cultural phenomena such as censorship is valuable work. This book provides case studies that advance our understanding of power and the ways in which those who possess it constrain free speech. But as much as I hope that my work feeds the research of other scholars, the stories in this book are unlikely to provide much opportunity for pushing the boundaries of sociopolitical theory.

Many of the most important advances in intellectual frameworks are driven by test cases at the margins of a concept. In my current field (environmental ethics and philosophy of ecology) the emergence of new ideas and the refinements of old ones occur during the pursuit of conceptual clarity: is technology natural, is the moon a wilderness, should we drive pest species to extinction, why is it bad for nonindigenous species to supplant natives (and just what does it mean to be native)? The richest cases come at the ragged edges of these categories. Likewise, marginal examples help to refine our understanding of censorship (e.g., do standards of public decency, film ratings, peer reviews, or art critics constitute censorship?). A scholar might use such cases to develop an argument about how a conceptual framework can account for events or how a particular theory needs to be modified. The argument I'm making is less sophisticated and so the stories in this book are intended to function in a different way.

It is my hope that the reader will consider critically the events in this book and follow the evidence to the conclusion that these are stories of censorship. "Censorship" is a serious accusation, and many people are understandably hesitant to levy this charge in a democracy that takes such pride in the liberty of its citizens. But these case histories are unambiguous, if sometimes clandestine, exemplars of censorship. If the reader comes to see the insidious forms of silencing in the modern world, then the book is a success in my professorial realm of teaching.

So while refining our understanding of censorship is unquestionably a valuable enterprise, I don't want to miss the moral forest while trimming the conceptual trees. Wherever the conceptual boundaries might be, I believe that for almost every reader these cases will illustrate clearly the suppression of free speech. And we must not delay our response to egregious cases that undermine human dignity and democratic governance while waiting for the marginal cases to be clarified.

Moreover, I am not a social scientist; I am an ecologist turned philosopher/ writer. What I bring to this book are long hours of reading the academic literature pertaining to censorship and an understanding of what scholars have written about its history, forms, and implications. I understand the conceptual issues, but I do not have the expertise or inclination to be (or pretend to be) a social scientist any more than I'd expect my colleagues in political science to practice ecology.

I also bring to this project the capacity to think critically, research carefully, document thoroughly, and engage authentically (much of this book is derived from more than sixty interviews with a tremendous range of people). In a crucial sense, I also have the ability to write honestly. In short, I am tenured and my job is protected through a social contract with the public. As such, I am obligated to pull back the curtain of censorship on behalf of those who have been silenced.

In some cases, these stories have been given a fleeting headline and a few inches of a newspaper column. But in no instance have the deeper nature and mechanisms of censorship been fully revealed. If one digs through the news archives, there are vignettes and snapshots, but not a complex understanding of situations, settings, and characters. Although the affected individuals wanted their stories to be told, for them to do so on their own was perceived as too risky, demanding, or inaccessible. They sought someone who would listen and have the wherewithal to speak—and this took far more courage on their part than on mine.

A poignant essay on "The Dangerous Silence of Academic Researchers" was recently published in the *Chronicle of Higher Education*.[8] A Columbia University professor wrote about her decision to speak out on the health hazards of sugary drinks (keeping in mind that annual soda sales are a $60 billion industry). Despite her anxiety about going public, she did so with this compelling rationale: "When [professors] absent ourselves from the public stage, we too often cede the conversation to those with the loudest voices or the deepest pockets. . . . Speaking out is not only our right, it is also our responsibility."

As a *New York Times* story noted, citizens in the energy-rich West have been "ignored, ridiculed, threatened, and paid settlements in exchange for silence." A typical example is the woman who angrily but silently attended the "One Million Barrels" celebration of oil in North Dakota, later telling a reporter, "I'm not that brave (or stupid) to protest . . . we're outgunned, outnumbered, and outsuited."[9]

And so this book is intended to provide witness to the injustice of censorship by the energy industry and their political partners, and in so doing to shift the balance of power ever so slightly to bring us closer to a tipping point of outrage, action, and change.

ACKNOWLEDGMENTS

A long-term project of this sort, extending into science, economics, politics, and philosophy, requires a great deal of research. I needed smart, curious, and incisive assistants to dig deeply into historical archives, newspaper accounts, web-based materials, legal documents, and institutional policies. They had to ask the right questions to the right people and in the right way so as to get the right answers. And they had to read my muddled mind when I wanted information on anything from atmospheric chemistry to political contributions to industry lobbyists. In short, this book couldn't have been written without the phenomenal work of Adrian Shirk, who was my brilliant researcher, insightful reader, and creative collaborator. I must also express my gratitude to Gretchen Heuberger, Hallie Stallman, and Molly Sublett, who also served as dedicated assistants during various phases of the project.

I should also thank the people of Wyoming who supported my work as a professor at the University of Wyoming. The public trust that is manifest in the practice of academic tenure provided the crucial protection necessary for me to delve into the nature of censorship and to tell the stories of silenced artists, educators, and scientists without fear of losing my job—at least in principle.

Of course, any department in a public university where external donations increasingly shape institutional decisions can be made to suffer the wrath of unhappy industries and powerful individuals. And so, I must thank my immediate administrators during the course of the project for their unwavering encouragement (Beth Loffreda, director of the MFA program in creative writing and Susanna Goodin and Franz-Peter Griesmaier, heads of the department of philosophy). Furthermore, I am humbled by my colleagues in creative writing and philosophy who courageously endorsed my work despite the possibility of political fallout and funding repercussions. As a colleague said in a faculty meeting during which my becoming the director of creative writing was under discussion, "If we decide that you must either drop your book project or decline to become the director, then we've self-censored, which means they've won."

Within the University of Wyoming, I am also deeply appreciative of the principled stand taken by the deans of the College of Arts and Sciences while I was researching and writing this book. Paula Lutz, the current dean, voiced her position to me in an e-mail response to my having given an interview about a politically sensitive topic regarding the energy industry: "I never worry about faculty—or anyone—exercising their 1st amendment rights!"

Vital, tangible support for this project was also provided by the Ucross Foundation, which granted me an artist's residency in an idyllic setting to write a portion of the book and conduct research on the people and happenings in northern Wyoming. I am also grateful to the Wyoming chapter of the Sierra Club and the Powder River Basin Resource Council for inviting me to share portions of the book with perceptive and critical audiences who asked thoughtful questions and provided valuable backstories. With regard to writing support, the folks at the University of New Mexico Press were extraordinarily professional. An author is truly fortunate to have an editor as capable, responsive, and encouraging as Clark Whitehorn.

The stories of censorship—including legal, financial, and physical intimidation—in this book could not have been told in such powerful or accurate ways without many courageous individuals agreeing to be interviewed. Most of the people who spoke to me did so on the record, but there were a few who felt their personal security or professional well-being would be put at risk by being named and I've honored their understandable desire for anonymity. I am also grateful to those individuals who agreed to speak with me despite their dubious roles in limiting the speech of others, particularly given that several such players declined to be interviewed. I will also put in an unapologetic plug for Avi Taub and his staff at Transcriptions for Everyone, who provided remarkably accurate and timely transcriptions of interviews, sometimes conducted under challenging auditory conditions.

I'd also like to express my thanks to attorneys who offered enormously valuable advice with respect to avoiding and, failing that, preparing for the possibility of a SLAPP (strategic lawsuit against public participation)—a tool used by the wealthy and powerful to silence the voices of those who offer dissenting views. Reed Zars, Rock Pring, and the Wyoming ACLU all provided clear and thoughtful recommendations.

Most importantly, I thank my wife, Nancy, whose enduring love, enormous patience, and unflagging support have made it possible for me to undertake and complete this project with all of its intellectual, emotional, and moral challenges.

Finally, I should hasten to add that while I've done everything in my ability to make sure that the information in this book is accurate, the scope of the venture is such that errors are possible. Perhaps it goes without saying, but my acknowledgment of any individual or organization should not be taken to mean that they agree with my interpretations or views. I apologize for any misunderstandings or misrepresentations of people, places, or events, but these are not the result of malice or meanness. Rather, my goal is to give voice to those who have been silenced.

Wyoming as a Lens into America

When you publish a book,
you do so in part to end the silence.
All censorship is silence.

—STEPHEN CHBOSKY

When my daughter headed off to college at American University, she understood that Washington, DC, was most assuredly unlike Laramie, Wyoming. Although born and raised in Laramie, Erin had various experiences with big cities and probably knew more about urban life than many of her classmates knew about living in a land with six people per square mile (the District of Columbia has 10,589 people per square mile). During a welcoming event, small groups of incoming freshmen were asked to share the places they called home. The listings included cities like Baltimore, Philadelphia, Richmond, and Los Angeles. When Erin said, "Laramie, Wyoming," one of her classmates remarked, "Wow, that's really far away," to which the fellow from Los Angeles noted, "Hey, California is farther." After a bit of discussion, the group agreed that the guy was only right geographically.

In many senses, Wyoming is much more distant from the bustle of DC than is Seattle, Portland, or San Francisco. A few years ago, Wyoming's tourism slogan was "Like No Place on Earth." Maybe this was a tad hyperbolic, but it is true that the state is pretty odd. Only 20 percent of the populace lives in cities (of which there are two that have at least 50,000 people) and there are no zoos, amusement parks, professional sports teams, twenty-story buildings, or Jaguar dealerships.

So what can the rest of the nation—or even my daughter's DC peers—learn from Wyoming's culture, economics, and politics? Wyoming might be anomalous in terms of its demographics, but this land of towering mountains and dry basins shares a great deal with the rest of the nation. Not only does Wyoming provide one-fifth of the country's energy, but it also offers a powerful window into how corporatocracy—the chimera of industry and government—is shaping the speech and lives of the people it no longer serves. Wyoming reveals aspects of American society that are obscured in places like Washington, DC, or Los Angeles.

And so, on one level, this book is about the censorship of art, science, and education by the energy industry in the state of Wyoming. While this might be of keen interest to the half million people in the state, the stories in this book are about much more. What is happening in the least populated state is no different than events across the nation where silencing of dissonant voices is harder to notice amid the cacophony of a metropolis.

The tales of corporate censorship in Wyoming are only about silencing voices in rural America in the same sense that jailing dissidents in Russia and suppressing protestors in China are only about silencing hooligans. There's far more to the stories of why members of the musical group Pussy Riot were sentenced to two years of imprisonment and why more than a thousand citizens were slaughtered in Tiananmen Square.[1] Squelching criticism of corporations, national leaders or political parties is a means of controlling society. When free speech challenges economic privilege or political power, then dangerous questioning must be suppressed to maintain the status quo. And such censorship is not limited to rural backwaters and foreign regimes. The silence on climate change during the last US presidential elections speaks volumes about the capacity of American corporations to control political discourse.[2]

Accounts of how art, science, and education have been censored are only about these endeavors in the same way that the destruction of Buddhist icons by the Taliban in 2001 and the burning of the Qur'an by Christians on September 11, 2010, were simply about religious differences.[3] These attacks were about obliterating competing values and belief systems. The message, not the medium, was the target. Those who benefit from the existing order cannot abide alternative systems of thought, whether these challenges are fostered by art, science, and education or, for that matter, journalism, literature, law, philosophy, and religion. The free flow of ideas is protected under the Universal Declaration of Human Rights[4] along with the First Amendment of the US Constitution, but unfettered speech is destabilizing to systems that depend on public complaisance to entrench social structures.

Likewise, focusing on the energy industry's efforts to silence critics is merely about fossil fuels in the same way that calling in the Pinkerton agents to crush labor strikes at the turn of the last century was about the production of steel or that, in recent times, keeping third-party candidates out of presidential debates is about election rules. Beneath the surface lies a common purpose—solidifying power. And in contemporary America, there is a rapidly diminishing difference between the concerns of corporations and the interests of governments. Wealth means power in a culture where everything—from sex and reproduction to pollution and prisons to jury duty and military service to information and communication—is a commodity.[5] Speech is no longer free but purchased by the highest bidder who then wields the power to decide what is created, researched, or spoken.

Finally, the stories from Wyoming in the last few years are only about this place and time in the same sense that the construction of the Berlin Wall was merely about a European city in 1961. Although the details differ and disanalogies exist, in the end these are timeless tales of controlling thought, suppressing speech, and imposing beliefs. For example, the iconoclastic burning of scrolls in the kingdom of Judah took place 2,700 years ago.[6] Perhaps in the age of the Internet and Twitter, governments can no longer easily quash the truth, but they can allow corporations to operate in secrecy. Communication technology has changed at breakneck speed, but the desire and capacity of those with political and economic power to suppress opposition is unchanged.

This book, then, can be read as an account of the insidious ways in which the energy industry has censored art, science, and education in Wyoming. But these are vivid symptoms of a virulent condition spreading across modern societies. In an important sense, this book is about any place where private wealth colludes with political power to silence dissent. In all likelihood, it's about where you live.

If censorship is an ancient story woven throughout human civilization, what's so special about the accounts in this book? Perhaps no other cultural and geographic context provides a more vivid and compelling view into the mechanisms of suppressing speech than does Wyoming. Few contemporary cases provide such lucid stories of how governments and corporations are colluding to silence voices that challenge political and economic power structures. The cases from Wyoming are not novel in terms of their fundamental features, given that, as meticulous research has shown, elected officials and business executives are busy silencing critics across the nation.[7] Rather, Wyoming provides a socio-politically unique lens—a kind of cultural microscope revealing the inner workings of money and power. In effect, Wyoming's simplicity, clarity, and transparency magnify what is happening elsewhere in modern America.

The first aspect of this lens is the simplified economy of Wyoming, which has led to the state being called an energy colony of the United States. Just how Wyoming came to such a place in American society is a story of opportunism, libertarianism, and power that is brilliantly told in Sam Western's *Pushed Off the Mountain, Sold Down the River*.[8] In this history of the state, Western recounts how Wyoming's leaders have long believed that natural resources bring wealth, even though the state's saga is one of chronic poverty with periods of acute prosperity. Although the people assert their fierce independence, the economic history of Wyoming is "working for the man."[9] In the 1920s, the state led the nation in petroleum production, which was more than 97 percent under the control of Standard Oil. Such a narrow foundation invited catastrophe, which arrived in the 1930s. And ever since the Depression, "Wyoming has stood where Ireland remained for centuries: a poor, friendly, hard-working state that exports everything, especially talent."[10]

The demand for petroleum increased during World War II, and by the 1950s the state was announcing that it was open for business—and exploitation. In the 1970s, Wyoming's coal industry, which began a century earlier to fuel the railroads and factories of the nation, grew at an enormous rate as the Clean Air Act created demand for low-sulfur coal in the country's energy plants. In the 1990s, a natural gas boom erupted in the western part of the state, which was echoed fifteen years later on the eastern plains. Today, the oil and gas industry promises untold riches thanks to fracking and coalbed methane production. Severance taxes (payments incurred when nonrenewable resources are extracted or "severed" from the land) have pumped billions into the government's coffers—at least sporadically.[11]

But every boom comes with a bust. Lacking a diversified economy, the state's only buffer has been federal funding, which further belies the myth of independence. Wyoming is consistently near the top of the list when it comes to receiving money from Washington.[12]

Fear breeds repression and Wyoming's politics are driven by the deep dread that the coal company will leave town, the natural gas boom will bust, or the oil revenues will stop flowing. So just how desperately does Wyoming need the taxes that are begrudgingly paid (and often evaded) by the energy industry—and to what extent does America need this state's energy?[13]

Wyoming produces nearly four hundred million tons of coal per year or twelve tons per second, which accounts for nearly one-sixth of the world's production. This single state provides 40 percent of the nation's output, which is delivered to thirty-seven other states in coal cars that, if strung together, would encircle the earth one and a half times. With India and China anticipating nine hundred new coal plants, Wyoming is planning to ship massive quantities of coal overseas.[14]

As for natural gas, Wyoming accounts for 9 percent of the nation's supply, making the state fifth in production. Its twenty-two thousand wells produce two trillion cubic feet of methane, which is about the volume of air exhaled by the human population of California in a year. Wyoming sits on $140 billion worth of natural gas and there are currently plans to develop the largest single gas field in the nation, which will cover an area the size of Rhode Island with nine thousand wells.[15]

Wyoming ranks ninth among the states in crude oil production, pumping out nearly seventy-five million barrels per year, enough to fill 4,800 Olympic-sized swimming pools. And there are plans to drill five thousand new wells over the next decade in the southeastern corner of the state.[16]

Wyoming's mines currently produce more uranium ore than any other state in the nation, with twenty-four more in the planning or permitting stage.[17] Should the United States decide to crank up nuclear energy, Wyoming has the country's largest uranium reserves.[18]

When it comes to wind, Wyoming's current production is 1,400 megawatts, which is enough to power 520,000 homes during peak hours. Ranked tenth in the nation, Wyoming is tapping into less than 1 percent of its potential wind energy.[19]

In short, the United States depends on Wyoming for about one-sixth of the nation's energy. No other state or country accounts for a greater proportion. Annual mineral royalties and severance taxes add up to about $1.36 billion, or about 60 percent of state revenues. If we include allied revenues (e.g., sales taxes from pipeline construction and mining machinery rentals), the income from fossil fuels accounts for at least two-thirds of the state's budget and up to three-quarters by some measures.[20]

And so it is that Wyoming serves as an economic lens revealing how

Gas wells sprinkled across the (in)famous Jonah Field, one of the richest natural gas deposits in North America. Since the early 1990s, fracking has allowed drillers to tap into otherwise inaccessible deposits, and this sagebrush-covered steppe in west-central Wyoming is expected to support more than three thousand wells before it is played out (painting by Travis Ivey, used with the artist's permission).

dependence on a single industry drives politicians and state agencies to battle any regulation hindering fossil fuels—and to silence anyone who might impede extraction by raising concerns for environmental and human well-being.

Lenses also allow us to see things more clearly, bringing aspects of the world into sharp focus. In this context, Wyoming avoids the blurring effects of sociological complexity by virtue of its relatively small and homogenous population. The state has 576,000 people, about the number in Baltimore or Milwaukee. Cheyenne and Casper are the largest cities in Wyoming with barely 60,000 people. Encompassing 97,000 square miles of grassy basins and forested mountains, Wyoming has the lowest population density (six people per square mile) in the lower forty-eight states. The state is overwhelmingly white (93 percent) and Republican (67 percent). However, the median income and home price are within 10 percent of the national average, and the educational level is similar to the rest of the country.[21]

Wyoming is like an experiment designed by a sociologist, insofar as a scientific experiment isolates particular features of a system while holding the others constant. The ecologist studies population dynamics using colonies of flour beetles in a laboratory so that the complicating factors of weather, predation, and disease can be excluded. For the sociologist, Wyoming is uncomplicated by competing industries, varied ethnicities, or diverse politics. Its inner workings are laid bare and we can see the machinations of corporate executives and government officials. But these social processes are no more unique to Wyoming than the entomological processes observed in jars of flour beetles. Wherever they are found, people and insects compete for resources.

A key feature of the Wyoming lens that allows us to see clearly the capacity of corporate power to silence dissent is the state's political transparency. This isn't to say that the libertarian conservatives who dominate the legislature (along with a growing number of Tea Party adherents) are forthcoming. In fact, Wyoming received an *F* in political ethics due to its weak open records and financial disclosure laws, along with its lack of restrictions on lobbyist and political action committee donations to campaigns.[22]

Although legislation is drafted in secret, the connections of politicians to the fossil fuel industries are not only conceded but are an overt source of pride. The state treasurer, former state auditor, past governor, and chief of staff for the current governor, along with any number of current state legislators, have worked for energy companies.[23] The citizen legislature is breathtakingly bold in demonstrating its fidelity to the state's corporate masters. Oftentimes, it is difficult to tell whether the openness of local politicians, state agencies, and institutional administrators represents an abundance of arrogance or a shortage of sophistication. While industry executives often (but not always) operate behind the scenes with untraceable communications, public officials frequently put their cards on the table. Whether from impunity or naïveté, what would be hidden as career-ending corruption in other states is worn as a badge of loyalty in Wyoming.

As long as those in power enjoy the protection of the energy industry, these elected and appointed individuals evince a shameless untouchability. As Phil Roberts, the state's preeminent historian, puts it, "No one who views the Wyoming political scene believes that the government—at any level—is a match for corporate power."[24]

Exploring the nature of censorship imposed by the energy industry, or on its behalf by the government, means coming to understand the features of this phenomenon in American life. Consider one of the more useful and practical definitions of censorship: "a variety of processes . . . formal and informal, overt and covert, conscious and unconscious, by which restrictions are imposed on the collection, display, dissemination, and exchange of information, opinions, ideas, and imaginative expression."[25] The scope of this concept is expansive, making no reference to who is enforcing the limitations. However, the stifling of speech by private parties traditionally has not been defined as censorship by social scientists. Some contemporary analysts have continued to sustain a narrow definition of censorship, restricting the term to the use of state power to suppress expression despite the reality that private entities are often as powerful as government agencies, if not more so.[26] The worry seems to be that if the concept pertains to less overt forms of privatized domination and control, then "censorship" is diluted and loses its substantive meaning.[27]

A few postmodern scholars go so far as to advocate abandoning the term altogether on the basis that any judgment about what is funded, published, or broadcast can be construed as censorship.[28] They contend that "the language of censorship is thus the language of professionalism, the language of expertise, the language of institutional competence."[29] But surely the intentions of the putative censor are crucial; upholding professional standards through peer review is simply not the same thing as enforcing an ideology via political retribution or economic pressure. This slippery-slope argument for scuttling "censorship" fails to recognize that meaningful concepts often come in degrees. While we can't identify the precise point at which we are no longer warm, healthy, or rich, and there is no moment at which diminishing light becomes darkness, these continuities do not mean that there are no cold, sick, or poor people wandering the streets at night.

Some of the difficulty in providing an uncontroversial definition of censorship arises from a historical perspective that is no longer applicable.[30] In the past, governments have been the enforcers of restrictions on free expression and these constraints often have been brutally imposed (e.g., Soviet Russia, Nazi Germany, Apartheid South Africa, and the Supreme Council's Iran).[31] State-sanctioned book burning is wonderfully unambiguous, but contemporary governments are rarely so direct.

While we often think of censorship as an act of the government, in contemporary society the distinction between business and state actions is increasingly blurred. An operational definition of censorship must track the nature of power in modern society.[32] As such, the concept "shifts from government silencing what powerless people say, to powerful people violating powerless people into silence and hiding behind state power to do it."[33] When corporations use their undeniable influence on public officials to reward or coerce authorities, who suppress forms of expression that the businesses find contrary to their interests, then this constitutes censorship by any reasonable standard. And, of course, corporations also directly limit what can be said, written, or otherwise communicated. However, as noted by the dean of the Yale Law School, these practices increasingly are considered normal: "Private restrictions on speech are enforced daily, are deeply rooted, and go unnoticed."[34]

More than two thousand years ago, Aristotle noted that "it is the mark of an educated man to look for precision in each class of things just so far as the nature of the subject admits."[35] And this insight applies today as well. Censorship is a complex phenomenon and its conceptual edges are fuzzy. Political theorizing, historical analyses, and linguistic deconstruction are all valuable endeavors given the importance of censorship to society. Conceptual clarity is surely a virtue. But we should also heed the admonition of Lotfi Zadeh, the father of fuzzy logic, who reminded scholars that, "as complexity rises, precise statements lose their meaning and meaningful statements lose their precision."[36] So, while a valuable line of inquiry consists of refining our understanding of censorship, this effort to clarify the concept should not impede our capacity to identify explicit cases that endanger our dignity and democracy.

Prior to the Enlightenment, religious and government leaders collaborated to oppress those who challenged the power structures of Europe. Although liberalism succeeded in divorcing church and state, this modern system of power married commerce and state. Instead of abolishing censorship, liberalism transferred "the office of Censor from a civic to a private trust. . . . The marketplace, not the priest or feudal lord, became the ultimate arbiter."[37] Understanding how censorship is woven into contemporary life is perhaps best approached through considering the ways in which speech, creativity, and inquiry are suppressed. A system of classification has emerged from social theoreticians, and this conceptual structure provides an effective means of understanding the collusion between the energy industry and government of Wyoming. Censorship can be roughly but effectively divided into explicit and implicit forms.

The explicit or active forms of censorship include destruction and intimidation. A censor with sufficient power might simply destroy an expression that is deemed offensive. In the 1930s, the Nazis burned books by Jewish authors. And in 2001 students at the University of California, Berkeley, incinerated copies of Daniel J. Flynn's *Cop Killer: How Mumia Abu-Jamal Conned Millions into Believing He Was Framed* in protest of the conservative author's views.[38] So, to be clear: no political ideology has a monopoly on censorship (as ably elucidated by the conservative pundit George Will).[39]

The most direct form of censorship is iconoclasm, a term derived from the Greek *eikon*, meaning an image (e.g., a religious icon), and *klastes*, meaning to break. The word was originally used in the late sixteenth century to describe mobs from the Eastern church who destroyed statues of Jesus and saints that were deemed to be idols.[40] In the mid-nineteenth century, as the principles driving the Industrial Revolution were becoming the cultural norm, iconoclasm broadened to include attacks on anything representing orthodox beliefs, including economic and political ideologies. The practice has continued into the modern day, as evidenced by the religious Right in the United States and fundamentalists throughout the Islamic world. In short, when seats of power collude, the destruction of heretical works may follow. For example, the conflation of Christianity and American politics led conservative Christians to burn the Qur'an in the name of patriotism.[41]

One of the most repugnant cases of iconoclasm in recent times was the Taliban's destruction of the massive 1,700-year-old figures of the Buddha in Afghanistan.[42] The extremist, Islamic political movement could not tolerate alternative belief systems, so the representation of the threatening alternative had to be destroyed. In modern iconoclasm, "One attacks the physical object in order to destroy the spiritual being that resides in it—or the system of belief to which it belongs."[43] Chapters 1–3 will elucidate how the energy industry pressured a public university to destroy a work of art that represented a challenge to fossil fuels by provoking viewers to think about the role of coal—and their own energy consumption—in the process of climate change.

The most direct form of intimidation is to kill, torture, or imprison the person responsible for an expression that threatens those in power. Of course, governments most often use military might for purposes other than censorship, but bullets also have been used to silence dissident speech. The goal of direct intimidation is not only to silence the individual but also to convey a message to others that similar acts will result in correspondingly terrible outcomes. The death threats issued by Muslim leaders in response to Salman Rushdie's *Satanic Verses* surely caused other authors to think twice about criticizing Islam.[44] In addition, artists in Russia must be intimidated by the jailing of performers of the musical group Pussy Riot, who criticized President Vladimir Putin's policies and his government's connection to the Russian Orthodox Church.[45] In Chapters 4–5 and 6–7 we'll see how the energy industry has pressured public administrators and elected officials to fire scientists and educators who raised concerns about fossil fuels—and the oppressive effect of these attacks on coworkers.

In the United States, punishment also can take the form of financial hardship, imposed through lawsuits intended to intimidate individuals who dare to speak in opposition to those in positions of authority and control. Corporations use the legal maneuver of a SLAPP—a strategic lawsuit against public participation—to silence activists by forcing them to pay the costs of a prolonged legal defense.[46] The plaintiff doesn't need a viable case and typically doesn't expect to win a court judgment; the goal is to exhaust the resources of the defendant, force a settlement of silence, and chill speech among potential critics. SLAPPs are allowed in Wyoming, where energy companies have used the legal system to silence environmental groups linking coal burning to climate change and energy magnates have sued citizens who obstruct mineral development.[47] Don't be surprised if you read about a gratuitous defamation suit being filed in response to the book you are holding.

However, overt acts of censorship can be self-defeating when they draw attention to the message they seek to quash. The alternative of frightening people into silence is a potent strategy, an advantage of which is that powerful individuals or corporations keep their oppression out of the limelight. This shift to more cunning forms of silencing dissent takes us to the second category of censorship: implicit tactics.

The forms of implicit or passive censorship are varied and blend into one another, but there are two reasonably distinct manifestations. In self-censorship, the individual decides not to speak, create, investigate, or otherwise act in a way that is likely to generate sanction from those in power. This phenomenon has been called "anticipatory compliance" to reflect the sense that an individual knows what is coming should he or she fail to act in accord with expectations. For example, in Rupert Murdoch's oppressive media empire, "one didn't need to be instructed about what to do, one simply knew what was in one's long-term interests [through] a collection of incidents and the atmosphere."[48]

Perhaps the most worrisome version is what is termed "foreclosure," wherein a person implicitly understands and unconsciously internalizes what is unspeakable.[49] In extreme cases individuals may not even allow themselves to think about certain possibilities, such that some concepts don't even occur to them. Whether we are unable to conceive or unwilling to communicate particular ideas, self-censorship requires continued reinforcement by those in power. A government that has vaccinated its people against having or expressing dangerous ideas will typically employ a booster shot by making a public example of an individual who dares to broach the prohibited concept. As such, it may appear to outsiders that the response by authorities is disproportionate to the offense, but the larger context of publicly reinforcing a prohibition makes such apparent overreactions explicable. This sort of brutal suppression and harassment is exemplified by corporate and political responses to the rather subdued voices of scientists and artists raising environmental concerns in chapters 8–9 and 10–11.

The other manifestation of implicit censorship is denying the individual access to an audience. Saying that a person has the liberty to speak inside of one's home when nobody is present to hear what is being said can hardly be construed as freedom of speech. Likewise, an institution that claims its scientists or artists are free to investigate or create anything they choose is disingenuous if the authorities deny the funding, space, equipment, or means for doing so. So-called market censorship is the use of commercial resources (e.g., print or broadcast media) to limit what can be made or communicated.[50] And when the press becomes big business, then its role as the Fourth Estate—the watchdog of illicit power—is undermined.

So it was that the British media empire of Rupert Murdoch was able to acquire the *Times* and the *Sunday Times* in 1981 without Margaret Thatcher raising any objections. He agreed to use his corporate bully pulpit to uncritically praise her government in exchange for her granting his business practices a free pass.[51] Likewise, when educational, scientific, and artistic institutions, which we might think of as being the Fifth Estate, become dependent on corporate funding, their capacity to critically examine socio-economic structures and engage in public communication is diminished. Throughout the book, the dark implications of such power dynamics for a vibrant democracy become evident.

In a sense, this book is the story of power, but this sociopolitical concept is too expansive to provide a narrative framework that holds together these accounts. That said, an understanding of censorship entails at least a brief consideration of power, insofar as silencing dissident voices is a manifestation of the capacity to control others. There are various definitions of power that refer to the ability of individuals, groups, or institutions to influence behavior, get things done, obtain some future good, dominate humans and the environment, and (perhaps most simply and compellingly) to shape the views and actions of people.[52]

The classic 1960 typology of power identified six forms: coercive (acting against one's will), reward/retribution (exchanging assets or liabilities), legitimate (exercising socially sanctioned influence), referent (desiring to be like another person), expert (possessing knowledge or skills that others want), and informational (providing or withholding valuable knowledge).[53] This framework has since been modified to distinguish between hard and soft power (coercion versus socially legitimized persuasion),[54] identify sources of power (ideological, economic, military and political),[55] and specify circles of power (e.g., celebrities, executives, military, and government).[56]

Today, corporations possess vast wealth and form a social network through which they exercise great power over the actions of governments. In the United States, political action committees (PACs) shape the course of campaigns, influencing both who runs and who wins. Just as the information is highly regulated by authoritarian governments, the media is effectively controlled by multinational corporations in the West through the processes of agenda setting (assigning content and importance to events and policies) and framing (providing templates for organizing experience).[57]

Political scientists recognize that a radical power shift is unfolding in the twenty-first century—the transfer of power to nonstate actors such as churches, terrorists, and corporations.[58] With the expansion of multinational corporations, economic cosmopolitanism may portend the end of state power.[59] Corporate power does not need to be won or legitimized politically, and it has no need of military might or democratic consensus.[60] As power flows from public to private entities, we see the emergence of a hybrid system of socioeconomic authority, the corporatocracy (a network of corporate-government partnerships that increasingly controls society).

As power shifts to multinational corporations, those with the greatest wealth and access to political structures will emerge as dominant, global forces. In this regard, energy companies have been on the rise for decades.[61] For example, in the years after World War II, the Arabian American Oil Company (Aramco) played a key role in Saudi Arabian territorial disputes. The company pressured the US government and deceived the British government to secure its position as the sole oil company in Saudi Arabia and effectively function as a state within the kingdom.[62] Or consider Nigeria, where oil companies conducted their business with impunity for decades, cut deals with officials, and "came to be seen as local government."[63] Since 1960, $300 billion in oil revenues have disappeared, while income and life expectancy for Nigerians have fallen.[64]

Fossil fuels molded American history, and there's no more meticulously researched story than that of how ExxonMobil shaped the nation.[65] To appreciate the power of this company, consider that its annual revenues now exceed $200 billion—more than the gross domestic products (GDPs) of the seventy-five poorest countries in the world combined. Today, the power of the energy companies takes a multitude of forms, such as the infamous "Halliburton loophole," which excludes fracking from the Safe Drinking Water Act, the Clean Air Act, and the Clean Water Act.[66] The revenue provided by fossil fuels—along with extraction, processing, shipping, and consumption—provides the means to suppress dissent.[67] Political action committees affiliated with fossil fuel companies pump $18 billion per year into political campaigns and spend $150 million per year on Washington lobbying (nearly as much as the lobbying budgets of Wall Street and the defense industry combined).[68] While political scientists are sounding the alarm in this century, prescient US leaders foresaw dismal consequences for the nation seventy-five years ago.

In 1941, in an era of tremendous global turmoil and national anxiety—a time strikingly similar to today—President Franklin Delano Roosevelt delivered his famous "Four Freedoms" speech to the US Congress.[69] He was deeply concerned about the future of democracy as totalitarian regimes waged campaigns of oppression through violence, propaganda, and censorship. Roosevelt's concerns apply to today's world in the form of the corporate-government alliances that, when taken to their political endpoint, become corporatocracies. Roosevelt's solutions, which were to promote the four liberties essential to human flourishing, translate to today as well. He spoke of the freedom to worship, the freedom from want, and the freedom from fear. But the first freedom he called for echoed the First Amendment of the US Constitution. Roosevelt maintained that the bulwark against tyranny was "freedom of speech and expression—everywhere in the world."[70]

One last thing. I had planned to donate the proceeds of this book to the Wyoming office of the American Civil Liberties Union. However, in 2015 the office closed, leaving Wyoming the only state without the protection of the ACLU. This is an extremely worrisome development in a state where censorship is so deeply woven into the social and political fabric. And so, I've decided to make my contribution to the PEN American Center, which is the US branch of International PEN, the world's leading international literary and human rights organization. The PEN centers form a worldwide network of writers dedicated to fighting for freedom of expression and acting as a powerful voice on behalf of writers harassed, imprisoned, and sometimes killed for their views.

The Case of
the Scuttling of *Carbon Sink*

*Censorship is to art
as lynching is to justice.*

—HENRY LOUIS GATES

CHAPTER 1

The Art of Making People Think
—and Industries Mad

University of Wyoming (UW) faculty had long perceived themselves as working for their students and the public. Their sense of service was something like that of town doctors or rural teachers (Wyoming still has one-room schoolhouses). But twenty years ago, this quaint, idealistic perception began to collapse.

The initial change began in the mid-1990s when legislators called for the dismissal of law professor Mark Squillace, who incensed the timber industry by doing pro bono work for an environmental group.[1] Others would trace the shift to the publication of a book by his colleague Deb Donahue in 2000. She proposed removing livestock from public lands in the West to protect biodiversity from the effects of overgrazing, and legislators responded by proposing to close the law school.[2] Although the controversy subsided, change was in the air.

The turning point came with the university's first major fundraising campaign that began in 2000 on the heels of an energy boom. Until that time, the institution had received just thirty-four gifts of more than $1 million over the course of 114 years.[3] By 2005 the institution had accrued $200 million from private donors, which, in Wyoming, meant energy magnates.[4] Local oil and gas executives had become multimillionaires, and Wyoming's coalbed methane industry was being valued at $140 billion.[5] Following the campaign, the university president got a half-million-dollar bonus, the head of the UW Foundation got a generous raise (via an apparent violation of institutional policy), and the university got a new mandate.[6]

Events in 2010 swept aside any lingering doubt as to who was in charge. William Ayers, a retired professor from the University of Illinois at Chicago and a 1960s antiwar radical, was invited to the UW campus to speak about social justice and education. The university received complaints, including a threatening message that those who had invited Ayers "should eat a mouthful of buckshot."[7] The event was canceled with the blessing of university president Tom Buchanan, who had been encouraged to do so by politicians and university trustees. He appealed to concerns about public safety in suggesting that while open dialogue was important, Ayers's proposed visit "demonstrates that we must be mindful of the real consequences our actions and decisions have on others."[8]

It soon emerged that those "real consequences" weren't about safety; the president hadn't even communicated his concerns to the campus police.[9] Rather, the issue was about threats—bordering on extortion—to the institution's bottom line. The most prominent figure was John Martin, cofounder of the McMurry Oil Company in Casper, Wyoming, who threatened to withdraw a $2 million donation in support of luxury boxes at the university's football stadium if Ayers appeared.[10]

After Ayers's visit was canceled, the university was sued and lost in spectacular fashion, with a federal judge explaining that the First Amendment applies even to people who may offend those in power.[11] So Bill Ayers spoke on campus to a modest crowd without incident. His lecture was titled "Trudge toward Freedom"—an ironic topic at an institution marching toward censorship.[12]

As a faculty member, I had begun to sense the pervasive reach of the energy industry by the time I met with artist Chris Drury six months after Ayers spoke at UW, but I had no idea that I'd be leading this jovial Englishman into what was to become the most notorious case of art censorship by corporate influence at an American university. On that cold November day in 2010, Drury wasn't looking chipper. Altitude sickness (Laramie lies at 7,200 feet) had transformed his normally ruddy complexion into something more akin to his wispy, white hair.

He had been commissioned to produce a piece of his renowned land art as part of an outdoor exhibit sponsored by the UW Art Museum. Using an anonymous donation of $50,000 to leverage another $25,000 from the Wyoming Cultural Trust Fund, the museum had lined up an impressive series of sculptors and land artists, including Jesús Moroles and Patrick Dougherty.[13]

Drury was looking for an ecological story to catalyze his project, and so I chatted over tea about the bark beetle outbreak that was being fueled by the abnormally warm winters, which allowed the insects to flourish.[14] Drury sipped his tea to alleviate nausea while I described millions of acres of dead and dying trees, including swaths of forest in the mountains above Laramie.

The *Carbon Sink* installation on the campus of the University of Wyoming. The logs, taken from beetle-killed trees, were interspersed with coal. The added subtitle for the sculpture, *What Goes Around Comes Around*, drew an implicit connection between the forest pest outbreak that was attributed, in large part, to unusually warm winters and the burning of fossil fuels (photo by Chris Drury).

I had no idea that he'd latch on to the relationship between fossil fuels, climate change, and beetle-killed trees. Had I known that Drury would become the energy industry's lightning rod, I might have been less forthcoming, but probably not. Although he looked like a gentle great-uncle, there was an unmistakable inner fortitude to him.

The following July, Drury returned to Wyoming with an evocative concept for his installation *Carbon Sink: What Goes Around Comes Around*. Along with a cadre of dedicated assistants, Drury laid out a thirty-six-foot-diameter vortex of charred logs from beetle-killed trees, interspersed with coal to give the sensation of a whirlpool spiraling into the blackened earth. The powerful piece had been given a site on the lawn to the south of Old Main, a stately stone building that housed the university's upper administration.

As construction began, the UW Art Museum issued a press release announcing that the installation would explore "the connection between Wyoming's strong oil and coal industries and climate change, which is contributing to pine beetle kill." Drury was staving off altitude sickness using a tincture of yarrow in his water bottle, but nothing was going to hold off political outrage once headlines in the state's newspapers proclaimed, "University of Wyoming Sculpture Blasts Fossil Fuels," and "New UW Sculpture Attacks Wyoming's Energy Industry."[15]

Stories in the *Casper Star-Tribune* and the *Gillette News Record* (Casper being the oil capital of Wyoming and Gillette being the coal capital) featured elected officials declaring that the sculpture, which none of them had seen, was "an insult to the tens of thousands of people across Wyoming that work hard to produce energy," and that politicians needed to "educate those folks [at the university] on where their paycheck came from."[16] The Republican legislators from Gillette left little doubt that the university was going to pay a price if *Carbon Sink* remained on the UW campus.

Balding and heavyset, Tom Lubnau looks more like a midwestern farm implement salesman who'd rather not be wearing a tie than a lawyer who presided over the state bar. In dealing with the media and other outsiders, the House majority floor leader used the "Ah, shucks" strategy.[17] He cagily prefaced his condemnation of *Carbon Sink* by saying, "While I would never tinker with the University of Wyoming budget . . . ," and his fellow Gillette legislator Gregg Blikre hedged with, "I don't know if I'd like it removed . . . it's up to the university."[18]

For his part, Drury insisted to reporters that he wasn't attacking the energy industry, noting that his own carbon footprint was "enormous" by virtue of airline travel.[19] He told the press that his goal was a beautiful piece of art that would suggest ecological connections and lead people to wonder what should be done about our rapidly warming world. On his blog, the artist was a bit more prickly, writing that the millions of dollars coming from the energy industry "doesn't mean they dictate what the University does nor will it be used to stifle a debate that needs to be aired, because it is the future of our children and grandchildren that is at stake here as well as the entire biosphere."[20]

In the days after the newspaper stories ran, the university was deluged with phone calls and e-mails from the energy sector. An official from Cloud Peak Energy demanded a copy of Drury's statement.[21] BP's director of government and public affairs sent a curt message: "I hope this isn't a permanent sculpture."[22] An Encana executive sent an ominous e-mail saying, "I don't want to suggest you need damage control, but I would say that the industry would like to hear from UW."[23] And the executive director of the Wyoming Mining Association contemptuously asked the director for governmental and community affairs, "Don, what kind of crap is this?" and declared that the artwork was "a stab in the back."[24]

The industry's political allies were likewise offended. State senator Phil Nicholas opined, "I fear that the perception is that UW promotes one view only"[25]—a valid point: every year tens of millions of dollars are spent on the School of Energy versus the $40,981.63 devoted to Drury's art.[26] But that's presumably not the singular view that concerned Nicholas. Meanwhile, Lubnau issued a warning to the university president: "I am considering introducing legislation to avoid any hypocrisy at UW by insuring that no fossil fuel derived tax dollars find their way into the University of Wyoming funding stream."[27] So much for his assurance that he "would never tinker with the University of Wyoming budget."

The shift from outrage to threats was subtle but unmistakable in messages from the industry. The president of the Petroleum Association of Wyoming e-mailed a who's who list of corporate executives and suggested that "the next time the University of Wyoming is asking for donations it might be helpful to remind them of this. . . . They always hide behind academic freedom but their policies and actions can change if they so choose."[28] But can a university renounce such a fundamental liberty and maintain its integrity?

The university adopted a strategy of pacification. The director of the School of Energy Resources (SER), panicked by the potential loss of industry monies, led the retreat. Prior to coming to the University of Wyoming, Mark Northam worked for more than twenty years at Mobil and ExxonMobil before moving to the world's largest oil and gas company, Saudi Aramco—and Northam knew who was in control.[29] Tall, meticulously groomed, articulate, and commanding, Northam also knew how to assuage corporate executives. He wrote to Encana, saying that "some folks [97 percent of climate experts] believe humans are responsible for global warming and that those who produce oil, gas, and coal are the heart of the problem."[30] And then Northam assured the company that *Carbon Sink* did not diminish the institutional commitment to provide them with employees and technologies. He reminded the company that "SER just this month committed $1.5 million additional investment in the Encana Lab,"[31] a public subsidy affirming the institution's loyalty. And to further demonstrate his own fidelity and contempt for free speech that was contrary to the interests of the energy industry, according to sources at the university, Northam privately bragged about sending an image of himself urinating on *Carbon Sink* to key members of the Wyoming legislature.[32]

Meanwhile, the central administration assembled a three-part apology. First, the e-mail sent to legislators began by asserting that the message of *Carbon Sink* should not be "embraced by all."[33] Just who should reject anthropogenic climate change was not made clear.

Second, the administration claimed to have been blindsided by Drury: "[There was] no indication that his work has been particularly politically motivated in the past."[34] In fact, Drury's *Winnemucca Whirlwind* (2008) had an explicit social message about the unjust appropriation of land from the Paiute people by the federal government.[35] The administration insisted that nothing about the project proposal hinted at climate change and quoted Drury's description from months earlier: "The work will connect the geologic and economic importance of Wyoming coal with the current pine beetle infestation surrounding Laramie."[36] Apparently nobody understood that the connection between coal and the insect outbreak was via climate change, despite this being a widely reported phenomenon.[37]

Drury had figured that those in charge would presume that art was innocuous and pay no attention to his proposal. "They can't ignore art anymore because art can sneak up and whack you when you're not looking," he chuckled.[38] As for a political motivation, Drury observed, "We live in a political world. [*Carbon Sink*] was definitely political because if you make work about land that's political. It always has been. Wars are fought over it."[39] He insisted that he didn't set out to generate controversy but to entice people into thinking and talking about our environmental legacy.

The third tactic in the university's placating communication was to describe *Carbon Sink* as a "distraction from the years of hard work by UW and with our partners."[40] As Drury noted with disbelief, "Distraction from what? What are they doing that's more important than what's happening around us?"[41]

The fossil fuel companies and politicians representing them weren't soothed. Indeed, the university's apologies seemed to aggravate the industry. A Peabody Energy vice president passed along a clear threat: "I discussed the University's response that you provided with our CEO and Sr. Management. They have directed me to talk further with President Buchanan. Our $2 million donation to the University is now in question."[42]

The classrooms and meeting rooms along the main hallway of the $25 million, 27,300-square-foot School of Energy Resources at the University of Wyoming feature the names of energy corporations that donated to the operation. The industry has poured millions of dollars into the university—matched by public funds—to shape its research and teaching programs (photo by Jeffrey Lockwood).

Kermit Brown, a legislator from the university's district, chose to align himself with the industry. He warned that *Carbon Sink* "almost seems to mandate that we have a second four year school in [Gillette] oriented toward the interest of those who make this state successful."[43] Of course, such a venture would be devastating to UW given the limited state funds for higher education. A fellow legislator ranted, "If you give someone money and they spit in your face, would you give them any more? . . . Artistic license is one thing, a spit in the face is another."[44]

The university was told to provide the legislature's Joint Appropriations Committee with "a detailed summary of all funds (from all sources) paid (1) to individual artists, (2) [for] outdoor art kept on UW or elsewhere, and (3) for other artwork shown on UW. . . . These requests are being made as part of the co-chairs' plan to prepare the committee for its upcoming budget work."[45] The message was clear: the university would pay for its effrontery.

Efforts by the energy industry and legislature to censor art were reported by dozens of media outlets, including the *Chronicle of Higher Education*, the

New York Times, and the *Guardian* (London). The tenor of the articles was consistent and exemplified by the international coverage: "[*Carbon Sink*] set off a debate about artistic and academic freedom, with the mining industry and Republican state legislators expressing outrage [and] accusing the university of ingratitude towards one of its main benefactors—in what some have seen as a veiled threat to cut funding."[46] E-mails came pouring in from around the nation and the world—and people were upset. The university handled most of these, but the most revealing responses were provided by Wyoming politicians. Lubnau, the House majority floor leader from coal country, replied to a dismayed citizen, "You see, from my perspective, your castigation was aimed at silencing my commentary on the art. . . . I anticipate that sending you this reply is not unlike teaching a pig to sing."[47] Evidently, Lubnau considered a punitive cut to the university's funding to be "commentary on art"[48] and any objection to this retribution as constraining his speech. But no matter how he parsed the controversy, Lubnau's dismissive response left no doubt of his allegiance to the energy industry.

By August, the SER director was complaining that the *Carbon Sink* fiasco had potentially cost his program $4 million.[49] Although e-mails among the university trustees mocked the sculpture (e.g., "my first thought was of a kum bye yah campfire gone up in flames"[50]), it was clear that something more had to done. So the president and his entourage headed up to Gillette to assuage the coal companies and their supporters.

The university's director for governmental and community affairs provided the president with a set of talking points emphasizing that Drury was merely an "artist under contract," that the university did not endorse his views, and that the institution had invested "tens of millions of dollars in research, seminars, and scholarship through SER."[51]

Between the angry letters to the editor from citizens who thought that they, rather than the energy industry, were supposed to be benefiting from the university and expressions of dismay from the readers of the major newspapers and viewers of national news programs, Wyoming's politicians were put on the defensive. In North Dakota, but not Wyoming, it's a felony for public officials to accept money from an individual or company with an immanent or pending procedure before them (even so, the law is not enforced for politicians with connections to the energy industry).[52]

Wyoming's politicians were continuing a tradition of comingling their personal financial interests and those of the state in what would be seen as a reprehensible conflict of interest in most other governmental settings. But this was the cultural norm according to Wyoming's long-serving public servant, Senator Alan Simpson, who described his time in state government between 1965 and 1977:

> I was a lost sheep when I was in the State Legislature. I tried to pass disclosure laws. I didn't get very far at all because [they'd respond] "Wait a minute, we're Wyoming, we all know what everybody's doing." Well, let me tell you, I'll buy the drinks if that's the truth. I mean there were guys sitting in that Legislature who owned stock in the Union Pacific and trucking companies and railroads and oil. Hell, you didn't know who the hell they were. Some of them, they listed their business in the little pamphlet as to who is on the floor of the House or Senate, but let me tell you I saw enough conflict there to last forever.[53]

Lubnau, whose political campaigns had been underwritten by the energy industry (Cloud Peak Energy, ONEOK, and the Williams Companies were all big donors and major players in coal, gas, or oil),[54] responded to public criticism with a bout of historical revisionism. In an editorial published by the *Gillette News Record*, Lubnau and fellow legislators thanked Drury for catalyzing "open discussions on a greater UW presence in Campbell County."[55] They explained that they'd simply been trying to educate those "pointy headed academic[s]" by letting them "know that between 60 and 80 percent of the state's budget is dependent on extractive industries."[56] What Lubnau failed to grasp is that the faculty are keenly aware that their salaries are linked to fossil fuels—and this complicity is exactly why I and others felt compelled to speak out.

Contrary to their private communications with the university (made public via the Freedom of Information Act), the legislators publically claimed, "We didn't ask the sculpture be taken down. We didn't take any steps to remove funding from the university. And we didn't engage in any form of censorship."[57]

Sensing an opportunity to take the offensive on behalf of academic freedom, I published an essay in WyoFile, an online news service that is Wyoming's main source for investigative reporting and in-depth analysis. I called out Lubnau for his bullying and argued that the legislature's plan for

developing an "energy literacy" program in the public schools on behalf of the
industry was shameful. My central point was the power of art: "Anyone who
has a soft spot for the underdog has to be doubly tickled by the fallout over
'Carbon Sink.' Most obviously, the Goliath of the fossil fuel industry was
thumped between the eyes. Even more delightful is that the rock was a piece
of art. Not a regulation, or a lawsuit, or a technical report. . . . Turns out that
art matters."[58]

The university's director of SER, Mark Northam, had become the industry's
bodyguard and the legislature's defender. In Northam's response to my essay,
he dismissed Drury as "an artist [who] probably knows as much about energy
and climate change as I know about sculpture," and then kowtowed to Lubnau,
calling him "a real sculptor . . . sculpting real solutions to carbon emissions."[59]
Lubnau defended himself, insisting that his words had been twisted into imag-
inary threats, but the university's top administrators clearly took them to be
real. He claimed to be a victim of persecution by "uppity eggheads," making
reference to my "uppityness, impertinance [sic] and arrogance."[60] His use of
"uppity" seems painfully revealing in terms of how he perceived the relationship between the legislature and the university. Whether Lubnau was fully
cognizant of the broader, cultural context (Wyoming is only 1.5 percent black),
many Americans would surely have sensed the meaning.[61]

As with previous stories in the state media, my essay elicited extensive
e-mail commentary among university administrators, state legislators, and
industry representatives. A member of the advisory board of the Wyoming
Reclamation and Restoration Center (WRRC, where scientists try to repair
the environmental damage of extractive industries) fired off an e-mail to the
dean of agriculture, asking, "How 'helpful' [is] this sort of crap . . . to our
efforts in trying to get the coal industry to support the WRRC. . . . Academic
freedom is one thing but here is a prime example of why the University needs
some oversight of this kind of activity."[62]

The dean forwarded the message to the central administration, and in
perhaps the most principled response during the entire controversy, the provost replied, "If [oversight] means that the administration should censor
what faculty members write, I don't agree. . . . Harm can be done when faculty members criticize important supporters. But the harm would be greater
if we undertook a program of censoring points of view that we think will hurt
our funding prospects."[63]

Chris Drury is a sixty-six-year-old British environmental artist who knows the evocative potential of natural materials and the political power of land. Reflecting on *Carbon Sink*, Drury said, "If the energy companies hadn't made such a fuss about an overblown headline in the *Casper Star-Tribune* all this would have been small beer," but key legislators chose to censor the artist's work (photo by Chris Drury).

In March 2012, seven months after the installation of *Carbon Sink*, political censorship became legislatively mandated. In the appropriation bill for renovating the university's recreation center, Wyoming politicians ordered that "the university shall require artwork which displays the historical, cultural and current significance of transportation, agriculture and minerals in Wyoming's history. Notwithstanding the provisions of W.S. 16-6-801 through 16-6-805 [which specifies community, artistic, and state participation] the proposals for artwork shall be submitted to the university's energy resources council and the governor for approval."[64]

Setting aside the convoluted wording, the legislature both decreed the content of art and nullified existing law. The politicos named the fossil fuel industry (seven of the nine voting members of the Energy Resources Council [ERC] are from private companies) and the governor as state-sanctioned censors.[65] Although *Carbon Sink* displayed the significance of minerals (climate change manifesting as dying forests is significant), that's surely not what the legislators meant. Lubnau found nothing wrong with giving industry veto power over art at the university.[66] And Phil Nicholas, a state senator who supported the legislation while representing the university's district, could offer no principled difference between the legislature mandating the content of art and the content of college courses—including whether a professor can talk about climate change.[67] Northam's view was that "clearly the legislative mandate for the ERC to oversee the artwork . . . was meant to send a message to UW leaders."[68] The takeaway is that a group of corporate executives were effectively empowered to decide if publicly funded art on a university campus sufficiently recognized the significance of their industry.

When Drury heard about this legislation, he put the situation into a global and historical perspective: "An artist can come in underneath and poke at power on a visceral level . . . that's why regimes the world over have always suppressed it. And you have a regime there. That's the richest of all of the ironies. That the most conservative state, the one that would be conceptually the furthest from totalitarianism, behaved as if it were a version of Soviet Russia."[69] Furthermore, the regime was not satisfied with merely censoring future speech. The politicians made sure they punished the arts for *Carbon Sink*. The Cultural Trust Fund had supported Drury's work, and now they paid the price: a plan to augment the fund by $2 million was deleted from the state budget through a simple motion that passed without discussion.[70] And to rub salt in the wound, the governor vetoed the selection of the UW Art Museum as a recipient of the prestigious Governor's Arts Award.[71]

So by the spring of 2012, eight months after *Carbon Sink* came to the UW campus, the provocateurs had been put in their place. The energy industry had been installed as censors to provide "assurance that *Carbon Sink* won't be repeated,"[72] and those who had supported the artwork had paid a price. There was just one problem. *Carbon Sink* was still on the university campus.

CHAPTER 2

Destroying Art to Preserve Political Privilege

The summer that *Carbon Sink* appeared on the University of Wyoming campus, tourists were streaming into Yellowstone National Park in the other corner of the state. There, the humans would encounter a creature more dangerous than a feisty British land artist. Bison thump an average of four visitors a year. The victims are rarely killed, occasionally gored, often battered, and invariably terrified.[1] Letting a kid pet a dairy cow at the county fair is sweet, but encouraging a child to touch a bison in Yellowstone is stupid.

Animals that have been domesticated through selective breeding can be trained to perform particular functions, but even a wild creature often can be tamed by rewarding desired behaviors or punishing those that are unwanted. The maxim "Don't bite the hand that feeds you" originated with Aesop's fable about an ungrateful dog whose owner saved it from a well, and it has become the guiding maxim for the people of Wyoming.[2]

Humans are meek toward authorities who pass laws, write checks, fire employees—and fund universities. The energy industry, along with its political lapdogs, was quick to frame Drury's *Carbon Sink* in terms of domesticated animals. The president of the Petroleum Association of Wyoming told his corporate compatriots to "remind [the university] of this and other things they have done to the industries that feed them."[3]

The state's newspapers picked up the theme: "The university appears to be biting the hand that feeds it. . . . Lubnau says those improvements [to university buildings] came from energy dollars, since up to 80 percent of the state's income comes from the energy sector."[4] And so the energy industry smacked the thankless curs at the UW Art Museum who sponsored *Carbon Sink*. Corporations withdrew their sponsorships from the gala that was the most important fundraiser of the year for the museum. The incoming chair of the museum board, a bank president, expressed doubts about his pending role, telling the director, "I truly love the Art Museum, and will always support it, but I don't agree with having the sculpture on campus."[5] Another well-connected member of the museum's board who had spoken with key executives at Arch Coal, Anadarko, BP America, and Cloud Peak Energy, reported, "I have been asked to request that this display [Carbon Sink] be removed from the University of Wyoming property."[6]

The sculpture had to go, but the university administration figured that some of the faculty might bare their teeth if they saw art being destroyed to appease the institution's masters. Even in the reddest state in the nation, the University of Wyoming has its share of dangerous liberals, edgy scholars, and cultural critics. Those in charge needed to muzzle the art without calling attention to an egregious act of iconoclasm with uncomfortable implications for political conservatives.

Dr. Tom Buchanan worked his way up the academic ranks to become the University of Wyoming's twenty-third president. Although he was hired through a bungled search process in which he—the internal candidate who'd spent his entire career at UW—was the only applicant left standing, Buchanan initially garnered the support of the faculty. With wire-rimmed glasses, a graying-and-balding pate, an easy crooked smile, and a sonorously authoritative voice, he projected confidence. And more important, the trustees knew that he wasn't the sort to get his hackles up when rich and powerful players intruded on university affairs.

Buchanan did well when there were no hard decisions, but he struggled during controversies. After he endorsed the censorship of Bill Ayers, Wyoming's conservatives were evidently pleased, but faculty wondered if their president had learned his lesson from the court's ruling. Unfortunately, he was a better teacher than a student. It's worth recognizing, however, that few administrators could stand up to direct threats to their institutions by vindictive politicians.

In January 2012 the director of the Art Museum informed Buchanan that Carbon Sink was not scheduled for removal until the summer 2013.[7] Under pressure from the legislature, the president sent a terse reply: "Given the controversy that it has generated, it would be best for UW if the fire pit (I've forgotten the name of the work) could be considered part of the Prexy's removal during the summer of 2012."[8] Between feigning amnesia to mock the artwork and using the phrase "best for UW" (which any at-will employee would interpret as "best for your future at this institution"), there was no doubt what was to be done. The museum director dutifully informed the president that removal had been accelerated and scheduled for May 21 with "no press planned."[9] The timing was brilliant. With graduation scheduled for May 5, the craven act of censorship would happen after the students had left and few faculty were on campus.

While the people of Wyoming weren't notified, the politicians who had demanded the suppression of speech were informed. The president's spokesperson trumpeted the destruction of *Carbon Sink* in an e-mail to the most ardent legislators from energy-rich counties, emphasizing that the artwork was being removed well ahead of schedule: "I want to inform you that today, the temporary 'Carbon Sink' artwork on UW's campus is being demolished. The artwork was always considered to be temporary, but it is being removed one year earlier than planned."[10] The politicians replied with condescending pats on the head. All would be well as long as nobody noticed that a circle of sod had been laid in the place of a world-class sculpture.

They say that it's very difficult to come up with a false alibi, particularly when several people are involved. Eventually the details get confused and the stories conflict. As one faculty member later observed, "If our University administration had simply said, 'They asked us to remove it, so we did because we're lapdogs of the energy industry,' then I would have thought at least they're being honest."[11] Instead of the truth, they opted for a bumbling cover-up that began with a story about plumbing.

In response to a concerned alumnus who noticed the absence of *Carbon Sink*, the university's director of government and community affairs explained in an e-mail that "an adjacent irrigation line recently broke and adversely impacted the sculpture. As a result, this sculpture was dismantled somewhat sooner than planned."[12] It was true that a sprinkler line had broken near the installation; however, the break occurred *after* Buchanan ordered *Carbon Sink* removed—and the minor damage was easily repaired by the university's physical plant, which hadn't been informed that the sculpture was slated for destruction.[13]

Unaware of this alibi, another administrator who was queried by Drury himself told the artist that limited financing and staffing had made removal necessary. Drury didn't buy this.[14] Logs and coal don't require a whole lot of maintenance, and any number of donors would've supported the minimal costs of curation.

Close-up of the simple but elegant construction of *Carbon Sink*, which required very little maintenance but demanded censorship. Some people took the outdoor installation personally, such as the executive director of the Wyoming Mining Association, who complained that the University of Wyoming "put up a monument attacking me, demonizing the industry" (photo by Chris Drury).

Top-level administrators scrambled to craft a more plausible explanation to an increasingly dubious public. The company line was that the removal had nothing to do with outside pressure and that the sculpture had always been viewed as temporary.

With regard to external demands, the special assistant to the president for external relations made the assertion to a perturbed citizen that "if UW had been concerned about the public reaction to Carbon Sink, it would never have been included in this exhibition in the first place. The University has experienced many controversies over the years precipitated by books written by faculty, guest lectures, visits by dignitaries, and dedications, to name a few. Through it all, UW has remained steadfast in supporting the most fundamental principles of higher education."[15] So in a dramatic reversal, an administration that first denied having any knowledge of the artist's message was claiming to have exhibited moral courage in approving the piece.

Like the porcine leader of the livestock in George Orwell's *Animal Farm*, the president of the university's board of trustees, Dave Bostrom, assured the public that "no constituency will override any other constituency [but] one of those constituents, a very major constituent, are the people of the energy industry."[16] In other words, all the animals are equal, but some are more equal than others. Then, in a move straight out of Orwell's *1984*, Bostrom declared, "academic expression will always be at the top of the list, from the standpoint of the board, from the standpoint of the administration, and I think that's been demonstrated."[17] How the destruction of art demonstrated the importance of free speech is a classic example of Orwellian doublethink.

As for the temporary nature of the artwork, just after the *Carbon Sink* was completed, the museum director told reporters, "There are no plans to uninstall it."[18] Drury had been led to believe that the piece would be allowed to "slowly rot back into the earth over the course of five to twenty years."[19] Yet the piece was removed after just eleven months.

In early summer only a few people were aware that the artwork had been destroyed and nobody knew about the inept cover-up. Encouraged by the editor of WyoFile—the statewide news service—I began to prepare a second essay. I contacted the director of the School of Energy Resources for his perspective. Mark Northam denied that the original controversy and subsequent censorship had anything to do with climate change, insisting that "it was about the university's benefactors' (industry and legislators) gut reaction to the university's support of protest against their existence. Clichés of 'don't bite the hand that feeds you' or 'dance with who brung you' come to mind."[20] For Northam, like so many other administrators who circle the campfire of corporations hoping that scraps will be tossed their way, the issue is "whether those who either directly or indirectly provide funds for the university have a reasonable expectation that they can control messages that the university sends."[21] Northam's view is that speech is for sale, and the energy industry is the highest bidder.

In my WyoFile essay, I expressed deep skepticism about the university's claim that political and industrial leaders played no role in the sculpture's disappearance. By connecting the dots, it seemed implausible that the Republican legislators had not coerced this shameful act of censorship. And I was appalled by the hypocrisy:

It's safe to assume that no conservative would countenance the policies of the former Soviet Union. [But art] "under Stalin developed under unique conditions of total state control which made all forms and means of artistic expression serve propagandistic purposes. The state proclaimed the arts to be its ideological weapon, established a monopoly over art production and distribution, and created a system of control over art with strict criteria of what kind of art society needs. All deviations from the state's demands, either in form or in content, were strictly forbidden and the violators prosecuted." Welcome to life behind the Carbon Curtain.

My exposé generated more traffic than any other piece in WyoFile's history and crashed the website. The university administration responded with an icy silence, although the rotating images on the opening page of the institution's website were updated to include a photograph of a student intern wearing a hard hat with ENCANA emblazoned on the front.[22] The timing could've been coincidental, but the message to the energy industry was clear: we're on your side.

E-mails sent to me by faculty, staff, and students were generally supportive ("it is because of people like you that I don't despair"), although some were less enthusiastic ("Perhaps we should not bite the hands that can help us?").[23] The continued framing of Wyoming citizens as domestic animals was evident in the response by a darling of the Tea Party who ran for US Senate in Wyoming: "If you accept handouts from the energy industry you may not want to bite the hand that feeds you."[24]

The problem was that I had only circumstantial evidence of a cover-up—absurd alibis but no smoking gun. However, Wyoming Public Radio picked up the story and used the Freedom of Information Act to acquire the e-mail communications sent to and from the university regarding *Carbon Sink*.[25] These documents confirmed that the sculpture had been removed prematurely under intense political pressure. Buchanan refused an interview, leaving his Art Museum director to twist in the wind.[26] When asked about his "suggestion" that *Carbon Sink* should be removed, she deferred: "I don't know what his reasoning was. . . . My feeling was it was not part of the pressure or whatever was going on, but I don't know."[27] But everyone else knew.

The state's largest newspaper, the *Casper Star-Tribune*, pushed further, saying that the university lied about both the timing and reason for *Carbon Sink*'s destruction: "University officials have maintained the sculpture was removed on schedule and because of water damage. However, e-mails between officials and others indicate that's not true."[28] An editorial was even more damning: "[The university] can be bought."[29] Ben Mitchell, the former curator at the Nicolaysen Museum who some years earlier had been run out of Casper for his support of an uncomplimentary photographic exhibit of coalbed methane, offered an incisive critique: "The journalists who uncovered the university's administrators' clumsy lies and the bone-headed, angry, intellectually dishonest cacophony of legislators' voices demanding its removal really didn't have such a tough job. But bless them for the good work."[30]

The sordid tale of censorship spread rapidly. A letter in the *Billings Gazette* suggested that a Republican candidate for Montana's governorship who advocated using severance taxes to fund education had drawn a lesson from Wyoming: "If education in Montana becomes dependent on taxes from natural resource development, as Rick Hill wants, we can expect similar efforts to control speech in our education system [about 24 percent of that state's government revenues come from severance taxes]."[31]

A New York public radio program, *Studio 360*, interviewed Representative Lubnau, who played the bumpkin card, referring to himself as "a simple, country legislator from the boondocks of Wyoming." The interviewer dismissed the ruse: "I've heard very powerful people say things like that in the past."[32] Contrary to Lubnau's fatuous claim that "no legislator ever called for the removal of the *Carbon Sink* sculpture,"[33] *Slate* magazine reported that "both industry representatives and state legislators weighed in on the sculpture, some threatening the university's funding in no uncertain terms."[34]

Marion Loomis, the director of the Wyoming Mining Association, told the *New York Times*, "We may have overreacted. We're over it."[35] Sure, they were over it, now that the artwork was relegated to the junkyard (the logs) and the university's power plant (the coal was burned, with no evident sense of irony).[36]

The *Index on Censorship*, a monitoring website for freedom of speech, put the Wyoming case in an international context: "In the UK, some of the most high profile arts sponsorship deals have been with the oil industry. . . . There are justified fears that long-standing sponsorship arrangements lead to self-censorship—one of the most pernicious enemies of freedom of expression."[37]

When training a dog, one school of thought is that the owner should become the alpha dog—the dominant member of the pack in the eyes of the animal. In a canine social system, the thinking goes, the lower-ranking individuals will defer to the top dog. In high school, I worked cleaning kennels and dis-covered the importance of exhibiting unwavering authority in dealing with menacing mutts who were quite willing to bite the hand that both fed them and cleaned their cages.

Buchanan wrote an op-ed piece in an effort to look undaunted, but the effect was more cringe-worthy than authoritative. He asserted that "no one demanded that the installation be removed"[38]—a ridiculous position given the e-mails from industrialists and politicians threatening the institution. Buchanan also claimed that he merely "asked the director of the university Art Museum to consider removing the 'Carbon Sink' installation"[39] (at least he remembered the name of the sculpture this time). As another of UW's at-will directors put it, "That's like the Godfather at the head of the banquet table saying, 'You know what I think you need to do? Not that I'm giving an order or anything, but . . . '"[40]

The *Casper Star-Tribune* pointed out how ludicrous Buchanan's claims were in light of the evidence.[41] But the university kept digging the hole deeper. A spokesman argued that the president didn't know that the public had been misled about the artwork being removed because of a water leak.[42] If true, this meant the president didn't read e-mails from his own director of govern-mental and community affairs concerning a matter that was potentially cost-ing the university millions of dollars.

Buchanan announced his retirement in September 2012.[43] The job announcement for his replacement listed a commitment to academic freedom last among the "additional preferred qualifications."[44] So much for the trust-ees' claim that this was the institution's highest priority.

In a move of breathtaking irony, the university named its new Center for Performing Arts after Buchanan, the man who ordered the destruction of art.[45] But then, UW also named its new science teaching facility after Sena-tor Michael Enzi, whose understanding of climate change is captured by this statement: "I barely made it back here because of a May [2014] snowstorm in Wyoming. They got 18 inches in Cheyenne. It's a little hard to convince Wyo-ming people there's global warming. We have 186 percent of normal snow pack. That's global warming?"[46] To complete the trifecta of irony, the univer-sity built the Cheney International Center to honor the vice president who countenanced torture and advocated starting a war over nonexistent weap-ons of mass destruction (at least Cheney donated to his own monument). Buchanan defended the naming of the International Center by saying,

"Whether you are Democrat or Republican, liberal or conservative, Catholic or Protestant, gay or straight, white or black, you are welcome at the University of Wyoming."[47] However, if you're a 1960s war protestor or a contemporary environmental artist, you'd best avoid the campus.

With Buchanan in retreat, the governor soon followed. He withdrew himself from the art approval process at the university.[48] The School of Energy Resources' advisory council decided to retain their role as art censors, but the students and faculty were emboldened.

In October I received an e-mail from Jack Clarendon, an undergraduate in the School of Environment and Natural Resources, who'd read my essay and wanted to take action. After a series of discussions with me, this bright and impassioned young man allied with a senator in the university's student government to craft a resolution titled "Support for the Preservation of a Censorship-Free Environment." Beginning with a series of statements about the value of free speech and the institution's having relented to political pressure, the document concluded: "THEREFORE, be it resolved that (the Associated Students of the University of Wyoming) express its disapproval of the University of Wyoming's administration having failed to preserve an academic environment allowing for dissenting opinions and intellectual creativity."[49]

The resolution was introduced in December 2012 and came to a vote when the students returned to campus after the holidays. The debate unfolded in the cramped quarters of the senate chambers, an elongated room on the second floor of the Student Union lined with portraits of past student body presidents. Advocates argued that the university existed for the students—not the energy industry—and that growing dependence on private funding was eroding free speech. The opposition contended that most students didn't even know that *Carbon Sink* existed and that the artwork had been on campus for long enough that its expedited removal wasn't really censorship.[50]

The most deeply troubling line of argument began with a student senator who said that after discussing the matter with state legislators, he was "warned against biting the hand that feeds us." Another senator put it in stark terms: "I agree with the principle [of academic freedom]; but urge a 'no' vote. Do you want to bite the hand that feeds you?"[51] Once again, the image of domesticated animals arose when the students perceived themselves as being well-fed through low tuition provided by energy taxes. The resolution failed to pass by a single vote.

The Naughton Power Plant outside Kemmerer, Wyoming, is fed by coal—the "hand that feeds" the people of the state (in terms of severance taxes). The annual output of carbon dioxide from this seven-hundred-megawatt facility approaches six million tons, and this plant ranked fifty-eighth on a list of the one hundred most polluting coal plants in the United States in terms of coal combustion waste (photo by Scott Kane).

The student body president was Joel Defebaugh, a thoughtful and articulate political science major. When I asked him whether the students had been tamed by the energy industry, he resisted the notion his constituents were what I called "fat and happy." But then he paused and sighed, "I do think there is a good number, and I could even say a majority of students, who are complacent. . . . They're well taken care of scholarship-wise, they want to come to class, get their education, and move on."[52] State-funded Hathaway Scholarships support about 40 percent of all Wyoming students at the university by paying 40–80 percent of their tuition costs, depending on high school grades and standardized test scores.[53] Understandably, students want to do well without the burden of wondering whether this means doing good. Which is to say, they're like most of us.

As for the allusion to "biting the hand" during the debate, Defebaugh initially avoided the metaphorical meaning and simply acknowledged that "energy feeds our economy in the state, and the state government feeds the university."[54] When I pressed him on what this phrase meant about students, he again paused. With a melancholy look beyond his years he said, "Now, sitting down with you, I'm thinking that does have serious implications. It is worrisome, and I'm glad you brought it up. I think it's huge."[55] That was one of my prouder moments as a university professor.

While the students were nipping at the energy industry, some feisty faculty wanted to take a bite out of their keepers as well. Despite my best efforts to entice the leadership of the faculty senate to step forward, the executive committee declined to support the development of a resolution, saying, "If we do something like this it should be worded in a positive sense."[56] In short, the pick of the litter didn't want to offend those who controlled the financial food bowls on campus. However, a gutsy professor took up the cause.

The senator who took the lead was Alexandre Latchininsky, a distinguished Russian entomologist with Old World charm and long experience under the Soviet system. In the course of his drafting a resolution to support academic freedom and censure the president, he evoked desperate efforts to avoid controversy among his colleagues. Fellow senators contended that academic freedom protected faculty (not invited artists), pertained only to "inquiry" (*Carbon Sink* didn't qualify as such), and didn't include sculpture (art wasn't a form of speech). Latchininsky's replies were incisive and diplomatic. He argued that academic freedom must extend to everyone on campus, that the sculpture was a form of inquiry asking us to think about our complicity in climate change, and that had a book about climate change, rather than the coal of *Carbon Sink*, been burned, surely there would be moral outrage.[57]

One professor questioned whether the faculty senate had the "moral authority" to declare the premature destruction of art as censorship.[58] Latchininsky saw the faculty as not only possessing the authority but also as having a moral duty. And when another maintained that because the state unwittingly funded the artwork, legislators had the right to destroy it, Latchininsky replied, "This is precisely the sort of argument that the principle of academic freedom is intended to refute. The state funds a university; it does not buy our speech or art. In fact, for us to be a university entails that the state and private donors are not within their rights to ask for the censorship of art or science."[59] The irony of Latchininsky, a former Soviet military officer, educating American professors about the nature of free speech was lost in the kerfuffle.

The final wording of the faculty senate's resolution was similar to that developed by the students. It chastised the administration and declared, "Academic freedom is of essential and non-negotiable importance to the integrity of a public university and to its duty to provide students and citizens with ideas, perspectives, and truths that are at the heart of a vital democracy and an open society."

When the resolution came to the floor of the faculty senate on January 28, 2013, the initial discussion was cautious as professors tried to finesse their positions and protect their departments from retribution.[60] Just as it seemed that the resolution would flounder, a professor of chemical and petroleum engineering unintentionally saved the day. This former employee of the oil and gas industry delivered a diatribe that incensed those who were otherwise tempted to put their tails between their legs and slink away: "The message from the piece of artwork was that the hydrocarbon industry is sending us down the drain. And I found that statement offensive, and I think a lot of people in the state, not just state legislators, found it offensive. . . . I don't think it was prematurely removed. I think it was removed about a year too late. . . . That's not censorship. It [*Carbon Sink*] amounts to hate speech really."[61] Once the engineer's jeremiad ran out of gas, a political science professor explained the First Amendment.[62] As she reminded the faculty that a vital democracy must protect all speech, her fellow senators realized that their votes would reveal where they stood—or skulked. The resolution passed easily, with a few barely audible nays.

It couldn't last. The emboldened students and faculty defended free speech, provocative art, and the integrity of a public university, but the energy industry and its loyal enforcers would return with a vengeance to muzzle these malcontents and deliver a series of harsh blows to art, science, and education. There's no room for tolerance when the stakes involve controlling a state's mind-boggling wealth. The political retribution seemed disproportionate to the threat of a bunch of academics, but a master cannot flinch when a defiant cur growls, lest others smell fear.

CHAPTER 3

Paying the Price for Free Speech

In 1991 I was a guest of the Chinese Academy of Sciences in Beijing, and one evening my hosts took me through Tiananmen Square. As we walked, a young researcher pointed surreptitiously to a pockmarked concrete lamppost and whispered, "That's where bullets hit." He was referring to the massacre that took place two years earlier, when the army descended on tens of thousands of students who had joined together to call for government accountability, democratic reform, and freedom of speech. After three weeks of protests, Communist hardliners ordered a military crackdown and mobilized a quarter of a million troops. At 10 p.m. on June 3, 1989, soldiers advanced on the square and used live ammunition against the unarmed civilians. In the course of the next twelve hours, more than a thousand protestors were killed.[1]

The government response had been ruthless, but both sides knew that the occupation of Tiananmen Square and its political cleansing were about much more than a particular protest. The events were about the people questioning authority and the government sending an enduring message to anyone daring to speak truth to power. Two decades later, Wyoming politicians took a page from the Chinese hardliners and sent a message—clear, reactionary, and extreme—to artists, educators, and scientists who might endanger the economic status quo. While the response to *Carbon Sink* by those in power was not militaristic or physically brutal, there is a fundamental similarity. Both governments felt threatened and acted to silence dissent. The response by Wyoming's leaders was meant to crush the spirit of anyone planning to challenge the hegemony of the energy industry.

The Wyoming legislature's initial retaliation had been to require that the governor and energy industry approve artwork at the university's new recreation center.[2] But this tit for tat seemed petty, and the politicians quietly struck the provision in their 2013 session. Rather than settling for a niggling payback crafted by a state senator who'd evidently never seen Drury's sculpture, the politicos had much bigger plans to quash dangerous discourse. Not wanting to bloody their hands, the legislature called in the trustees to protect the industry and consumers from difficult questions and provocative art. Lacking the courage of their conservative convictions, the politicians required the university's overseers to develop a policy for the approval of public art, making the trustees into mandated censors.[3] But the trustees weren't keen on taking the heat.

To avoid openly admitting that they were tasked with silencing dissent, the board shifted the discussion to aesthetics, saying that that they wanted to "avoid the problem of us becoming art critics," adding, "no one agrees on what is good art."[4] Of course, this rhetoric sidestepped the fact that nobody had ever suggested that *Carbon Sink* wasn't "a singularly beautiful, visually powerful, aesthetically subtle, and conceptually profound piece of work," as one art critic observed.[5] It wasn't aesthetic judgment that the trustees sought to avoid, but the dirty work of censorship.

So the supreme leaders of the university passed the buck. The trustees decided that they'd just approve the guidelines for a Public Art Committee and shove the president into the line of fire when it came to final approval.[6] Each layer of political power wanted censorship, but nobody would take responsibility. And for their part, the faculty didn't ask whether a policy for approving science, philosophy, journalism, or history would be next.

The Public Art Committee is chaired by the vice president for governmental and community affairs (a former Wyoming legislator and long-term player in state politics), with the balance of the group consisting of the vice presidents for administration and the University of Wyoming Foundation, along with the head of the art department and the director of the Art Museum.[7] The seven-page policy guiding their decisions includes provisions for the energy industry to weigh in: "The Committee . . . may require artists, donors, or sponsors to engage stakeholders [a euphemism for corporations] to discuss any proposed installation (both its physical nature and its content)."[8] The word "heritage" appears on virtually every page, with the goal of the approval process being to select art that "preserves and acknowledges history, heritage and culture."[9] In a state where the Wyoming Heritage Foundation is an obsequious advocate of coal and a loyal skeptic of climate change,[10] "heritage" is a code word for extractive industries, big businesses, and political apologists.

Wyoming is not alone in developing a public art policy for its university campus. However, most other guidelines do not circumscribe the content or purpose of art (e.g., Carnegie Mellon University, University of Arkansas,

University of Indiana, University of Montana, and University of Washington),[11] and review committees are typically stacked with art experts rather than administrators.

During the occupation of Tiananmen Square, discordant voices sought to negotiate with officials and defy the authorities. But during the chaos of the military assault, one individual stood out. "Tank Man" stood courageously in front of an armored column, blocking the advance until bystanders pulled him aside, evidently figuring that a lone human could stalemate the Chinese army for only so long.[12]

Sometimes a single person or a simple question can stop the authorities in their tracks—like the gentle but principled British artist who asked, "What's the role of the university if it can't speak the truth, if it can't talk about what's important? You can live a very good life in Wyoming because of coal and oil. You can go to university for free, but is the price worth paying?"[13] While Chris Drury wondered aloud if the cost of silence was too high, Wyoming's commanders moved to decisively restore social order.

The political corruption behind censorship in Wyoming and much of the rest of the nation echoed elements of the socioeconomic discontent in China during the Tiananmen protests, where protestors objected to private companies exploiting lax regulations and cozy relationships with the government.[14] In Wyoming, the government crackdown on *Carbon Sink* and what it represented deepened the bonds between political and economic power. The message was clear: there will be no reform. As the university broadened corporate connections, the sorts of questions that researchers could ask were commensurately narrowed.

In an effort to remake the UW College of Engineering and Applied Science into a "Tier 1" enterprise, the university set a fundraising goal of $115 million.[15] So the governor, a cadre of politicians, the president of the University of Wyoming Foundation, and other university-affiliated luminaries met with energy executives at the Dallas Ritz Carlton in early 2013. They came away with a few million bucks, which the people of Wyoming matched to assure that some of the world's wealthiest corporations wouldn't have to bear the entire burden of their own research and development.[16]

If Wyoming governor Matt Mead struck a rich vein in Texas, he evidently figured that the mother lode for university funding was in the Middle East, where he met with executives from Saudi Aramco.[17] Why he chose this

The Energy Innovation Center on the campus of the University of Wyoming. The building houses the Peabody Energy Advanced Coal Technology Laboratory, the Arch Coal and Marathon Oil Research Offices, the Shell 3-D Visualization Research Laboratory, the BP Collaboration Center, the Encana Auditorium, and the Ultra Petroleum Corporation Student Area (photo by Jeffrey Lockwood).

particular company appears obvious: it is the corporate alma mater of Mark Northam, the director of UW's School of Energy Resources.[18] One might wonder whether Northam has financial connections with his former employer such that publicly subsidized research would be to his personal advantage. That is, should he have substantial holdings in Saudi Aramco, the profits of the company through Wyoming-funded research could have a personal payoff. However, the university administration assiduously avoids asking this question, despite policies regarding conflicts of interest.[19]

In 2014 the university hired Richard Horner to coordinate the effort to become a top-tier engineering (read "resource extraction") institution. His former employer also happened to be Saudi Aramco. Although the administration is unable to recount the hiring process, it seems that Horner was the only candidate brought to campus.[20] One of the concerns of those who gathered at Tiananmen Square was that acquiring a lucrative position within the state-run bureaucracy was a matter of political favoritism. University students and graduates were frustrated by a system in which connections and nepotism had become more important than qualifications in the hiring process.[21] Whether plum positions are through corporate or political associations, those on the outside looking in will become fractious.

Chris Drury's sculpture was subtitled *What Goes Around Comes Around*, which became perversely prescient in terms of industry influence in Wyoming. Dick Cheney, alumnus of the University of Wyoming and six-term US representative from Wyoming, had also been the CEO of Halliburton, where he received a $20 million retirement package when he ran for vice president.[22] So few were surprised when Halliburton chipped in $3 million to support the UW School of Energy Resources, a gift that state officials described as "underscor[ing] the close collaboration between the energy industry, state government, and the university."[23] Halliburton's current CEO was refreshingly frank, saying that his company expected a return on the investment. And Wyoming's governor Matt Mead gushed, "we've got a legislature that absolutely supports the mineral industry, and is completely behind this," as he handed the CEO a UW football helmet to seal the deal.[24]

Evidently, Halliburton figured that they'd purchased not only the public university but the state's media as well. When the *Casper Star-Tribune* requested an interview, the company required the newspaper to sign an agreement that it would not "portray Halliburton in a negative light." The reporter was dumbfounded, saying, "I've never seen a [media release] with such a requirement."[25] In effect, the company dismissed any notion of a free press. When corporations brazenly expect to censor journalists, something has gone dreadfully wrong in America.

Today, the Communist Party of China controls all media allusions to the Tiananmen Square protests. One of the "Seven Demands" of the protestors had been an end to the ban on private newspapers and to the censorship of the press.[26] In the ensuing years, the government has made sure that the massacre remains virtually unknown to Chinese youth. In a similar vein, who decides what cannot be said at American universities? In Wyoming, the government is passing ever more control to the energy industry. A particularly revealing statement regarding corporate-political alliances came from Eli Bebout, a state senator and the president of Nucor Oil and Gas. He told reporters that the energy industry looks to UW for assistance, "and sometimes we don't feel it's there."[27] "We"? The use of this pronoun, probably unintentional, reveals who Bebout perceives to be his constituency.

The legislature told the trustees to consider whether the Energy Resources Council—an industry-dominated advisory group for the university's School

of Energy Resources—should approve the school's hiring.[28] State senator
Drew Perkins (a Republican from Natrona County, one of Wyoming's energy
empires) left no doubt that this was continuing payback for *Carbon Sink*: "So
you had a university that was in large part funded though the mineral industry [and has] hindered and caused problems [by displaying subversive art] in
the furtherance of the state in the use of those resources."[29]

Just as the university's trustees were poised to debate whether hiring in
the School of Energy Resources should be overseen by Arch Coal, Shell, and
PacifiCorp (companies with seats on the Energy Resources Council), the item
disappeared from their agenda. Although one trustee called the legislative
meddling "distasteful,"[30] the others had been willing to swallow the bitter
pill of self-censorship. A trustee put the matter bluntly: "I don't want to fight
the people who write the checkbook for the university."[31]

Edmund Burke—a defender of the American Revolution and democracy—
asserted in the late 1700s, "All that is necessary for the triumph of evil is
that good men do nothing." Burke's words were used to underscore the courage of the Tank Man on Tiananmen Square. And yet, years later, university
leaders chose to do nothing.

Behind closed doors, the Chinese government consolidated its power after the
Tiananmen protests by rewarding party loyalists and installing stalwart
Communists in important positions. In the autumn of 2012 the University of
Wyoming trustees began their search for a president to replace Tom Buchanan
by adopting a confidential process. When Wyoming media challenged this
approach, the legislature rushed to pass a bill allowing such secrecy. While
the issue was being wrangled in the courts, the trustees hired Robert
Sternberg.[32]

The legislature was assured that Sternberg would "continue building programs focused on research and workforce preparation in collaboration with
the energy industry."[33] Sternberg, the former provost at Oklahoma State, was
keenly aware of the hazards of free speech and early in his tenure condemned
a controversial initiative by saying, "The last thing we need is another *Carbon
Sink*."[34] When asked directly about the artwork, he replied that academic
freedom was important, but "we don't necessarily want to stick our finger in
the eyes of those who support us. We would go out of business. We are one of
the top energy producers in the country; if you don't like the energy business,
don't turn on the lights."[35] For this Yale-educated scholar, then, the options

were appallingly simpleminded: support fossil fuels or live in darkness. To prove his fidelity, Sternberg decided that the School of Energy Resources would report to him rather than to the vice president for academic affairs, saying, "I'm going to work directly with [the director] to serve the energy industry in the state."[36] To show that he shared the legislature's disdain for academia, Sternberg purged the administration. He fired the provost and replaced him with a fellow who had ties to the energy industry and enjoyed what amounted to a courtesy appointment in the College of Business. A cascade of resignations and firings followed.[37] But no change was as revealing as the shake-up of the law school.

The president announced that, based on informal conversations around the state, there would be a review of the UW College of Law to assess its shortcomings "with regard to energy, natural resources, water, and environmental law."[38] The review was to be conducted by a task force stacked with energy industry supporters. Subversive UW law professors had previously challenged the forest and grazing industries, so any incipient criticism of the fossil fuel companies had to be crushed. Outraged by the duplicitous politics that provided no voice for his faculty, the dean resigned in protest, writing, "I cannot continue to serve as your dean while critical decisions are made about the College of Law without the input of the administration and faculty of the College."[39]

A savvy bit of investigative journalism by a reporter soon revealed that Sternberg's plan to reeducate law students was based on demands from a single trustee with connections to the energy industry through his law practice, which counted Sinclair Oil and Rocky Mountain Power among its clients.[40] However, nobody in power objected to Sternberg's deceit. And the official who orchestrated the disingenuous review is now the president of the board of trustees.[41]

The party elites were evidently pleased with their new puppet's capacity to stifle discourse. Unfortunately, the qualities that allowed Sternberg to be an unreflective authoritarian on campus didn't play well in the rest of the state. On November 14, 2013, just 137 days into his presidency, Sternberg resigned and was provided with a $414,000 severance package.[42] The trustees declared, "The board fully accepts and endorses the personnel changes and changes in the direction at the university that have taken place in the last several months."[43]

Ignoring institutional bylaws, the trustees bypassed the Faculty Senate and appointed the interim provost as the new president.[44] Although he lacked a record that would have qualified him to be an assistant professor, Dick McGinity found himself in charge of the university;[45] however, he didn't lack the experience that impressed the energy industry. McGinity had been the chairman of Canada Southern Petroleum, a company sitting on nearly a trillion cubic feet of natural gas. They became a subsidiary of Canadian Oil Sands, a company with enormous reserves of tar sands, which require a huge amount of energy to be transformed into usable oil that will flow through the Keystone XL pipeline if it is ever built.[46] In short, he had fossil fuel credibility.

Early in his tenure, McGinity criticized previous administrations for being unresponsive to the "needs of the state"—meaning the university had slipped in its commitment to the energy industry.[47] Although he tried to backpedal, politicians took the opportunity to endorse censorship. Alluding to *Carbon Sink*, a state senator said that the legislature was frustrated by the university having "lost its balance" between supporting academic freedom and supporting the mineral industry.[48] Another Republican legislator was willing to throw the US Constitution under the bus (or the coal train), saying, "There's a happy medium between your First Amendment rights and the rights of the [industries] who are paying the bills."[49]

McGinity insisted that he wouldn't sacrifice academic freedom "even if it offends the industries."[50] He might have considered that the general secretary of the Communist Party was denounced for being soft on the Tiananmen protesters—and was forced to resign.[51]

Whether McGinity's successor will have the courage to defend free speech during the coming years of economic turmoil as energy prices plummet is anyone's guess. Laurie Nichols, the university's next president, arrived in 2016. During her interview, she applied a rather creative interpretation of the federal legislation that established the land-grant institutions, contending that energy research and corporate partnerships were part of the land-grant mission. However, Nichols also maintained that while she wouldn't "put big energy companies aside . . . they are not all of your state."[52] Exactly what this means in terms of protecting academic freedom waits to be revealed. What we do know is that she hired a provost—the chief academic officer of the university—whose career began as an Amoco (now BP) development and exploration geologist.[53]

After crushing the Tiananmen protests, the Communist government subjected Chinese youth to a massive reeducation program of hardline political philosophy to prevent a repeat of the turmoil that came with unfettered thought and speech.[54] Such approaches to forcibly indoctrinate students were less brutal than the practices of "re-education through labor," which dealt with "undesirables" on anniversaries of the protests.[55] When a hegemonic power seeks to silence dissent, education is a wickedly effective tool—as the energy industry and its political minions well know.

Although Wyoming's politicians failed to act on legislation concerning high school dropouts and math standards in 2013, they managed to pass a bill supporting the initial development of an energy and natural resource literacy curriculum.[56] The legwork behind the bill was provided by Devon Energy, and the legislation allocated $75,000 for an industry consultant.[57] According to the Petroleum Association of Wyoming, the target of the educational program was fifth and sixth graders,[58] presumably to preempt their asking tough questions, organizing protests, or making provocative art when they are older.

While Devon Energy was getting paid to plan curricula, ExxonMobil was paying the UW School of Energy Resources $100,000 to "advance Energy Literacy Education in Wyoming,"[59] and Chevron soon joined the venture. The goal of the program was to "enhance the workforce pipeline and promote general energy literacy among all students."[60] The School has since promoted the ExxonMobil Challenge day, established middle and high school energy clubs, fostered an energy academy, and hosted teacher workshops with lessons provided by a Chevron representative.[61]

Meanwhile, a plan for an energy and natural resources curriculum in the public schools was developed by a hodgepodge of industrialists and administrators. They emphasized a "balanced approach," but teachers weren't fooled. Responses to the plan ranged from skeptical ("In Wyoming's energy based economy, I worry that efforts to improve energy literacy will focus on mineral extraction more than on conservation and stewardship") to hostile ("I'm highly opposed to what would otherwise appear to be an attempt by industry to abuse the political process into brainwashing students into thinking unscientifically").[62]

Continued development of an energy literacy program is still awaiting state funding, but its form can be inferred from legislators' enchantment with

Oklahoma's "Petro Active" curriculum, which is an unapologetic infomercial.[63] The Campbell County School District's website featured Wyoming's gifted-and-talented sixth graders singing the praises of the Powder River Coal Company. Under "Environmental Issues," one could discover that "coal mines provide a kind of refuge for wildlife [protecting] animals that are living on the mine site [from hunters]."[64] As for the effects of carbon dioxide on the climate, there wasn't a word.

When it comes to anthropogenic climate change, Wyoming politicians are willing to exchange public education for industry indoctrination. The Next Generation Science Standards (NGSS) were developed over the course of a rigorous, two-year process by the National Academy of Sciences, the National Science Teachers Association, and the American Association for the Advancement of Science, while garnering the unanimous approval of a thirty-member committee of Wyoming educators and school administrators.[65]

Nobody would have foreseen a problem unless they had been privy to e-mails from the chairman of the State Board of Education in February 2014. Ron Micheli objected to the inclusion of climate change as "fact" rather than "theory" in the NGSS, and he insisted that "the ice pack is expanding [and] the climate is cooling," based on reports from the right-wing Fordham Institute.[66]

In the waning minutes of the spring legislative session, Wyoming's politicians passed a budget footnote prohibiting the use of state funds to implement the NGSS. The bill's author explained that the standards treat "man-made climate change as settled fact. . . . We are the largest energy producing state in the country, so are we going to concede that?"[67] At issue was not the veracity of the science but the vitality of the energy companies. The governor defended the use of ideological indoctrination with a rhetorical question: "Are the Next Generation Science Standards . . . going to fit what we want in Wyoming?"[68]

When the Wyoming Board of Education subsequently solicited input from citizens, legislators insisted that the meeting was illegal. The politicians maintained that they had the authority to quash dissent and demanded that the board "obey the law" and silence the crowd.[69] To his credit, Micheli allowed public comment; however, he might have been wise to remain mum at the public meeting, as he insisted that the discussion had to be "fair, balanced" and "based on the economy of this state"[70]—not the findings of science. His voice rose as he declared that "Wyoming's entire educational system is based on fossil fuels . . . and any attempt to derail that or change that is not in the best interests of the state!"[71]

When it comes to knowing the inner workings of energy and education, few are better positioned than Jim Verley, a science education specialist with the Wyoming Department of Education who looks like a thin Tom Selleck. I first met him more than a decade ago when he was a graduate student at the University of Wyoming, and even then it was clear that he was politically astute. Verley figured that the censorship of the science standards was continuing payback for *Carbon Sink*. Noting that the then state superintendent of public education was a Tea Party ideologue, Verley understood that climate change was a test case for the role of government in regulating industries—and teaching children.[72]

After the story of Wyoming's politicians censoring educators made national headlines, science advocacy groups launched a campaign calling for the rights of American students to "explore the causes and consequences of climate change."[73] Similarly outraged, faculty at the University of Wyoming signed on to a position paper titled "Why the Critics of the Next Generation Science Standards Are Wrong," which was sent to the state Board of Education.[74] This report might suggest a glimmer of academic freedom, except that a quarter of the forty-six signatories were retired and only three untenured professors signed their names. Meanwhile, the university's trustees refused to take a position, explaining that the standards were "a fairly hot potato."[75]

In 2015 state lawmakers drafted a bill to require the Board of Education to "independently examine and scrutinize" science standards to ensure that they "promote excellence," thereby tacitly allowing the Next Generation Science Standards and permitting climate change to be taught. However, before the legislation was passed, the Senate majority floor leader tried to amend the bill to prescribe that the standards would be "unique to Wyoming," as if an abundance of fossil fuels makes the science different. The conference committee killed this amendment, along with language requiring that the standards promote "independence," which was a code word for the state defying scientific consensus on climate change.

With the state allowing the possibility of climate change into public school curricula, at least one Wyoming school district took matters into its own hands. After an eighteen-member committee spent two and a half years reviewing texts for adoption, a group of Tea Party members from the school board and community put the kibosh on buying materials that mentioned evolution, race, and climate change. Although the majority of the community evidently supported the texts, the opposition managed to halt the purchase through a bureaucratic maneuver. A leading opponent on the school board wrote, "I will NOT authorize any of the $300,000 allocated for this purchase to include supplemental booklets about 'global whining.' . . . Our Wyoming schools are largely funded by coal, oil, natural gas, mining, ranching, etc. This junk science is against community and state standards."[76]

In at least some parts of the United States, the government worries that if the youth learn about anthropogenic climate change they will question the wisdom of burning fossil fuels. So maybe when they're in their twenties they'll just be quietly perplexed by persistent droughts, massive storms, and other such events, while their peers in China remain completely unfamiliar with the events of June 4, 1989.[77] Censorship can erase awareness, but it can't change reality.

In the midst of the Tiananmen protests, students from the Central Academy of Fine Arts built a thirty-three-foot statue. *Goddess of Democracy* became a rallying symbol when spirits were flagging among the demonstrators, and it drew more than a quarter million people into the square. The authorities declared the artwork to be illegal. When the army forced their way into Tiananmen Square, a tank was dispatched to topple the *Goddess*.[78]

Less than six months after the destruction of the thirty-six-foot-diameter *Carbon Sink*, the university announced a $6 million leadership gift toward building the Marian H. Rochelle Gateway Center.[79] The Rochelles made their riches in various enterprises, including oil and gas. A few more million dollars were added by the McMurrys of Wyoming energy fame. The stated purpose of the Center was as a place to welcome students and alumni, along with "prospective employers [and] industry leaders."[80] The political purpose of the building was to serve as a monument to fossil fuels. Mick McMurry wanted visitors to know that "the lifestyle that the world enjoys is all because of hydrocarbons and coal."[81] This message was delivered with the subtlety of an army tank, using a "three story graphic illustration of the Wyoming energy industry and the impact it has had on the state and the university."[82]

In Tiananmen Square, the government didn't install a new sculpture to dominate the empty space left after the destruction of *Goddess of Democracy*. They just left behind bullet-pocked lampposts as reminders of the cost of free speech.

The University of Wyoming's Gateway Center houses the institution's alumni association, admissions, career services, foundation, and the McMurry Foundation UW Legacy Hall. And, of course, "the impact of Wyoming's energy industry in advancing Wyoming and UW is celebrated in a permanent exhibition." At sixty times the area of *Carbon Sink*, the monument to fossil-fueled wealth sends a clear message (photo by Clayleen Rivord).

Having done what I could to reveal how my institution had colluded with the energy industry and state politicians to censor artistic expression on campus, I was ready to settle back into my teaching and scholarly work. However, my published essays and conversations on campus had marked me as someone who was willing to tell the story of oppression. I started receiving e-mails and phone calls that revealed partial tales, telling glimpses, second-hand accounts, and other leads into the experiences of Wyoming artists, scientists, and educators who had been silenced.

One of the first fragmentary accounts communicated to me involved a scientist at the University of Wyoming whose work and career had come under fire from the energy industry. Artists can be controversial, and dissenting views can provoke those in power; however, scientists labor to reveal the world as objectively as possible—they are looking for answers, not trouble. What follows is the story of a researcher who worked hard to benefit the energy industry but dared to share his knowledge with the public—and paid the price.

The Case of
Shoot the Messenger

When silence is a choice,
it is an unnerving presence.
When silence is imposed,
it is censorship.

—TERRY TEMPEST WILLIAMS

CHAPTER 4

Science Fails to Mind Its Own Business

Geoffrey Thyne was used to relocation. When he was two, his father abandoned his dream of teaching college English, moved the family from New York to Florida, and started a general contracting firm. The business was successful; Thyne and his younger brother settled into middle-class life. When not working for their father, the boys wandered the beaches of Sarasota, where Thyne's fascination with the natural world presaged his becoming a scientist.[1]

The wickedly smart young man was bored in school and ranked 423rd out of 427 in his senior class. But Thyne's exceptional SAT scores convinced the University of South Florida to take a risk on him—an act of benevolence that he'd never forget. After earning degrees in zoology and chemistry, he pursued a master's degree in geochemistry at Texas A&M. Upon graduation, the divorced father of two young sons needed well-paying, stable employment.

Thyne parlayed his A&M Aggie connections into employment as a research geochemist with Arco Oil in Plano, Texas. After seven years he took early retirement and headed to the University of Wyoming to work on his doctorate in geology, where he developed an interest in hydrology and the movement of contaminants into aquifers.

As a freshly minted PhD, Thyne took a tenure-track position at Cal State Bakersfield, but his love of research was misaligned with the teaching focus of the university, so he resigned when a Norwegian oil company offered him a lucrative contract that allowed him to set up shop in almost any research institution. Thyne chose the Colorado School of Mines, where he was welcomed as a research professor. The Norwegians were pleased to funnel their money through a high-powered research university, and the school was delighted to have his expertise. Everybody was happy until 2003, when Thyne responded to a request for assistance from environmental activists.

Thyne feels indebted to society because public universities gave him a chance and a first-rate education. His deep gratitude drives a sense of duty: "The least I can do when the public asks a question is to provide the best possible answer."[2] He also notes that the Thyne family history involved an unspecified but evidently serious conflict with government, which motivated his ancestors' hasty emigration from Scotland to New York. As he frames it, "Apparently there is a family trait for confrontation with authority," and then he pauses, saying, "Stupid authority, is the way I'd put it. Smart authority I don't have a problem with."[3] It seems that the US Environmental Protection Agency (EPA) qualified as the former.

The Earthworks' Oil and Gas Accountability Project, an environmental nonprofit organization, knew of Thyne's industry experience and academic expertise. He was hardly a tree hugger, but the man had what they wanted: credibility. So they asked Thyne to review an EPA report on hydraulic fracturing or "fracking"—the process of injecting water, sand, and a cocktail of chemicals under enormous pressure into the earth to break apart rock and release oil or natural gas.[4] The agency had asked states for cases that irrefutably linked fracking to degraded water quality, and having received none, the agency decided that there was no impact (definitive evidence required baseline data, which was generally lacking). Thyne recalls, "They concluded there was no problem based on there being no data, whereas I concluded there was no data." The environmental group held a press conference and Thyne was quoted as saying that the "absence of proof is not proof of absence."[5]

The university administration was unimpressed with Thyne's reasoning, and his department head told him, "You can't say that because you're representing the Colorado School of Mines," where the energy industry was a major funding source. The head explained that "the smart thing would be to never say anything about this again, even as a private citizen."[6]

Having been told to remain silent about interpreting the lack of data, Thyne figured that fracking research was a golden opportunity for the School of Mines. Being sympathetic to the challenges of industry, he suspected that problems were likely to be rare, detectable, and manageable if somebody would actually do the research. Just as Thyne was transitioning into a leadership role in the school's Energy Research Institute, Delta County erupted into controversy over the impacts of fracking.[7] He led a project to evaluate water quality and reported to the county commissioners that there was no evidence of contamination.

A couple weeks later, Thyne was called into the office of academic affairs. Thyne figured that he was going to be congratulated for having served the public interest through good science that had exonerated the industry. The reality was that important donors and other influential figures didn't want anyone rummaging around fracking sites. The vice president told Thyne, "I won't sign your next contract unless you drop this research on hydraulic fracturing."[8] Thyne was taken aback but agreed to the political censorship. Case closed, or so it seemed.

A short time later, Thyne's boss informed him that his contract was being cut to half-time. The Colorado Oil and Gas Association had marked him as a troublemaker. So when news broke a few months later that he was involved in another controversy, the industry was ready.

To supplement his diminished income, Thyne began private consulting for Garfield County to analyze groundwater quality near gas fields.[9] He reported that a dozen of the 220 wells in the county showed elevated chloride and methane. Unbeknownst to Thyne, a coalition of energy and state interests hired a team of consultants at a cost of a couple hundred thousand dollars to comb through his report and find a flaw—anything to undermine his research. And when Thyne appeared at a public hearing, the trap was sprung.

In one figure in the report, he'd simplified a complicated statistical analysis for the public, and this graph became the singular topic of discussion. Although the rest of the findings were uncontested, he'd violated a statistical assumption, which was a legitimate concern. However, for four hours they focused solely on the flawed figure, never mentioning the contaminated sites. "That's when I became convinced that maybe I shouldn't stop talking in public," Thyne recalls.[10]

After he did an interview with National Public Radio, School of Mines officials decided that Thyne couldn't be silenced and told him that he wouldn't be reappointed. Thyne, however, had given an award-winning paper on his method for detecting groundwater contamination at a meeting of the American Association of Petroleum Geologists, which caught the eye of the Enhanced Oil Recovery Institute at the University of Wyoming. Perhaps industry figured that his relocation would keep him out of their hair in Colorado, where environmentalists were far busier than in their ultraconservative northern neighbor. Thyne was happy to be back in Laramie, where he'd earned his doctorate, and had no plans to go anywhere near "the whole fracking thing." But the best-laid plans sometimes go astray.

Understanding just how Thyne's new research program functioned in terms of its corporate connections and funding model is a bit of a challenge. So,

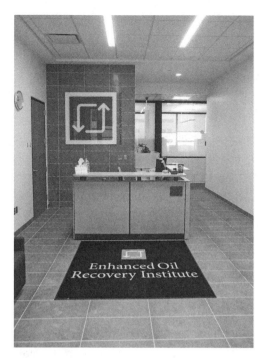

The entryway to the Enhanced Oil Recovery Institute (EORI) within the School of Energy Resources at the University of Wyoming. Overseen by a governor-appointed commission, EORI is legislatively mandated to assist energy companies in extracting "stranded oil" from reservoirs where conventional methods have taken easily obtained petroleum (photo by Jeffrey Lockwood).

imagine a small town where the primary source of income is apple orchards. The trees are so tall, however, that the townsfolk must rely on a multinational harvesting company that tears up the land while using enormous machines to pick apples on the outside of the trees—leaving four-fifths of the fruit behind. When the townspeople complain about the waste, the company says that the locals will have to use their meager income to fund an Augmented Apple Extraction Institute to develop a new machine to pick a bit more of the crop—otherwise, they'll just move on to the next valley. That's pretty much how the Enhanced Oil Recovery Institute (EORI) functions in Wyoming.

The Institute is embedded in, and reflects the workings and mission of, the University of Wyoming's School of Energy Resources (SER),[11] which was established in 2006, when then governor Dave Freudenthal worked closely with the legislature in allocating state funds to "initiate a major energy agenda for UW."[12] Twelve years earlier, the university had started its School and Institute of Environment and Natural Resources with a $40,000 budget; SER was initiated with three hundred times the support.[13] According to the president of the University of Wyoming Foundation, with the development of

SER "the university suddenly had immediate alignment with the state's energy industry"[14]—which was taken to be a good thing. In the following decade, the state invested $440 million in energy programs at the university, along with $60 million in private funds. By the institution's own accounting, 20 percent of the money provided by the legislature to the university had been plowed into energy-related ventures.[15]

In effect, the legislature used public money to build an enormous research and development center for the wealthiest business enterprises in human history—and then provided a dollar-for-dollar match when companies pumped in $150 million to fund ventures of particular value to them. The architect for the massive new SER building worked hard to create a sense of environmental sensitivity in a structure devoted almost exclusively to fossil fuels, incorporating planters out front with trees and an interior featuring barnwood paneling along with incongruously sleek Scandinavian accents, as well as other greenwash touches.

Governor Freudenthal was at that time a key player in promoting corporate welfare. A lawyer by training, he was an expert in converting political power into cash. Shortly after leaving office, he signed on with a major international law firm representing the energy industry, joined the board of Arch Coal at a salary of $186,000, and taught a seminar on energy, law and economics for three semesters at the University of Wyoming's College of Law for a salary of $150,000.[16] He continued to work behind the scenes to funnel resources into the university's energy-related programs based on his philosophy that "we need to have a university that matches our economy."[17]

Most of the scientists in SER are devoted to coal, oil, and gas, while a council dominated by the fossil fuel industry oversees the organization.[18] The director of EORI insists that industry does not "influence the outcomes of the research."[19] However, there's no doubt that industry decides what questions are asked—and which lines of inquiry languish.

After the School of Mines decided to dismiss Thyne, he was hired by EORI to research how changing the chemistry of the water injected into aging petroleum reservoirs could improve the flow of oil. His expertise complemented EORI's singular purpose.[20] The initial surge of easily obtained oil from a new field represents about 20 percent of a reservoir. After skimming the cream, the energy company moves on to a new site. "That's the glamour; that's where the money is," explains Thyne.[21] The oil that's left behind requires sophisticated technologies to extract, and only another 10 percent can be economically recovered. So companies balk at developing these methods.

David Mohrbacher, the director of EORI, is a burly, well-groomed fellow who exudes self-confidence. He strongly defended his program, which is entirely paid for by the people of Wyoming: "We've generated around 20 million barrels of incremental oil, which would translate to about $160 million in increased revenue and severance taxes, and we've spent $3 million a year. So simple math says the state netted $130 million."[22] It's a sweet deal for an industry to have its research and development programs funded by the state. Moreover, if a technique works for a particular company, the information can be declared confidential as an enticement to do business with EORI.[23] In effect, the public pays to generate industrial trade secrets.

Although Mohrbacher had worked for major companies, he had a soft spot for what he called "the little guys," which he exemplified with companies that didn't seem particularly diminutive, including BreitBurn Energy ($876 million in acquisitions) and Merit Energy Company ($5.5 billion in acquisitions), along with True Oil and Wold Oil Properties (namesakes of two of the wealthiest families in Wyoming).[24] However, Anadarko Petroleum, with nearly $15 billion in annual sales, is also a beneficiary of EORI.[25] Mohrbacher's program touted having goals that "align with the oil industry's priorities and values."[26]

Alignment is the name of the game. The commission that oversaw EORI included the governor and a state senator who was an oil and gas drilling contractor from energy-rich Fremont County. The technical advisory board had representatives from Anadarko, ConocoPhillips, and Marathon.[27] And amid all of this power and money, Mohrbacher hewed to the notion that EORI was untainted: "We want to maintain our third-party objectivity."[28]

Whatever was meant by "the little guys," Mohrbacher took pride in Wyoming's being a major player: "The governor's office, when I first got here, showed us being number one in coal production in the US, number two in the gas production, number seven in oil, number one in uranium, and in the top five of wind. . . . If we were an independent country, we'd be one of the top ten energy producers in the world and our peers would be Mexico and Norway."[29] But there are small annoyances in the world of big energy.

In 2011 the Niobrara Shale in southeastern Wyoming was supposed to be the next big thing—a humongous expanse of prospective oil fields that would feed corporations with profits and the government with severance taxes. However, the oil was trapped in rock, which meant fracking, which meant trouble.

The *Wyoming Tribune Eagle* dug into the environmental risks of the pending boom. The story described "pumping millions of gallons of water, sand and a concentration of chemicals" into the ground, noting, "Typically, only 30 percent of these chemically laced fluids are recovered from the formation."[30] State officials offered carefully hedged reassurances:

> "I am *pretty assured* all the way that there won't be any path back to the surface for this fluid," says Tom Doll, supervisor of the Wyoming Oil and Gas Conservation Commission. . . . John Wagner, administrator of the Water Quality Division of the Wyoming DEQ [Department of Environmental Quality], adds, "That's not to say that anything couldn't happen. But there's a very wide vertical separation that is *pretty protective. As long as it's done right, people shouldn't be too concerned.*"[31]

When Thyne was contacted by Shauna Stephenson, a reporter from the *Tribune Eagle* who was asking about the well hole connecting groundwater to the fractured rock thousands of feet below, he felt obligated to provide his expertise. He was quoted as saying, "Casing can leak; cement can leak."[32] He hastened to explain that 99 percent of wells were properly constructed, which should've pacified industry. But it wasn't what Thyne was quoted as saying that put him in the corporate crosshairs; it was an unattributed photo caption.

The reporter asked Thyne how much water would be needed for fracking, but he was reluctant to provide a specific estimate without knowing the actual geological properties of the Niobrara Shale and the number of fracks planned for each well. When pressed, he offered a range of figures based on the available scientific literature.[33] Stephenson assured him that his name wouldn't be associated with the numbers and then reported the worst-case scenario. The newspaper story included a picture of a pump jack with the caption: "The energy industry has 150 permits to drill in Laramie County and it could take between 48 to 70 million gallons of water to drill and frack one well over its litfetime [sic]."[34]

The university's vice president for government communication and community affairs e-mailed the directors of SER and EORI to notify them that

A typical fracking operation requires two to eight million gallons of water (along with 40,000 gallons of various, often toxic, chemicals, including acids, alcohols, salts, and heavy metals). The outpouring of tainted waste water is dumped into lined evaporation pits. Behind the pit can be seen the drill rig and tanks that provide fracturing fluid for the drilling (photo by Ted Wood).

Noble Energy (a Houston-based oil and gas company with $3.8 billion in annual revenues)[35] and the Petroleum Association of Wyoming were on the warpath, having traced the offending figure to EORI. Amid a flurry of e-mails, Thyne explained to the frenzied administrators that he'd "made the comments based on my experience as a member of the scientific advisory board for the current EPA hydraulic fracturing study. . . . I told [the reporter], EORI is not involved in fracking and I do not represent EORI or UW in any capacity when discussing fracking. . . . I would be happy if someone has better numbers based on actual data from the Niobrara. . . . I used the most recent data from the Apache frack in Canada."[36] In response, Thyne was informed that he'd been summoned to a gathering of university officials and industry representatives. Before the meeting, Mohrbacher told Thyne that Noble Gas had extracted his name from the *Tribune Eagle*. Mohrbacher was nonplussed by industry's strong-arm tactics and the newspaper's lack of ethics, but Thyne felt betrayed.[37]

In fact, Stephenson was never contacted by the industry, contrary to their claims. Rather, the Petroleum Association of Wyoming evidently squeezed the name from an editor. When asked if she would've revealed her source, Stephenson took a deep breath and said enigmatically, "Energy is a power to reckon with." She contended that Thyne's numbers were consistent with values offered by other experts she'd interviewed. As for choosing the high-end values, she said, "We were looking at potential effects. It's a scary business when you can't talk about possibilities."[38]

At this point, Thyne wasn't intimidated, even though he'd worked for industry and had a sense of what he was up against. He knew of the energy companies' sense of privilege and entitlement and described their view thus: "we are going to give the United States energy independence; we are the most critical people in this country, and we cannot be impeded in any way."[39] Thyne says he now understands their willingness to silence dissent: "The energy industry's strategy is not to steer around a bump in the road but to bring in a grader followed by a steamroller." And if the bump can't be scraped away, he notes that it can be paved over by funding university institutes "that are so intimately connected they can spread no other message than the one industry wants."[40]

It would've been easy to pick out the "bump" at the meeting of university and industry executives. Thyne was the athletic-looking guy with wire-rimmed glasses, a salt-and-pepper beard, and no suit. The Petroleum Association of Wyoming—a major political supporter whose members were beneficiaries of EORI—was represented by Jonathan Ekstrom of Noble Energy and Jody Levin from a lobbying and public relations firm. The university contributed two vice presidents and the directors of the School of Energy Resources and EORI.[41] After initial pleasantries, Ekstrom got down to business and told Thyne that he was wrong about the amount of water that would be used for fracking the Niobrara Shale. As a scientist, Thyne said that being wrong was an occupational hazard—and then he asked for the data. The industry representative simply insisted that Thyne was off by an order of magnitude and offered no evidence.

Exasperated by the fruitless back-and-forth, Thyne asked, "So is there something you guys want?" Ekstrom demanded that he write a retraction. Thyne replied that he would repeat that his statements didn't represent the university, but without data he wasn't going to change his mind about the water demands. He understood that he wasn't endearing himself to the attendees, but he also knew that the industry had information on water requirements, as well as the components of fracking fluids and the chemistry of water wells near gas fields, all of which they kept secret.[42]

The energy industry had drawn a line in the sand. Scientists were about to see what happens to troublemakers. But to understand the ultimate fate of an irksome researcher, it's essential to grasp the ways in which energy corporations wield power in Wyoming.

When asked about external pressure, the director of EORI gives the university's party line: "I haven't been told by anybody what to do because of politics." But it's difficult to stay on message when the message is unbelievable. When pressed, Mohrbacher lets slip that when an oil company is unhappy, "we're in deep shit immediately because they all call their state senator." In a state with a population less than that of Akron, Ohio, political connections assure that power plays happen fast. Or, as Mohrbacher put it, "The closure time is remarkably small, kind of like the speed of a bullet."[43]

Morhbacher's boss is Mark Northam, the former Saudi Aramco executive and director of the School of Energy Resources. Northam has worked hard to get the School aligned with the Saudis, bringing along the Wyoming governor on a junket in 2013.[44] He has been ruthless in suppressing dissent, hiring an off-duty police officer to evict troublemakers from a fracking conference and then personally heckling a presenter who recounted a drilling disaster.[45] Northam maintains that those who provide money to the university rightly expect to "control messages that the university sends."[46] At the university, speech is not free—it's bought and paid for by the energy industry.

Consider just one of the major companies pumping money into the School of Energy Resources. Arch Coal was there at the birth of SER, with two of their corporate executives on the governing council. The company's vice president of western affairs is a former University of Wyoming trustee. When Arch Coal dumped a $1.5 million "gift" into the Clean Coal Technology Center, the state matched the contribution with public monies.[47] The legislature had already put $17 million into clean coal research, presumably because the corporate giant couldn't fund its own research and development (Arch Coal had $4.2 billion in revenue in 2012).[48] And the Wyoming governor's seat wasn't even cool by the time Dave Freudenthal left office in 2011 and joined the board of Arch Coal for nearly twice his public salary.

The university's trustees understood power. In March 2013 the governor appointed Dave True to the university's board of trustees. True is a joint owner and senior manager for the True companies—a massive conglomerate of enterprises involved in oil and gas trucking and pipelines, oil-field equipment, drilling operations, and crude oil exploration, production, marketing, and trading.[49]

Quite appropriately, True Oil has benefited substantially and directly from EORI research (True's brother is on the Institute's Technical Advisory Board).[50] Thyne affirms that while employed by EORI he "did work for the benefit of True Oil [and] I know of projects with direct benefit to True that yielded . . . advice of direct economic impact."[51]

But quite unbelievably, after being appointed as a university trustee, Dave True filed a disclosure statement declaring, "I am aware of no actual, apparent or potential conflict of interest (including known interests of my family members)."[52] Northam described True's prevarication (his company clearly benefited from EORI, a direct conflict of interest with his role as a university trustee) as nothing more than "an oversight." No other university administrator rushed to the defense of the trustee.[53]

Rather ironically, the founder of True Oil (Dave True's father) is quoted on the company's website as saying, "I have always considered integrity and ethics to be the most important part of a business decision."[54] Even more incongruously, True gave a lecture to his fellow trustees on "cowboy ethics," which evidently included the admonition to "remember that some things aren't for sale"—although just what these things might be is not terribly clear.[55]

True mirrored the conflict of interest found in the state legislature. In 2012 state senator Kit Jennings proposed legislation that would have favored a natural gas extraction method being developed by only two firms—one being the business paying him as a Washington lobbyist. Feeling pressure from energy companies disadvantaged by the political machinations, no other lawmaker signed on. The bill was withdrawn, and there were no consequences for Jennings—a lesson about the abuse of power that he learned well, as we shall see later.[56]

Despite dramatically declining fossil fuel revenues, as of 2016 the University of Wyoming continued its attempts to secure $115 million to bolster its College of Engineering and Applied Science to provide energy companies with even better and cheaper research and development, as well as employee training—the largest single venture in the university's history.[57] The effort began when Governor Mead assembled a task force to direct the institution's

effort to tap the bank accounts of wealthy industrialists, corporate foundations, and energy companies—and to determine the programs that will be at
the end of the funding pipeline. The group's cochairs were Freudenthal (the
coalcuddling ex-governor) and Chad Deaton, the executive chairman of Baker
Hughes, one of the world's largest oil-field service companies. The rest of the
body was dominated by the likes of executive vice presidents from Shell,
Encana, and the Hess Corporation (a Fortune 100 oil and gas company). In
their initial report, the task force proposed that the university identify a few
areas of comparative advantage: "We have a bias for the energy industry but
believe strongly other niches are certainly appropriate."[58]

In February 2013 the dean of the College of Engineering and Applied Science underwent a review that revealed strong support by his faculty but
included an ominous allusion to his relationship with the governor's task
force: "Some were of the opinion that the demands of the Governor's Task
Force may have exposed a weakness in the Dean's stewardship of the college."[59] Six months later the dean, a civil engineer, resigned and was replaced
by a petroleum engineer from Oklahoma State University.[60]

When a respected dean can be tagged for removal by virtue of having
failed to show proper deference to the likes of Freudenthal, Deaton, and True,
things can't look good for a mere scientist such as Thyne. Although True was
appointed to the board of trustees after Thyne's fate had been sealed, it's
worth noting that the oil man is on the board of directors of the Petroleum
Association of Wyoming—the organization that had the scientist in their
sights when the university pulled the trigger.[61]

CHAPTER 5

Reloaded and Fired Again

Geoffrey Thyne was in trouble. Readers of the *Wyoming Tribune Eagle* might have inferred that this researcher was representing the University of Wyoming (he wasn't) and that he knew what he was talking about when he provided information about fracking (he did).[1] The energy industry and its university supporters found this intolerable. The Petroleum Association of Wyoming took the untenable position that after their interrogation of Thyne, "he took it upon himself to write a letter to the paper."[2] In fact, Thyne was ordered by his boss, David Morhbacher (director of the Enhanced Oil Recovery Institute) and his boss's boss, Mark Northam (director of the School of Energy Resources) to write a letter stating that Thyne did not represent their organizations—and that he was wrong.[3]

Northam's initial concern about freedom of speech quickly faded and he told Thyne, "I will edit your letter and you will sign it. You shouldn't have said anything and don't say anything ever again."[4] The director rewrote the letter, striking references to Thyne's expertise about fracking and allusions to human error in fracking, and spotlighting the safety of industry. Thyne relented to the changes, but he refused to retract his estimates of water usage by the energy industry.

Of course, the university's anxiety and the industry's apoplexy weren't of much interest to the paper, and the letter was never printed. There's really nothing newsworthy about a scientist not speaking for his institution and not changing his mind. But there was something extremely newsworthy about groundwater contaminated with fracking chemicals—and this story was grabbing headlines.

Pavillion is a town of 231 stalwart souls living in the desolate reaches of the Big Horn Basin in central Wyoming. The farming and ranching community sits atop an unusually shallow natural gas field that has been belching methane into the water supply since the 1880s. However, in 2008 it begun to burp up industrial toxins.

Natural gas extraction in the area began in 1960, with Encana purchasing the rights to the fossil fuel in 2004. Shortly after the company started fracking, local residents complained about the quality of their drinking water, which triggered a series of tests by the company, the Wyoming Department of Environmental Quality (DEQ), and eventually the US Environmental Protection Agency (EPA). In 2011 the EPA released a report that linked fracking to Pavillion's groundwater contamination.[5]

The industry denied all responsibility. Encana insisted that the cocktail of chemicals, including thirteen used in fracking, had leaked from production pits that the company inherited as part of its acquisition. Under pressure by industry allies in the US Congress (including the former ranking member of the Senate Environment and Public Works Committee), the EPA turned tail. The agency passed the whole matter over to the state of Wyoming, which teamed up with Encana to conduct further investigations.[6]

While the Wyoming Department of Environmental Quality worked with a private consulting firm to dismiss any link between fracking and groundwater contamination,[7] a 2016 scientific study reported that chemicals used in fracking fluids were also in the aquifer, leaving no doubt that improperly cemented gas wells were the source of contamination (the technical journal used seven experts to review the work, rather than the normal two).[8] Encana continued to deny the veracity of peer-reviewed science and expected the state of Wyoming to fall in line. This would be more shocking if the story wasn't being echoed two thousand miles to the east.

Dimock Township is to Pennsylvania as Pavillion is to Wyoming—a sparsely populated area sitting atop an enormous supply of natural gas. In both places, Encana was busy fracking while explaining away flammable water. In Dimock, the folks also complained about contaminated water, but little was done until an elderly lady's well exploded and authorities subsequently sampled homes throughout the area and found methane at high, but not "unsafe," levels (at least in terms of drinking the water—fire balls being another matter).[9]

The company blamed a cracked pipe, the EPA retreated (again under political pressure), and drilling resumed. When researchers found methane-contaminated groundwater throughout the region, the industry asserted that the gas was naturally occurring from shallow sources, despite chemical evidence that the methane had come from deep underground.[10]

A cloak of censorship descended on Pennsylvania. The corporations paid off families driven from their homes by methane and industrial chemicals, but only if they signed lifetime nondisclosure agreements complete with nondisparagement clauses (a kind of legal censorship that precluded the plaintiffs from saying anything negative about the companies).[11] Meanwhile the state legislature required companies to reveal the chemicals used in fracking—unless the companies decided the information constituted trade secrets. And when physicians treating potentially poisoned residents were provided with the names of the industrial toxins, the doctors were prohibited from sharing the information with their own patients, other physicians, or the community.[12]

As Thyne put it, "The companies insist there has never been a proven case where fracking has been a problem. So why do they buy people out and make them sign nondisclosures?"[13] But his rhetorical questions weren't what pinned a target on Thyne's back—it was his precise answers.

In the Fort Worth suburbs of Parker County, Texas, drinking water began bubbling like champagne with the onset of fracking. By 2012 the gas had been identified as methane, the energy companies had painted themselves as

Hydraulic fracturing of rocks to release natural gas and oil is a method used throughout the world. This operation is on the Bakken Shale of North Dakota. The profitability of this extraction method is undeniable, but the contamination and depletion of groundwater, noise pollution, degradation of air quality, and triggering of earthquakes are potential costs (photo by Joshua Doubek, Wikimedia Commons).

the victims of a witch hunt, state officials had rushed to the defense of the persecuted industry, and the EPA had abandoned its investigation.[14]

All of this should sound familiar, except that this time Geoffrey Thyne was a key player. Functioning as a consultant for the EPA, a role allowed by the university, he conducted the chemical analyses and directly linked the methane in the water supply to the nearby fracking operations. The company responsible for the contamination dismissed Thyne as being anti-industry, as if this refuted the science of geochemistry.[15] Six months later, he was facing the wrath of Wyoming's energy companies.

With the gas industry's agenda disrupted in Texas and its authority challenged in Wyoming, the problem scientist had to be dealt with. Thyne was called into Mohrbacher's office and told, "We're not going to renew your contract." When Thyne asked for an explanation, his boss replied, "I don't have to tell you why." He was right, having been tutored by the central administration. When Thyne suggested that the issue was being blown out of proportion, Mohrbacher became angry and gave the explanation that the scientist was seeking but that the university wanted to deny: "Mark Northam gets a lot of money from these oil companies and you are screwing with that."[16] Private honesty notwithstanding, the energy industry and the institution worked hard to shape the public story of Thyne's dismissal.[17]

The *Boulder Weekly* caught wind of the former Colorado scientist getting the boot in Wyoming and started asking questions. The newspaper put the obvious interpretation up front: "It's likely that when an EORI staffer says something that upsets the industry the institute serves, it's a problem."[18] Thyne was the first-ever EORI scientist to be fired, so the paper asked the Petroleum Association of Wyoming about its influence at the university. John Robitaille, vice president of the association, admitted that his organization had "a conversation" about Thyne's estimates of the amount of water used in fracking, saying, "we felt it was necessary to correct those figures, which never happened." But Robitaille denied any role in Thyne's dismissal: "We don't have any reason to get into any of their [the university's] personnel issues." When he was asked whether a major donor or funding source could persuade the university to stop its faculty or staff from doing something, Robitaille stuck by his untenable position, saying, "I don't believe so."[19]

Wyoming would starve without energy revenues, the caloric equivalent of trying to survive on a cheeseburger and diet soda as your only meal each day (two-thirds of Wyoming's state funds are derived from energy extraction). Likewise, the University of Wyoming would go hungry without state funding—nearly three-quarters of the university's base funding comes from the state.[20] How could anyone believe that industry lacked the power to silence an untenured scientist who was creating problems?

Mohrbacher had no respect for the intelligence of the faculty or the readers of the *Boulder Weekly* either. He maintained that "the reason for not renewing [Thyne's] contract was not related to his participation with the press. . . . It was based on EORI achieving their technical, strategic objectives. We chose a different way to go."[21] This explanation was nearly as implausible as Robitaille's denial. Altering injection-water chemistry to enhance the flow of oil was Thyne's expertise, and this remained a strategic focus of EORI after his dismissal. Contrary to Mohrbacher's claim of changing course, EORI continued to pursue this objective, according to their own website (ironically, Thyne wrote the text EORI featured on its website to explain and justify this research).[22]

At first, Thyne was reluctant to connect the dots. As a hardheaded scientist, he wasn't one for persecution complexes and conspiracy theories. But in time he understood why the commissioners overseeing EORI offered no comments or questions when Mohrbacher "revealed" Thyne's dismissal. They already knew.

The payoff for industry went far beyond getting rid of a misbehaving scientist. Thyne's dismissal had a chilling effect among EORI researchers, who all had one-year, at-will contracts. "I know my colleagues got the message," Thyne says. "'You want to be like him?'"[23] The risks of a brazen act of censorship were more than offset by the benefits to the academic-industrial complex.

Not satisfied with being able to censor researchers at the university, industry leaders in 2015 extended their capacity to silence dissent by convincing the Wyoming legislature to pass a sweeping law prohibiting citizens from collecting data on "open land" outside of towns and subdivisions without permission of the landowner.[24] In theory, you would face a stiff fine for taking photographs without permission in Yellowstone National Park if you intended to share the images with the state or federal government (e.g., documenting a dangerous bridge or a rare bird). But the real concern was that citizen scientists would collect environmental samples or census wildlife populations on private, state, or federal lands and then use the information to draw attention to problems and petition the government to take action. The legislation was led by the agricultural industry, which didn't want people figuring out bacteria loads downstream from public land grazing allotments. However, the energy industry also would stand to gain by keeping people from monitoring air, water, soil, and wildlife.

An ongoing case against an environmental activist who was charged under the new trespass law appeared to deflate the hopes of resource extraction industries. In a pretrial hearing, the judge ruled that punitive damages would not be allowed.[25] But he also refused to dismiss the case based on the defendant's claim that the case constituted a SLAPP (strategic lawsuit against public participation), intended to punish the defendant and intimidate others from engaging in environmental monitoring and advocacy. The judge had little capacity in this regard, since Wyoming lacks anti-SLAPP legislation.[26]

Justin Pidot, an attorney affiliated with the Western Watersheds Project—an organization with a keen interest in tracking water quality—contended that the law was blatantly unconstitutional because "it singles out speech about natural resources for burdensome regulation and makes it a crime to engage in a variety of expressive and artistic activities."[27] Environmental, animal welfare, and media groups filed suit in US District Court to challenge the law.[28] Pidot provides a stark indictment: "By enacting this law, the Wyoming legislature has expressed its disdain for the freedoms protected by the First Amendment." The result is an insidious silencing of public discourse: "The mere fact that you have a criminal statute that applies to this conduct sends a real chilling message to citizens."[29] The industry's payoff comes with this unsettling effect, as scientists and other citizens self-censor within private organizations, across state institutions, and throughout the nation's academic communities.

Katie Keranen, an assistant professor of geophysics at the University of Oklahoma, knew about self-censorship. Her research involved the relationship between fracking and earthquakes, and she confided, "I have to be careful what I say." She was not yet tenured in the university's ConocoPhillips School of Geology and Geophysics, where a $6 million investment by the company bought top billing, valuable research—and silence.[30] Nor was Keranen merely paranoid, as recently released e-mails reveal that billionaire oil man (and major donor) Harold Hamm told university officials that he wanted certain scientists dismissed who were studying the link between oil and gas development and the state's nearly four-hundred-fold increase in earth-quakes.[31] Even tenured faculty can be made miserable and their departments starved for resources, so it's safer to quietly avoid pursuing certain lines of inquiry, publishing controversial ideas, or speaking about politically danger-ous subjects.

How, then, are faculty supposed to behave? Ask Timothy Considine. He was involved in a string of pro-fracking studies published by the American Petroleum Institute, the Wyoming Mining Association, and the Cato Institute (founded by Charles and David Koch, who have spent millions to oppose cor-porate taxes, social services, industry oversight, and environmental regula-tion). The industry-funded disciple was safely ensconced at the University of Wyoming's School of Energy Resources when it came to light that he and colleagues had issued a report, wrongly described as "peer-reviewed," through the Shale Resources and Society Institute at SUNY Buffalo. The report failed to reveal his ties to the gas industry and touted the safety of drilling in Pennsylvania, when in reality the number of major violations had actually gone up.[32]

The SUNY institute had been formed when an influential player in the natural gas industry proposed that his colleague, a consultant with an abun-dance of industry connections and a shortage of academic credentials, be put in charge. And then the institute let the university know that if it so hap-pened to publish a favorable article, "they would attract additional resources from the gas industry."[33]

When the faculty of SUNY Buffalo expressed outrage at the corruption of their institution by industry, the board of trustees launched an investigation, and the university president closed the Shale Resources and Society Institute in order to salvage the university's reputation.[34] Entangled in the contro-versy, the University of Wyoming's administration worked hard to deflect criticism of corporate largesse: "We regard [industry's] willingness to fund our faculty's work as evidence of its relevance to real-world problems," said the provost.[35] Those problems, however, didn't include an exorbitant demand for water to frack the Niobrara Shale.

So where does Thyne's story fit into the academic-industrial complex that has arisen across the country? In the end, the companies drilling in south-eastern Wyoming were right about water—and wrong about oil. The unusual geology of the Niobrara Shale meant that fracking required much less water than was typical.[36] The industry had the data when they confronted Thyne (the state allows such information to be kept secret for eighteen months), but they weren't about to let their adversary set the terms. For the energy industry, being right was not as important as being powerful.

As for oil, the president of the Petroleum Association of Wyoming admitted that the boom "didn't pan out the way folks thought it would." In other words, it was a bust. Nevertheless, industry analysts insisted that "someday that place is going to be littered with oil rigs. . . . There's plenty of oil there, they're just trying to figure out how to get it out."[37]

We might imagine that Geoffrey Thyne was an exceptional case. Having created problems for frackers in Colorado, Texas, and Wyoming, perhaps he had it coming. But other scientists at the University of Wyoming stayed in their own backyard and still provoked the censorial wrath of the energy industry.

Larry Munn, a sagacious, down-to-earth soil scientist, and Ginger Paige, a spirited, no-nonsense water scientist, managed to incite the ire of the natural gas companies.[38] While fracturing shale was the key to extracting gas in southeastern Wyoming, coalbed methane was the goose laying the gaseous egg in the northeast. And while fracking pumps fluids into the ground, coalbed methane (CBM) extraction pumps water out of the earth to release the trapped gas. The problem is what to do with the "produced water," which is often loaded with salts.

In 2005 Munn and Paige—whose job descriptions included providing direct service to the people of the state—came to the aid of a rancher whose valuable bottomlands were about to be flooded. When these professors provided state authorities with evidence of the environmental damage of dumping CBM wastewater on the afflicted ranch, the Wyoming Department of Environmental Quality (DEQ) was incensed. The DEQ's water quality administrator lambasted the scientists for interfering with the work of a regulatory agency. Such a response raises the question of whom the DEQ serves. The answer became apparent when the agency began a review of their water quality standards later that year.

To revise their regulations, the DEQ assembled a committee that included two of their own, two industry consultants, and Paige. After one of the industry representatives subverted the process and convinced the DEQ to issue standards without involving the committee, Paige cried foul. When she insisted that neutral scientists review the new rules, the agency's environmental program manager turned bright red, pounded the table, and shouted, "This has nothing to do with science. It's all about policy!"[39]

While Paige was aggravating the regulators, Munn managed to outrage the energy industry by again fulfilling his duty to serve the public. He provided pro bono testimony for the plaintiffs in a case in which the court was deciding whether the Northern Cheyenne tribe was being harmed by CBM wastewater flowing onto their lands. The gas company lawyers were baffled when Munn explained to them that he was doing his job as a professor.[40]

Once Munn returned to campus, he was called into the provost's office and told that a legislator had contacted the university about the scientist's testimony and demanded his termination. Munn was assured by the administration that he wouldn't be fired because he was protected by academic freedom. However, the provost later maintained that Munn couldn't have been fulfilling his faculty duties because expert testimony was a form of consulting (although the university attorney was not able to produce a policy to that effect or provide a compelling rationale for the institution's position)—and academic freedom evaporated under such circumstances.[41] Setting aside the institution's evident confusion, which state legislator had the audacity to censor a university scientist on behalf of industry?

The best guess comes from the School of Energy Resources. When SER's director, Mark Northam, reported to the board his efforts to recruit faculty in 2012, Kit Jennings (the powerful state senator who tried to pass legislation favoring his own energy firm) recommended that new faculty be excluded from earning tenure. The state senator went on to explain that having asked top university officials to fire a tenured professor, he was disappointed to learn how difficult it was. When a reporter asked Jennings whom he'd wanted fired, the senator clammed up.[42] Larry Munn would be a good guess. Meanwhile, Paige was learning that Jennings was a big cog in a well-oiled political machine.

During Wyoming's natural gas boom in the first decade of this century, the industry was drilling 2,500 wells annually,[43] and the DEQ was allowing companies to dump the wastewater with abandon. Paige found herself in a no-win situation; a prolonged debate was almost as good as weak regulations for the industry. She had no doubt that DEQ was under orders from the governor's office, who was under pressure from the energy industry, to keep drilling permits flowing as freely as brine from CBM wells.[44] In other words, if the governor wanted to keep the companies happy and the state's coffers filled with severance taxes and mineral royalties, then his regulatory agencies had better not be interfering with the energy industry.

Thyne, Munn, and Paige are in good company. Faculty at Cornell and Duke Universities have also come under fire for their research on the CBM industry. In 2011 Anthony Ingraffea made headlines with a peer-reviewed study showing that using natural gas may be worse for global warming than burning coal, particularly if the rate of gas leakage exceeds 3 percent (the actual rate of loss is a matter of intense debate). He then went on to famously debunk a number of myths about fracking and natural gas. The American public was being duped into believing that fracking was a safe, long-standing, well-proven technology for extracting a clean fossil fuel.[45]

Unable to silence Ingraffea, the next best thing was to discredit him. An industry website posted pictures of the scientist's home and "revealed" that he was a consumer of natural gas, as if this somehow refuted his science.[46] The industry also twisted the words of Cornell administrators to suggest that the university supported fracking (the article actually said, "We cannot put this genie back in the bottle"—hardly a ringing endorsement).[47]

A few months later, Duke University professor Robert Jackson authored a peer-reviewed study linking gas drilling to methane contamination of water and homes across five counties in Pennsylvania.[48] Jackson and his colleagues detected markedly elevated levels of methane in wells near fracking sites, and their analysis showed that the methane had come from deep underground. The industry attacked the scientists' credibility and pointed out that the investigation had failed to find fracking fluids in the water (the incoherence of both dismissing the researchers and embracing their study evidently didn't occur to corporate PR departments).[49] It is true that toxic chemicals weren't found, but this is tantamount to declaring to a TSA agent that your luggage is safe because although it is filled with explosive gas, there are no poisons inside.

The question of how to understand the obligations and allegiances of our public institutions, particularly America's universities, which have long been held as sources of reliable information, is increasingly urgent. And the answer is all the more troubling when we consider the role of corporations—the energy industry being an exemplary case—in shaping research and teaching.

The Department of Geology and Geophysics is one of the oldest and most renowned academic strengths at the University of Wyoming. Although many of the senior faculty are involved in basic studies, the greatest growth has been in economic geology, particularly in fields such as petroleum geology, with funding from the School of Energy Resources (photo by Jeffrey Lockwood).

The University of Wyoming restarted its petroleum engineering program in 2006 and saw the number of majors increase nearly tenfold in the next eight years, while national enrollments in this field increased by 250 percent.[50] With petroleum engineering being the most lucrative undergraduate degree in the country, students and money were pouring in.[51] So while legislatures were cutting funding to public universities, industry was on a buying spree.

For pennies on the dollar, energy companies have convinced universities and colleges to shift their dwindling public monies into subsidizing corporate educational programs. Rather than employees being paid to receive on-the-job training, they are paying for their own training at public institutions such as New Mexico's San Juan College, North Dakota's Williston State, and Utah's Uintah Basin Applied Technology College.[52]

The enticements to align with corporate education and research objectives include industry payments of $49 million to the South Dakota School of Mines, $30 million to Colorado State University, $25 million to Colorado School of Mines, and $10 million to the University of North Dakota, to name a few.[53] Administrators saw no problem with cutting these deals. The vice president of research at the University of Wyoming viewed energy extraction as simply and unconditionally good for an institution that depended on state revenues. He maintained that what benefited industry benefited the public, shrugging off concerns of impropriety: "Wyoming is Wyoming."[54]

Universities have bought into the business metaphor (the University of Wyoming refers to its president as the "chief executive officer"),[55] with their quasi-private foundations functioning as a sales force.[56] So when a buyer offers a few million dollars, the salesman takes his commission, promises a customized product, and tells the factory to crank out the goods. But to conceive of educational institutions—or hospitals, fire departments, or social service agencies—as being businesses is to make a tragic mistake. College art departments are not profit centers, school lunch programs are not money-making ventures, and state-funded research institutes are not shills for the energy industry.

And so universities disguise backroom deals that citizens might view as using their tax dollars to subsidize the wealthiest business enterprises on earth. The universities and their foundations tout the money as "gifts" or "donations," rather than as down payments for programs that result in the public paying the mortgage. Sometimes the charade fails and the corporate minions are exposed. Consider the failure of the University of Wyoming's Timothy Considine to disclose his connections to the gas industry while declaring that fracking was safe in the report from the Shale Resources and Society Institute at SUNY Buffalo.

Or consider the desperate effort of SUNY Buffalo's dean of arts and sciences to avoid answering questions about whether the institute had received industry funding. First the dean said that there was no such financial tie, but when pressed he said, "you've asked a question that's a complicated sort of issue" and proceeded to not give an answer.[57] Consider the lame excuses that the chancellor of the SUNY system gave for why university foundations, such as the one that evidently funded Considine's work, needed to keep the identities of their corporate backers secret: "[Donors] have people competing for their money."[58] Not to mention that money laundering through foundations formalizes the tactics of willful ignorance and plausible deniability by university administrations. Not to single out New York, consider the University of Texas, where the director of their Energy Institute conveniently failed to mention his $2 million stake in a gas company when his organization produced a whitewash of fracking.[59] And the list goes on. The undermining of academic integrity and the shaping of speech is not limited to the United States. Oxford, Cambridge, Manchester, and Imperial College London are busy cashing checks from industry, passing out honorary degrees to senior executives from BP and Shell, and hosting putatively academic talks that amount to corporate advertisements by company insiders.[60]

Advertising has always been part of the game. However, the energy industry didn't stop at trumpeting its message; corporations now silenced their critics. Drowning out alternative views is a dubious tactic in the marketplace of ideas, but gagging your opponent undermines the foundations of our democracy. The American Association of University Professors puts the problem in stark terms: "Where the financial resources of an academic department are dominated by a corporation there is the potential, no matter how elaborate the safeguards for respecting academic freedom and the independence of researchers, for weakening peer review both in research and in promotion and tenure decisions, for distorting the priorities of undergraduate and graduate education, and for compromising scientific openness."[61]

Shauna Stephenson, the reporter who interviewed Geoffrey Thyne and unwittingly provided the ammunition that the energy industry needed to dispatch their nemesis, framed the concern for free speech in terms of the public good. She regretted what happened to Thyne but even more what it means for society. When she was in journalism school, "Academia was supposed to be on its own shelf," she said wistfully. "Not anymore." As for her effort to understand the implications of fracking, Stephenson offered an understated assessment typical of Wyomingites: "The idea that academics are beholden to people with a profit motive is not a good place to be."[62]

Thyne is now a consulting geochemist and doing reasonably well. Having been blackballed from academic positions, he's unsure where Stephenson or others can go for unbiased information. In his experience, federal agencies and state regulators operate within strict, political imperatives. He considers what happened to him at the Colorado School of Mines and the University of Wyoming as vivid instances of the energy industry's "distorting and subverting" the mission of public institutions.[63]

Now that self-censorship is not a part of his job description, Thyne has begun to speak out. The energy industry cost him his job but ironically gave him his freedom. As he explained in an interview with Josh Fox, director of the Oscar-nominated documentary *Gasland*, being hunted by corporations drove him into the open.[64] He insists that his science is solid and is more than happy to go toe-to-toe with critics in the way of all good researchers.

Thyne continues to frame his life in terms of his duty to repay society for his years of public education and sees his growing activism as fulfilling that obligation. In a reflective moment, he paraphrases the ancient wisdom of Plato: "The price good men pay for indifference to public affairs is to be ruled by evil men."

In a chilling way, 2011 was a watershed year for censorship, leaving no doubt as to the collusion between industrialists and politicians. One month after the *Wyoming Tribune Eagle* ran their story about fracking, the state's largest newspaper announced, "Wyoming Legislators Support Plans to Convert Natural Gas, Coal to Gasoline." The former story was Thyne's professional death knell, the cost of speaking to the press about the downsides of fracking. The latter story led the director of a rural, higher education center to write letters to the editor of his small-town newspaper questioning the wisdom of a coal-to-gas plant. Although covert (if poorly disguised) acts of censorship were becoming part of Wyoming's culture, few people could've imagined that these letters would lead the county commission to publicly demand that the education center director who opposed Big Energy be silenced—or fired.

The Case of
the Carbon County Controversy

If liberty means anything,
it means the right to tell people
what they do not want to hear.

—GEORGE ORWELL

CHAPTER 6

Silencing Dissent in Coal Country

If the middle of nowhere had a marker, it might well be a pair of concrete pads the size of a double-car driveway in front of a suburban home. They're set amid sunbaked rocks and leathery sagebrush outside of Medicine Bow, Wyoming, a town made famous as the setting of Owen Wister's *The Virginian*.[1] Like the western tale, the story behind those two slabs involves far greater wealth and power than the desolate landscape would suggest.

When a person is heading west across Wyoming on Interstate 80, Carbon County is the gateway to the Red Desert. Vast stretches of scoria-crusted, alkali flats are virtually devoid of plant life, and the gray-green sagebrush is dwarfed by the winds that whip up blinding ground blizzards in winter and suck the moisture from the soil in summer. This is also the location of the state penitentiary, where people joke that escapees take one look at what's outside the wall and climb back into the prison.

Fewer than sixteen thousand people live in this southern county of nearly eight thousand square miles (about the area of New Jersey). Most of the folks are white (95 percent) and few of them are college educated (17 percent have a bachelor's degree). While there's a treasure chest of energy resources, including fossil fuels, uranium, and wind, not much of that treasure is held by the residents of the county, whose per capita income of $27,962 is lower than any state in the nation (Mississippi is the lowest at $33,073).[2]

But the people, or at least the ones who choose to stay, love their homely homeland. One resident insisted, "This a fun place to live. You fish and hunt. If you get sick of people, drive over any hill."[3] While it's not a pretty place, there is an enchanting, austere beauty in all that emptiness.

The first town in the county was Carbon, established in 1868 and abandoned twenty years later when the coal ran out. Today, the political hub and county seat is the town of Rawlins, population 9,203. If Rawlins is the figurative company town for the region's fossil fuel industry, just ten miles to the east is the literal company town of Sinclair. Named for the oil company, the houses are overseen by a superstructure of refinery towers, tangled pipes, and enormous tanks that rise like a postapocalyptic movie set. In recent years, Sinclair has become known for its spectacular industrial accidents and hefty fines. The refinery exemplifies Wyoming's dismal worker safety record.[4] In 2009 three million gallons of fuel spilled and ten thousand pounds of hydrogen sulfide gas were released; three fires in 2011 led to evacuations but no injuries; and six workers were burned by flash fires in 2012.[5]

None of the towns in Carbon County are wealthy, but the eastern part of the county is in dire economic straits. One community leader put the situation in stark terms: "Medicine Bow and Elk Mountain are struggling. They can't keep their kids. You graduate from high school over in Hanna, and then what are you going to do? If you want to earn a living, you're going to have to go to work in the mines, and if you don't want to do that, you're screwed."[6]

This brings us back to Medicine Bow, its 283 stalwart souls, and those two concrete slabs. The pads might be a pair of forlorn parking spaces awaiting the arrival of semi trucks, except that the nearest highway is five miles to the north. In fact, the concrete was poured in 2010 by DKRW Advanced Fuels. It represents either ground zero of what will be the first coal-to-liquid (CTL) conversion plant in the nation or a cynical token of the Wyoming Industrial Siting Council's requirement that construction begin within two years of their granting the permit.[7]

Like *The Virginian*, the tale of DKRW is supposed to be a classic Western with a bit of conflict and a happy ending. Their $2 billion facility will provide clean fuel to America and lucrative jobs for Carbon County. At least that's the company's story. But there's another, murky tale.

"I am writing this letter in hopes you will stop his foolish, self-serving attempt to cast doubt on the DKRW project which is very important to Carbon County, The state of Wyoming, and out [sic] entire country. . . . Please address this issue with Dr. Throgmorton as it is very important to the way we in Carbon County appear to the rest of the world."[8] This letter from the Carbon County commissioners demanding that the board of the county's Higher Education Center censor their director was sent on May 1, 2012. The irony of their view that obstructing industry would be more shameful than suppressing speech was not lost on Gilbert Archuleta, the self-effacing chair of the board who played a pivotal role in what eventually transpired. When interviewed, the county commissioners agreed that their chairman, Terry Weickum, wrote the letter—hence the use of "I" in the text. However, their stories diverge when it comes to the conversation that culminated in all three

These two concrete pads, poured in late 2010 a few miles from Medicine Bow, Wyoming, are the only physical evidence yet of DKRW's project, which was first announced in 2004. The coal-to-liquid refinery will purportedly produce more than four million barrels of low-sulfur gasoline each year, based on a process that has never been commercially employed in the United States (photo by Allen Best).

signing the document. How a group of elected officials came to publicly call for silencing a critic of a major energy project is important in understanding censorship in contemporary America. This chunk of Wyoming might seem to be geographically isolated and culturally unique, but every state has at least one Carbon County.

Exactly what the commissioners expected to happen isn't entirely evident, although their target was obvious. David Throgmorton is a slightly rumpled, soft-spoken, gracefully graying academic with an incisive wit whose politics fit into Rawlins about as well as the ballet would fit into the state penitentiary south of town. He grew up in Cheyenne, attended Casper College (one of the seven community colleges in Wyoming that complement the state's sole four-year university in Laramie), and eventually earned a doctorate in sociology from the University of Illinois. He returned to Wyoming to direct the

Higher Education Center in Rawlins after an academic and administrative odyssey took him from the Bible Belt of Louisiana to rural Iowa to the outskirts of Chicago; from a funky nonprofit in a Colorado hamlet to the sunshine of California. Throgmorton signs his correspondence "Pax" (meaning "peace")—except for his regular column in the *Rawlins Daily Times*.

It was a series of these columns, along with letters to the editor of the *Casper Star-Tribune* (the state's largest newspaper), that incited the commissioners. Throgmorton was asking some very unsettling questions about DKRW's project. Although one of the politicians admitted that they'd discussed the possibility that Throgmorton would be fired by his board[9] (grossly underestimating the gumption of the chairman), the commissioners have since offered kinder and gentler interpretations of their aspirations: "The letter was intended to be a statement of support for potentially 2,000-plus construction jobs and 400-plus permanent jobs in an extremely economically depressed region of Carbon County, and an undetermined amount of tax revenue for our county and state of Wyoming."[10] However, if the commissioners' purpose was to express support for industry (which is served by the Higher Education Center's training programs), it's not clear why they didn't simply do so without making threats.

The commissioners could make life easier or harder for just about any public entity in the county. So when Terry Weickum said of the Higher Education Center's director, "it would be a good idea just to keep your mouth shut until you know what you're talking about,"[11] then the implications were clear for an organization that had plans for a new campus at the edge of town.

When pressed, the commissioners begrudgingly admitted that they had tried to suppress free speech—an uncomfortable admission for political conservatives who claimed to defend constitutional rights. But their position was that Throgmorton was crying "Fire!" in a crowded theater, and they feared DKRW would find a venue with a more appreciative audience. As one commissioner put it, "We thought that it was an abuse of that power—the power of the pen—that [Throgmorton] could impact Carbon County negatively."[12] Evidently, these politicians failed to see the consequences of their own pens.

There's a saying that in Wyoming everything's political except politics— and they're personal. Terry Weickum, the chair of the county commission, had an ax to grind with Throgmorton. One of the director's letters to the newspaper referred to Weickum's claim that 97 percent of county residents favored the CTL plant as "pure fiction."[13] Weickum was not one to back down from a fight, although one also gets the sense that this fiercely pro-business exterior hides a soft heart. That this gruff sixty-one-year old former automotive mechanic owned a food and beverage distribution operation called Candy Mountain said something. As did his dismissal of Throgmorton as a man who's "got all those letters behind his name."[14]

The second commissioner, Jerry Paxton, could have passed as the town marshall in a Western. He proudly traces his Wyoming roots back to a great-great-grandfather who came to the territory as a trapper in the 1840s.[15] Paxton taught agricultural education before becoming a principal, and after taking early retirement he won a seat on the county commission. He's as Republican as Carbon County is arid (nine and a quarter inches of precipitation per year in Rawlins), and this formed the basis for his conflict with Throgmorton, who believed such malarkey as the burning of fossil fuels causing climate change.

Leo Chapman was the most distinguished of the three commissioners, looking the part of a conservative, well-groomed, retired banker, which he is. But Wyoming politics are personal; Chapman is Throgmorton's brother-in-law. In the understated way of Wyomingites, Chapman chuckles, "We've had some interesting Thanksgiving dinners."[16]

While the commissioners weren't exactly clear on what they wanted to happen following their letter, Throgmorton summed up his assessment of what they were hoping to accomplish: "I don't think Terry was thinking, 'I'm going to drive this SOB out of town.' Paxton was the guy who thought, 'We don't need your kind here,' and he made no bones about that. Leo, I don't know what the hell he was thinking."[17] Presumably they were all thinking about the power wielded by Wyoming's county commissioners, who were tight with the movers and shakers. In Carbon County that meant the energy industry: BP, Devon Energy, Sinclair Oil, and, of course, DKRW. In brief, the county commissioners controlled land-use planning—and everything that happened in Carbon County had to do with land.

The story that the energy industry did not want told includes some shady characters, a convoluted plot, and a disturbing setting. Like much of the land in Carbon County, the deeper one digs into the DKRW venture, the more stygian things become.

In the commissioners' letter, they complained that Throgmorton "states doubt in the company and basically calls Bob Kelly [the K of DKRW] and his partners crooks. He writes about the fact that they worked for the now defunct Enron and insinuates their involvement in wrong doing."[18] Before the mortgage fraud disaster, the collapse of Enron in 2001 was the most devastating corporate bankruptcy in US history, with 5,600 lost jobs, $60 billion in stock market losses, and $2.1 billion in vaporized pensions.[19]

DKRW Advanced Fuels is named after four Enron refugees who decided that converting solid coal into liquid fuel would be a great commercial venture. Jon Doyle is CEO of the company; at Enron he worked under a couple of the company's other partners "in an executive capacity."[20] One of his superiors was Robert Kelly, a West Point graduate with a Harvard doctorate in economics. He was smart enough to sell his stake in Enron Renewable Energy Corporation for $20 million before the collapse.[21] Doyle also worked for H. David Ramm, president of Enron Wind Corporation and managing director of Enron Renewable Energy Corporation. Although not a graduate of West Point, Ramm served nine years as an army officer and earned a master's degree in management at MIT.[22] Thomas White, former vice chairman of Enron Energy Services, is a graduate of West Point, where he rose to the rank of brigadier general and into the ranks of America's multimillionaires through Enron stock and options. He managed to avoid indictment for his corporate misdeeds by virtue of being appointed secretary of the army by President George W. Bush in 2001 just as federal prosecutors were closing in.[23]

While this cast of characters might be grounds for suspicion, Throgmorton's real concern was the unfolding plot—or the lack of one. The commissioners' letter to his board correctly noted that "[Throgmorton] has cast doubt on scientist's [sic] ability to turn coal into liquid fuel."[24] Weickum remained dismayed with the skeptics: "It's not a new thing. Of course you can do it!"[25] Notwithstanding Weickum's confidence, the technical issues of profitably converting coal into liquid fuel were substantial.[26] And in the newspaper, Throgmorton sardonically observed that, "like Enron, its predecessor, DKRW has never produced anything but paper. This corporation has absolutely no track record of success. In fact, it has no track record at all. It is not an energy producing corporation like those in our community that know how to dig and drill and haul and refine. It is essentially a speculative finance company."[27] He also pointed out that previous coal-to-liquid projects, such as the one in Schuylkill County, Pennsylvania, had been abandoned.[28] Despite DKRW's insistence that their operation would simply combine off-the-shelf technologies that had been used for decades, the plant still would be the first commercial-scale operation of its kind in the United States.[29] Although the basic process was developed by the fuel-starved Germans in World War II, the only significant CTL operation in the world today is found in South Africa. The plant's output is about twice that of the modest refinery in Sinclair, Wyoming.[30]

At present, the entire CTL plant in Carbon County consists of those two concrete pads. Although not much has changed on the desert landscape, little has remained the same in terms of the company's technical plans. In 2004 DKRW announced that they would produce 33,000 barrels of diesel fuel a day (it takes about 1,000 pounds of coal to make a barrel of diesel).[31] By 2009 the daily output was supposed to be 21,000 barrels of gasoline, which then slipped to 18,500 barrels. Although a 2013 report pegged output at 11,686 barrels per day, which is about one-sixth of what the Sinclair refinery was producing,[32] a year later the figure was back up to the 2009 estimate.[33]

The change in volume suggests considerable technical uncertainty, but Throgmorton latched onto the switch from diesel to gasoline. In his column he argued that DKRW "completely changed the process they're going to be using. They're going to use a process that has been designed in China. So it has nothing to do with any of the original documents that they have submitted [for permitting]."[34] According to Mary Throne, the attorney handling permitting for DKRW, Throgmorton was entirely mistaken—or upon further consideration, maybe half-wrong.[35] She admitted that although the original permit request specified the German Fischer-Tropsch process, which is designed to generate diesel fuel, the application was later changed to the ExxonMobil methanol-to-gasoline (MTG) process. State agencies were evidently unperturbed by this dramatic technological shift. Throne insisted that DKRW was sticking with their current plan.

In his column, Throgmorton recounted a meeting in Medicine Bow hosted by DKRW in 2007 where "they said, very proudly, 'This is going to be an entirely private-investor funded operation.' They were going to get no public money for this at all." As Throgmorton pointed out in the newspaper, it didn't quite work out that way.

> The project is estimated to cost a bit over $2 billion. DKRW has
> applied for a $1.75 billion dollar loan guarantee from the federal govern-
> ment as a key component of its financing. It has also asked the State of

Wyoming, through the Wyoming Business Council, to underwrite about
$300 million in industrial development bonds, an arrangement that must
be approved by the State Legislature. DKRW has also asked the Carbon
County Commissioners to endorse the $300 million industrial develop-
ment loan plus an additional $245 million in tax exempt bonds to com-
plete the deal.[36]

Now, in 2016, the financial state of DKRW has stalled. The loan guarantee
from the US Department of Energy has been in limbo for six years, pending
environmental review and the fiscal mess created by the Solyndra failure.[37]
At the state level, the company reduced the $300 million taxpayer-backed
bond to $100 million, thereby avoiding the need for legislative approval.[38] The
state funding is contingent on the project passing an economic and technical
review by the Idaho National Laboratory, which is still pending, given that
DKRW doesn't seem anxious for a third-party analysis of their plans.[39]

In DKRW's desperation to secure financing, they joined up with Sinopec,
the construction and engineering branch of the gigantic, state-owned China
Petrochemical, Inc.[40] "DKRW claims that Sinopec actually has a coal-to-
liquids plant that they built in China somewhere," says Throgmorton, "but
nobody from here has ever seen it."[41] The good news for DKRW is that they
contracted for the sale of their entire fuel output to a company that actually
exists. The bad news is that in 2012 Vitol Inc. was investigated for skirting
US sanctions in its dealings with Iran.[42]

While DKRW's financial situation is a hazard only to speculative investors, their operation would represent a danger to human lives. Throgmorton
wrote, "I hope our commissioners have the answer to the question Rita Clark
[a local landowner] asked at one of the initial public DKRW meetings: 'Do our
first responders and medical personnel know what chemicals are used in this
process so they can be prepared in case of an accident?'"[43] The answer has
been "no" since 2007.[44] Throgmorton, however, has a potent ally in raising
questions about the safety of the CTL plant and its associated coal mining
operation.

Jason Lillegraven is a retired paleontologist from the University of Wyoming. Having spent countless hours in the deserts of Carbon County, he
became enchanted by the rocks and their stories. He scoffs at DKRW's claim
that the closest fault is 240 miles from the mine site. Lillegraven's research
has revealed that the land is laced with faults and slippages, and when

Jay Lillegraven is a curmudgeonly, retired paleontologist of international standing—
and the leading scientific opponent of DKRW's coal-to-liquid plant. His passion for
the region's ecological integrity and geological story, as well as his affinity for the
people of this desert landscape, make him a potent and incisive "David" to the energy
industry's "Goliath" (photo by Allen Best).

miners are going to be hundreds of feet underground, such instability is a
recipe for disaster.[45]

With an abiding love of this desolate landscape, Lillegraven is also concerned about the plans—or the lack of planning—for the infrastructure that
will arise from the emptiness of the desert to accommodate construction and
plant workers. Remarkably, there appear to be no provisions for utilities,
health care, or schools for what will be the largest town within fifty miles of
the plant,[46] though the company's permit application did specify that "all of
the rooms will have a WI-FI system, flat screen televisions, and cable."[47]
There is also the absurd assertion that "the construction population has
additional incentives to reduce criminal incidences"— presumably not amus-
ing to local law enforcement, which consists of two marshalls in Hannah,
Wyoming (think of Mayberry RFD without the charm).[48]

If Throgmorton's account of the characters and plot in the DKRW tragicom-
edy isn't sufficiently aggravating to the industrial-political cabal, Lillegraven

describes the setting as a stage in the theater of the absurd. He has scrupu-
lously documented his concerns in carefully referenced letters to the Wyoming Department of Environmental Quality (DEQ), but the agency has not
responded. Their position mimics that of DKRW's attorney for permitting,
who used to be the DEQ's attorney and is now a state representative. Mary
Throne contends that "the decision has been made [and] you can't come in
after the fact and ask questions."[49] When pressed about this as a legal principle, she's less adamant but insists that nothing would change if Lillegrav-
en's concerns were taken into consideration. Based on the chumminess of
politics and energy in Wyoming, she's probably right, but not because Lillegraven is wrong.

One might imagine that a company planning to convert coal to gasoline
(or diesel) would have figured out whether there's sufficient raw material to
do so. Given that Arch Coal has a 24 percent stake in DKRW and Arch Coal
is highly proficient at digging up coal, it would stand to reason that somebody
would have run the numbers.[50] Even figuring on just 10,600 barrels of gasoline per day (the lowest estimate available), DKRW would need sixty million
tons of coal over the lifetime of the plant. Unfortunately, the planned mining
area has only forty-four million tons of recoverable coal.[51]

But if coal is in short supply, water is an even bigger problem. The state
engineer's office approved DKRW's water production plan based on a report
from the company's consultant, who had drilled a single well into the Mesa-
verde aquifer and measured the flow rate for twenty-four hours. Extrapolat-
ing that one test to more than a dozen wells producing for thirty years is a
stretch.[52] Along with quantity, Lillegraven pointed out a water quality issue
in his letter to the Industrial Siting Division. Because the water from this
aquifer is brine, he asked, "Can the high-pressure/temperature, superheated
facilities planned for construction be expected to operate safely and effectively using the low-quality waters?"[53] He also wanted to know what would
be done with the heavy metals and salts that would be left behind along with
the daily allotment of 430 tons of slag and fly ash.[54]

To make matters still worse, excavating all that coal and pumping all that
water means dramatic changes in the region's ecology. As the water table
drops, pockets of wetlands will disappear. The mining also will convert the
uplands into thousands of acres of "pot-and-kettle" topography (imagine the
land as scarred flesh after a bad case of acne). As the surface slumps into
ten-foot deep pits that reshape the hydrology of the land over the course of

fifty years, one has to wonder at what point officials will admit that their prediction of "no effect on surface waters" was part of an incoherently fragmented analysis that merely greased the skids of the energy industry.[55]

To be fair, Throgmorton is a liberal sociologist, and Lillegraven is one of those conservationists who manage to find beauty in places like Carbon County. While DKRW might have lacked objectivity concerning the viability of CTL technology, surely the county commissioners could find some reliable source of information. As much as Wyomingites loathe the federal government (while depending on the feds to prop up the state's economy),[56] the US Department of Energy published a brochure endorsing CTL projects.[57]

In a series of terribly mixed messages, the Department of Energy provided a list of issues that their research and development would resolve. The agency said that they were working to "advance construction of first-of-a-kind pioneer plants to demonstrate the overall technical feasibility and operability" (which seems odd, given their claim that this is a proven technology that has worked for decades) and "develop and implement the preferred financial incentive package including investment credits, tax breaks, low cost financing alternatives and loan guarantees to reduce financial risk and encourage industry development" (subsidies for a proven, flourishing industry would hardly be necessary).[58] Evidently, the energy industry has been far more effective in shaping policy in Washington, DC, than they've been in building a CTL plant in Rawlins, Wyoming.

Maybe the critics are wrong. Perhaps David Throgmorton is mistaken in his assessment: "I don't think [DKRW] have the financing. I don't think they'll ever have the financing. I don't think that they have the technology, and I don't think that they have the expertise."[59] Let's assume that his newspaper columns and letters to the editor were misguided. After all, the issues are complicated. But when did having a different perspective, even a mistaken view, become grounds for political censorship? The answer is, when Wyoming became no longer a far-flung community of independent malcontents but a dispersed and obsequious company town.

CHAPTER 7

Corporate Coercion and Public Courage

This is the vital question for Carbon County—and for the rest of us who recognize elements of their struggles in our own communities: how did censorship become the solution to conflict? The answer lies in understanding corporations—whether DKRW, Bank of America, ExxonMobil, Microsoft, Monsanto, Pfizer, or Wal-Mart—and their capacity to shape political perspectives.

The ways in which energy companies manifest their influence are often duplicitous, unless someone points them out. When DKRW announced that unless the Carbon County commissioners granted the company hundreds of millions of dollars in bonding authority the company would not submit their engineering and financial plans for review by the Idaho National Laboratory, Dave Throgmorton raised an objection in his newspaper column: "Shouldn't this equation be reversed? Shouldn't our Commissioners know the results of that analysis before they commit themselves to endorsing the bonds? Or does DKRW think it is calling the shots in Carbon County?"[1] The answer was provided by Commissioner Terry Weickum: "The energy industry in Wyoming offers opportunities you can't get anyplace else. Honestly, I love the bucking horse [the state's iconic image]. But it should be an oil well."[2] Say what you will about Weickum, the fellow is a straight shooter.

Leo Chapman harbored no illusions about the county commission's impotence in relation to the demand for energy: "It's steamrolling over us . . . I mean, we can't stop it so let's make them do what we want them to do by making them follow our land-use plan." After a moment of quiet reflection, his bravado faded and he acknowledged, "We are probably a pretty small peg in that cog."[3]

While fossil fuels are the engine of the modern world, don't think that those developing alternative energy sources are reluctant to shape politics and speech. According to Carbon County's third commissioner, "Regardless of how you feel about whether or not wind energy is green, it's a freight train coming at us out of Washington, DC." Jerry Paxton figured that "you have a

The $4.8 billion Chokecherry and Sierra Madre project in Carbon County, Wyoming, will be the largest onshore wind farm in the United States. Scattered across 230,000 acres (360 square miles), the one thousand turbines will produce ten million megawatt hours per year, enough to power as many as one million homes in Arizona, California, and Nevada that have renewable-energy standards (photo by Scott Kane).

choice of either standing in front of that train and getting run over, or standing at the switch and make sure it gets on the right track. That's what we were elected to do, to try to get it on the right track."[4]

Even if DKRW gets derailed, Carbon County is slated to host the largest wind farm in North America—an expanse a thousand wind turbines with power lines draped across the landscape. And the Creston Divide natural gas project will bring 8,900 wells to the county.[5] Psychologists have a term for how the people of Carbon County respond to years of seeing their land drilled and mined by corporate giants: learned helplessness.

Corporations were spawned in their present form when the US Supreme Court ruled in 1819 that they had the rights of individuals, and legal personhood was achieved with the *Citizens United* decision in 2010.[6] Today's energy giants derive their staggering power in large part from an ethical void. We've created corporations to be amoral beings—persons even—with the sole function of making money.[7] And no corporation more vividly exhibited this singular goal than Enron. When Enron's CEO learned his company's oil traders were doctoring bank records, Ken Lay's message was clear: "If you're profitable, you can break the rules."[8]

In one of his columns, Throgmorton recounted a scene from *The Smartest Guys in the Room*, a documentary about Enron. When Thomas White (the W in DKRW) was asked how he was going to cover gigantic losses as the company's scam unraveled, he answered, "California." Enron played a pivotal role in the financial meltdown of the Golden State, which was the world's seventh-largest economy. Throgmorton's somber warning: "I would hate for Carbon County to be the punch-line in the next Enron documentary."[9]

And there's reason to believe that energy corporations would have little compunction about sinking Wyoming, based on how they treat their employees. From 2000 to 2010 Wyoming was first or second in the national rate of workplace fatalities. In 2010 the fine for illegally killing a deer was three times greater than the average fine for safety violations related to workplace fatalities.[10] The executive director of the National Council for Occupational Safety and Health put the corporate mindset in stark terms: "As companies decry regulations and emphasize profits over safety, workers pay the ultimate price."[11]

It's hard enough for citizens to battle corporations, but when the CEOs are allied with congresspersons, the struggle can seem hopeless. In February 2011 Wyoming Senator John Barrasso (R) asked Energy Secretary Steven Chu to push forward federal aid for DKRW's project. That October, Barrasso hypocritically castigated President Barack Obama for picking "winners and losers" in the field of alternative energy and argued from the Senate floor that the failure of Solyndra (the manufacturer of solar cells) showed that the administration shouldn't "be betting with the taxpayer's money." According to Barrasso's spokesperson, he supports only those projects that are "financially sound, transparent and based on sound science"—and somehow DKRW met these criteria in the senator's mind despite the rather straightforward argument given by energy experts that "if [Solyndra and DKRW] were an economically viable solution already, [they] wouldn't need a loan guarantee."[12]

That same year, Barrasso teamed up with Jim Inhofe (R-OK), in an attempt to circumvent environmental guidelines blocking the military's purchase of coal-to-liquid-generated fuel (the prohibition was based on the production of these fuels resulting in much more greenhouse emissions than conventional fuels—50 to 100 percent more carbon dioxide than from making diesel out of crude oil).[13] Lifting the restrictions might have been a boon to DKRW and other producers if a commercial plant ever squeezed the first drop of gasoline from a lump of coal; however, Pentagon leaders killed Barrasso's plan.

The war on free speech demands an alliance between corporations and government. And Wyoming is not the only the battlefield. The *New York Times* has reported evidence of "the unprecedented, secretive alliance Republican attorneys general have formed with some of the nation's top energy producers to push back the Obama regulatory agenda."[14] E-mail exchanges reveal that attorneys general in nineteen states are colluding with energy companies to challenge the federal policies through lawsuits and other tactics—in exchange for the industry providing a record $16 million in political contributions for the lawyers' reelection campaigns. So perhaps we shouldn't be surprised when the flow of corporate money into the political system has the downstream effect of pumping funds back into private ventures.

The Wyoming Infrastructure Authority is charged with fostering energy projects through their billion dollar bonding capacity. In one of his columns, Throgmorton expressed frustration about the Infrastructure Authority meeting at an exclusive resort in Jackson, Wyoming, to consider DKRW's venture: "When [the residents of Carbon County] know that crucial information is being traded between public employees and industry representatives but is being withheld from them by location or cost, they get cranky."[15] And in a letter to the *Casper Star-Tribune*, Throgmorton reminded readers that Wyoming received a failing grade in "public access to information" in a national survey of government accountability.[16]

Many Wyomingites perceive that the state government is primed to facilitate the industry and impede the public.[17] Although one should not ascribe to malicious conspiracy what can be explained by bureaucratic incompetence, landowners opposing DKRW's project contend that the bumbling of the Wyoming Department of Environmental Quality (DEQ) "masks an underlying bias in favor of developing fossil fuels at the risk of long-term environmental protections."[18]

Lacking relevant expertise, the DEQ's Industrial Siting Council (ISC) dismissed evidence provided by Jason Lillegraven, a state-licensed geologist, on

The Sinclair Oil Refinery in the eponymously named town of 450 stalwart souls. The Wyoming plant processes crude oil at a rate equivalent to the output of about ten fire hoses running twenty-four hours a day. In 2013, the Wyoming Occupational Safety and Health Administration levied a $707,000 fine for workplace safety violations—the largest such penalty in the state's history (photo by Scott Kane).

the basis that it was "nothing other than his professional advice" and accepted the testimony of DKRW consultants.[19] This position echoed that of Mary Throne, DKRW's attorney, who regarded Lillegraven's technical analyses as "opinion based on misinformation" and offered her reassuring opinion: "This is a highly technical project that's been in the works for a number of years and has lots of really good engineers working on it."[20] In other words, trust us. In fact, industry engineers are so good that Throne can't recall a single instance of the ISC denying a permit in her twenty-five years of practice in Wyoming. If the police in a small town never issue a speeding ticket, either the residents are unbelievably law abiding or the radar gun is rigged. Lillegraven summed up the proceedings: "The ISC exhibited a dazzling expression of unbridled trust in corporate motivations and technical capabilities."[21]

With profound dependence on a single industry, the balance of political power shifts dangerously. By almost any account, the Carbon County Higher Education Center is an enormous asset to the community. The center provides high school and adult education in various trades, adult basic education, industry training programs, community education classes, college-level courses, academic testing services, and tutoring. But when Throgmorton reflects on his $5.5 million annual budget derived from taxes on energy-rich lands and fees for training Sinclair and BP workers at the center, he admits, "We are whores for the industry."[22]

Throgmorton and Weickum might not agree on much, but they both recognized the capacity of the energy companies to shape public discourse and decisions. Weickum put it bluntly: "Why do we love them? Because they pay a tremendous amount of taxes and have some really good paying jobs. Other than that we wouldn't want these gaping holes in the earth, these pipelines and stuff like that."[23]

When you hear Carbon County commissioners reflect on the conditions of their constituents, it's easier to understand their effort to censor a critic of DKRW. "You take Hanna, and Medicine Bow, and to some degree Elk Mountain, a lot of people are up at the last rung," Chapman said. "They're starting to look at their dog's tail for soup . . . I've had people with tears in their eyes saying, 'What can you do to keep them coming?'"[24] So if DKRW doesn't succeed, the politicians can save face and rest easy knowing that the government was "cocked, and aimed, and ready to make them be successful in any possible way, shape and form that we could."[25]

The only economic good news for the people of eastern Carbon County in recent times has been that the sawmill reopened in Saratoga in 2013, thanks in large part to Commissioner Jerry Paxton.[26] The painful irony is that the mill is processing trees killed by a massive outbreak of bark beetles, resulting in large part from the abnormally warmer winters that allow the insects to survive.[27] So the climate-changing carbon emissions from CTL fuel might be a perverse means of providing jobs for the forest industry, at least until the trees worth harvesting are gone.

The Carbon County commissioners knew that silencing dissent on behalf of the energy industry undermined democracy. They were deeply conservative in Wyoming's traditional, libertarian mold, which keeps government out of the boardroom and the bedroom. So what went wrong? The short answer is that they were outmatched, overly trusting, and just plain scared.

When it comes to shaping public policy, the energy industry's biggest bang for the buck comes from state and county governments. Getting the US Congress to favor extraction requires expensive lobbying and campaign contributions. The return on investment is much better when three county commissioners, a few understaffed state agencies, and a handful of gubernatorial appointees set the agenda for eight thousand square miles of energy-rich land.

Carbon County selects its commissioners from a pool of 12,000 eligible folks and the state legislature is drawn from a population of 440,000 people over the age of eighteen.[28] Wyomingites are proud of their "citizen legislature," but bumpkinism has a cost.[29] Bob LeResche is the former commissioner for Natural Resources and director of Policy and Planning in Alaska and is now active in Wyoming politics and conservation, so he's able to compare the two energy-rich states. Up north, legislators have staffs and legislative committees have million dollar consultant budgets; they don't need to rely on industry lobbyists for information. As for the Wyoming legislators, "they're totally lambs," LeResche says, noting that the state's political vulnerability is "not just because there's so few people, but because they don't give importance to the intellectual function of the government."[30]

So it's not hard to figure out why local and state politicians are outmatched by multinational corporations. Just how much savvy, experience, and capability can we expect from schoolteachers, local bankers, and small business owners? Weickum came to appreciate this vulnerability: "[When] there's no experience on [the commission], it scares the hell out of me. It isn't that they are bad people, or mean people, or any of that. It's that, if you don't know, you don't know."[31]

When a politician ventures into the unfamiliar territory of multinational energy corporations, he understandably falls back on his experience of small-town trust. As Weickum put it, "People up here, if they say they're going to do something, almost always they'll do it. And if they're not going to, you already know they're not going to because everybody in town's been promised something they haven't done."[32] What he failed to recognize is that Enron executives excelled at not doing things they'd promised. In Paxton's estimation, DKRW was "honestly trying to do the right thing."[33] The problem was he didn't consider that the right thing for DKRW wasn't necessarily the right thing for Carbon County.

Finally, the commissioners were scared—and for good reason. Go into an

The Rawlins Residential Historic District is listed on the National Register of Historic Places; the bell tower of St. Joseph's Catholic Church is seen in the distance. With 9,259 residents, Rawlins is the county seat of Carbon County, created in 1868. The county was named for the extensive coal deposits in the area, which fueled the Union Pacific Railroad (photo by Jeffrey Beall, Wikimedia Commons).

economically depressed rural hamlet with jobless, hungry people, and maybe Weickum's explanation of why he drafted the letter to silence Throgmorton is understandable if not defensible: "It's the duty I thought I had at the time, to do everything I could do to protect Carbon County and its citizens from having something that was really good and coming to them being chased away."[34] Scared, yes, and maybe a little bit angry when others suggest you're being outgunned and bamboozled by the industry.

In old-time Westerns you could find the villain by looking for a black hat. Jerry Paxton wears a black cowboy hat, but he wasn't the villain of this contemporary saga, nor were his fellow commissioners. When decent people are in high-stake situations where they are outmatched, deceived, and scared, very bad decisions are often made. If you want to find a villain, look for the guy wearing the tailored suit and power tie.

Finding the villains in this Western tale may be difficult, but finding a hero is easy. Gilbert Archuleta never finished high school, but he managed to earn an MBA and raise three daughters on his own.[35] Archuleta was the finance manager at a car dealership in Rawlins—and the chair of the Carbon County Higher Education Center (CCHEC) board.

When he received the letter from the county commissioners demanding that the CCHEC silence their director, he was incredulous. His reply to the county commission, endorsed by his entire board, provides an object lesson in courage and integrity. In standing up to the most powerful political body in his county, Archuleta was diplomatic but direct: "We share a common goal of acting in a manner that serves the needs of all the county's citizens. . . . A distinction has to be made, however, between opinions expressed as an individual citizen and those expressed in an official capacity. . . . We are certain you agree with the premise that it is a fundamental duty or right of any citizen to question the actions of our governing bodies, regardless of who the individual is."[36] And as for the commissioners' assertion that "there is no doubt that Dr. Throgmorton's negative attitude and lack of factual comments have damaged the Higher Education Center permanently,"[37] Archuleta left no doubt that the director was an asset: "We could list the numerous positive impacts our current director has had while employed at CCHEC, but suffice it to say we believe Dr. Throgmorton's actions have been nothing but exemplary."[38] When the commissioners' letter and Archuleta's reply were made public by the *Casper Star-Tribune*, the political fallout was substantial. Weickum attacked Throgmorton in the article, comparing him to "the people who would cut your tires and key your paint: They don't do it to your face, they take cheap shots and do it to your back."[39] And if there was any doubt about whether the commissioners intended to jeopardize Throgmorton's employment, Weickum's rhetorical question made his position clear: "Should that kind of person be in charge of our higher education center?"[40]

Although Weickum said that he was misquoted,[41] his aggression put the rest of the commissioners in an awkward position, particularly Throgmorton's brother-in-law. Leo Chapman responded with a letter to the editor of the Rawlins paper: "I condemn that kind of statement about a person with the moral fiber of (Higher Education Center Director) David Throgmorton, and I can say that Weickum is not speaking on behalf of me. He is not authorized, at least by me, to be speaking as chairman of the commission in that manner, and in the future I hope he will clarify that he is speaking only on his own."[42]

Chapman's insistence that Weickum should have made clear that he was speaking as a private citizen is particularly ironic given that both Paxton and Weickum insist that such a difference didn't pertain to Throgmorton.

According to Weickum, "There are not several Dave Throgmortons. There's not Dave Throgmorton the guy that runs the Higher Ed, and then Dave the personal guy, and then Dave the columnist. Oh and then another one Dave, Leo Chapman's brother-in-law."[43]

Maybe Chapman was influenced by his relationship with Throgmorton, but he's not one to offer excuses. When asked if the commissioners were acting out of fear of losing DKRW, he admitted that they felt strongly that the plant was important to the county, but he didn't use that sense of desperation to justify their effort at censorship: "The fact of the matter is, as a county commissioner, I cannot jawbone with a threat of somebody's job. . . . It's not ethical, it's not proper, it's not right. We had lots of ways that we could have put our point across. In his position, he [Throgmorton] might carry a lot of influence, but in our position we do too."[44] These days, humility from a politician is an even rarer resource than gasoline from coal.

One might reasonably wonder why the players in DKRW continued to push this seemingly fruitless venture. Surely it doesn't compare to the profitability of Enron. Presumably, some venture capital is flowing in and this isn't the only project that the executives have in the works. Maybe if the thing gets off the ground (or the concrete pad), there's big money to be made from investors—at least enough to generate paychecks for those at the top while the project grinds its way toward completion. Or perhaps there's some other angle that will become apparent in the course of more a thorough federal analysis that is being planned.

Under public pressure, the US Bureau of Land Management announced in 2013 that it would develop a full-scale environmental impact statement to assess the effects of the DKRW project.[45] Although in 2016 this assessment is still pending, such a thorough analysis will likely take at least two years, which would typically put a project on hold. But in this case, DKRW could build the plant on private property[46] and assume that the government will conclude that there are no intolerable harms to adjacent public lands—a safe bet if the analysis were conducted by the state of Wyoming, but a riskier wager with federal agencies.

In December 2013 Wyoming's ISC approved a thirty-nine-month extension to DKRW's venture, even though the company only asked for another thirty months. Before this decision, the county commission was on the verge of recommending against the extension, but DKRW's attorney and vice president made an end run of the published agenda, arrived in Rawlins unannounced, and captivated the commissioners with a two-hour infomercial, which was sufficient to generate a split vote. One commissioner admonished, "You guys can't just come flying in every once [every] couple of years and try to sell us 'snake oil.'"[47] Well, maybe not oil from snakes, but the council bought the idea of gasoline from coal.

Recent public meetings with DKRW have become even more fractious.[48] The ISC directed the company to hold semiannual meetings in Carbon County to keep the people informed of developments. In the December 2014 meeting, Throne, the company's attorney and a state representative, arrived fifteen minutes late with a DKRW executive in tow. They brought cookies and something less palatable. She opened with a declaration that discussion would be constrained to issues pertaining to the ISC. However, the agency had imposed no such restrictions, and Dave Throgmorton saw this as a way for Throne to narrow the scope of the meeting and "intimidate people into obliging silence."[49] DKRW's senior vice president for finance (another Enron refugee) could offer nothing about the company's progress in the last six months and sat down after fifteen minutes of rambling.

Without anything substantive from the company, Jay Lillegraven stepped into the breach and began to address DKRW's lack of ownership of the property on which they were proposing to build. At this point, Throne yanked the microphone away from the geologist and declared to the crowd of fifty people that they didn't need to listen to him. She judged that his concerns were outside the scope of the meeting that she had established (without any authority to do so). Censorship is rarely manifested with such physicality and clarity.

Fed up with corporate bullying, a woman in the back row stood up and challenged Throne: "Who are you to tell us we cannot listen to this man? He's told me more in five minutes than DKRW has told me in five years. I want to hear what he has to say." And so the people of Carbon County were allowed to hear from a fellow citizen—a small victory for freedom of speech, although nobody is counting on being heard by the US Department of Energy as it decides whether to provide $1.2 billion in public funds as a loan guarantee to DKRW.

The subsequent report to the community in early 2016 by a senior vice president of DKRW avoided a reprise of the conflict by keeping the presentation to under four minutes. He summarized the previous six months of progress: "I'm sorry to say not much has developed with the low oil prices that have ensued since we got back in June. We continue to monitor the project internally and do studies and kind of think about how we can make this project work. We really haven't had any substantive discussion with any contractors or vendors and we really haven't talked with DOE. . . . I don't want to leave you with the impression that we've given up on the project, uh, you know, our investors have spent almost 100 to 120 million dollars to get to this point."[50]

Even if energy prices improve and the US government agrees to back the company, DKRW has another financial impediment. After Sinopec delayed construction for reasons known only to insiders,[51] DKRW canceled its contract with the Chinese petrochemical giant and announced that it was seeking a new partner.[52] A mostly new set of Carbon County commissioners seems to have had it with the diddling. The now-five-member commission asked the ISC to deny DKRW's request for an extension, essentially calling for the company to "put up or shut up."[53] There was one dissenting vote. Leo Chapman, the only one of the three former commissioners still serving, wanted energy companies to know that Carbon County was open for business.

Paxton is now in the state legislature, and when asked about the conflict with Throgmorton, he equivocates in the way of all politicians who aspire to move up: "In retrospect, it probably wasn't the smartest thing we ever did. . . . If I had to do it over again, I don't know whether I would or not."[54]

Weickum wanted nothing more than to continue as a county commissioner, but he lost his bid for reelection by fifty-three votes—and didn't leave his house for three days.[55] His self-esteem came from being a well-liked commissioner, and he worked tirelessly at the job. The Carbon County district attorney told him, "You're one of the best commissioners I've ever worked with—and one of the worst politicians I've ever known."[56] Weickum figures that the DA was probably right. While he won't apologize for how he handled the conflict with Throgmorton, he admits that the fallout probably cost him the election. The gruff businessman tried to salvage a childlike victory: "I wanted him to quit writing crappy letters. He quit writing crappy letters." But when pushed as to whether Carbon County lost an experienced and devoted commissioner along with an impassioned and articulate columnist, he says, "I don't know if we all lost, but I'll tell you nobody won."[57]

Dave Throgmorton did stop writing his column. He's been pouring his energy into the CCHEC's new seventeen-acre campus—a source of tremendous civic pride and a huge improvement over their single building near the fairgrounds. That's not the whole explanation but, in a sense, his devotion to the CCHEC is why he quit writing. "I have a responsibility to the Carbon County Higher Education Center to have a good relationship with British Petroleum, and a good relationship with Sinclair, and a good relationship with Devon Energy, and all these places," Throgmorton says. And then his voice softens: "Every time I sit down to write about something (controversial), I'm suddenly thinking, 'Who am I going to alienate with this one that is going to do us damage?'"[58]

Political censorship is unconscionable, but self-censorship is an insidious silence that eats away at the integrity of a community. When people stop speaking for fear of reprisal from corporations or their political allies, we are in deep trouble. "I'm legitimately worried about putting Carbon County Higher Education in a position where they can't do their job . . . they did a great thing for the First Amendment. [But] I don't want to put them in a position of having to defend me."[59]

Throgmorton is torn between the price that others might pay for his words and the moral cost of silence. "I wrestle with who I'm letting down by not writing, because I think that I gave people permission to think things and say things that they couldn't think or say if they hadn't seen it in the paper," he says, then lays bare the aspirations of an educator: "I'd like to think that there were students out there who said, 'Okay, this is how somebody who doesn't think like everybody else in town thinks.'" Embarrassed by his hopefulness, Throgmorton smiles and laughs at himself saying, "I know better; they don't read the paper."[60]

Not even Dave Throgmorton, who loves the dry and craggy landscape, would describe Carbon County as being pretty. Likewise, Katharine Hepburn at ninety years old was not pretty, but she was beautiful. Had Ted Wood, an acclaimed photojournalist, been photographing Hepburn instead of the roughnecks working on coalbed methane wells two hundred miles northeast of Rawlins, maybe he wouldn't have found himself in as much trouble as Dave Throgmorton. But as moving as Wood's portraits of leather-tough men were, it was his images of the wastewater and well pads that outraged the fossil fuel corporations. The pictures of the industry's legacy on the land of the Powder River Basin were deemed so defamatory by one enormously wealthy and powerful magnate that Wood's images were censored—along with the photographs of three other documentarians—at the state's largest art museum.

The Case of
an Epitaph for Photographs

As to the evil which results from censorship,
it is impossible to measure it,
for it is impossible to tell where it ends.

—JEREMY BENTHAM

CHAPTER 8

A Picture Is Worth a Thousand Words
—or a Million Bucks

Casper has something of a Rodney Dangerfield complex. Just like this comedic icon of self-deprecation, the Wyoming city doesn't get much respect—even if it gets plenty of visitors. Being in the middle of the state and straddling Interstate 25, the major north–south highway in the Rocky Mountain West, Casper hosts lots of meetings and events, but geography, not ambience, is the attraction. Casper is Wyoming's "second city," with barely 60,000 people (Cheyenne, the capital, claims 62,000). The downtown is mostly aging brick-and-concrete buildings largely devoid of character, giving the place a gritty, utilitarian flavor mixed with the aroma of petroleum.

The city named its American Legion baseball teams the Oilers and the Drillers. And Casper's amenities include the Three Crowns Golf Course named for the three grades of gasoline available from Standard Oil service stations years ago. The fairways blanket Amoco's former oil-field site, thanks to BP (which merged with Amoco) contributing funds for reclamation. Oil drill bits serve as tee box markers, and oil rig models mark the holes. Generations of golfers can savor petrochemical vapors as oil recovery is ongoing with groundwater treatment being planned for the next one hundred years.[1]

There's a kind of eerie, Stepford quality to Casper. There's money flowing through town supporting gentrified neighborhoods. The community college is flourishing and the North Platte River flows as serenely as the disposition of the populace, who seem lulled by whatever concert, tournament, gun show, or RV gathering is happening at the events center. But despite a veneer of everyday normalcy, there is an odd silence about who's paying the bills.

You could wander quite a while in search of a decaf cappuccino, tofu stir-fry, or funky gallery. Head north of the city center, to find the tomblike Dick Cheney Federal Building, named for the city's most famous son. And if you wander a couple of blocks east of the not-very-bustling downtown you'll find

The Nicolaysen Art Museum in Casper, Wyoming (one of the state's only two "cities" with 60,000 residents), began its development in 1967. The current 25,000-square-foot location was established in 1990 after an extensive renovation of the Mountain States Power Company building. The museum's focus is on contemporary art of the Rocky Mountain region (photo by Jeffrey Lockwood).

the Nicolaysen Art Museum, housed in the renovated Mountain States Power Company building.

Go inside and you'll enter a spacious lobby filled with natural light, an entryway befitting the state's largest art museum. From there, the main gallery is through a pair of towering glass doors that draw your eye upward. Etched into the lintel is "McMurry Foundation Gallery," letting the visitor know who paid for the industrial-chic space that features multifarious art—within limits.

The constraint is not the size of the gallery, which is voluminous, but the sensitivity of the museum's benefactors. You see, the McMurrys and Casper's elites acquired their wealth from oil and gas. Mick McMurry parlayed an enormous windfall into an Italianate villa outside of town and a portfolio of holdings in construction, real estate, agriculture, and, of course, energy

The McMurry Foundation Gallery at the Nicolaysen Art Museum is named after one of the wealthiest families in Wyoming, who made their fortune in natural gas, having sold the Jonah Field in 2000 to Encana, Canada's largest natural gas producer in 2000; the company recently sold the gas field for $1.8 billion. The McMurrys are the museum's largest benefactor (photo by Jeffrey Lockwood).

(including plans for a natural gas-to-gasoline conversion plant heavily subsidized by the state).[2] So when contemporary artists offended fossil fuel magnates, freedom of speech gave way to the interests of industry—as was vividly documented in 2006.

The Ucross Foundation Art Gallery will open its 2006 season with an exhibition of photographs, *THE NEW GOLD RUSH: Images of Coalbed Methane* . . . [with] over 40 images that document coalbed methane development in Wyoming . . . [the show] will travel in the fall to the Nicolaysen Art Museum in Casper. [According to] Sharon Dynak, Executive Director of the Ucross Foundation, "These photographs and satellite images offer a striking portrayal of the recent changes that have taken place in the Powder River Basin due to CBM development."[3]

The intent of the show, sponsors and artists say, is to educate people about how the land has changed in the decade since drilling began taking off. . . . Some in the industry have written off the show as an attack, even before seeing it. Karen Brown, coordinator at the Coalbed Natural Gas Alliance, questions whether the exhibit will prompt a free-flow of ideas. She said the industry is already highly regulated and responsible.[4]

Casper's Nicolaysen Art Museum & Discovery Center canceled a photo exhibit featuring coalbed methane development in northeastern Wyoming amid criticism that it's meant to give the industry a black eye. Nicolaysen director Holly Turner said . . . there was no pressure from the museum's supporters in the oil and gas industry to drop the exhibit. "I've heard a lot of comments that people didn't like it," Turner said.[5]

Ted Wood was one of the artists whose work was featured in *The New Gold Rush*, and as a photojournalist and former director of photography for the *Jackson Hole News*, he had his finger on the pulse of Wyoming's energy politics. Wood was fascinated by how the coalbed methane (CBM) boom had "created all of these strange pressures and bedfellows in the Powder River Basin—strongly conservative ranchers aligning with conservationists to protect private property rights."[6] But even with his years of experience, Wood didn't expect that his work would be squelched. With a mixture of shock and pride, this Ted Scripps Fellow in Environmental Journalism announced on the fellowship website, "I am now an officially censored photojournalist in Wyoming!!"[7]

In 1963 President John F. Kennedy admonished, "If art is to nourish the roots of our culture, society must set the artist free to follow his vision wherever it takes him."[8] Under the presidency of Ronald Reagan, religious fundamentalists made significant inroads in suppressing works that they deemed to be immoral. While it's not hard to understand those who were offended by a crucifix immersed in urine, it's difficult to muster empathy for today's energy magnates censoring art that reveals the human and environmental costs of their extractive practices.

But this is not merely the story of wealthy industrialists in one company town. When corporations provide more than five times as much funding to art museums as the combined annual budgets of the National Endowment of the Arts and the National Endowment for the Humanities,[9] then the free search

The Teapot Dome, seen
in the background of this
gushing oil well, was the
site of an infamous scandal.
In 1922, this Wyoming oil
field was designated as a
Naval Oil Reserve and leased
to Mammoth Oil under
suspiciously favorable terms.
The interior secretary, Albert
Fall, was found guilty of
accepting bribes (Photofile:
Petroleum—WY—Teapot
Dome, American Heritage
Center, University of
Wyoming).

for truth and its unfettered expression are at grave risk. Corporations have
bought speech across America—and when it serves their interests, silence.

The Powder River Basin in eastern Wyoming is a sublimely desolate landscape, but the paucity of people has not translated into a lack of human
conflict. This is the land of Crazy Horse, the Johnson County War, Butch
Cassidy's Hole-in-the-Wall gang, and Teapot Dome.[10]

    The scandal over federal oil leases at Teapot Dome augured the fractious
future of fossil fuels in the region. In 1910 the federal government comman-
deered a chunk of the Powder River Basin to provide fuel for the navy, and in
1922 Interior Secretary Albert Fall leased the field's reserves to private oil
companies at low, no-bid rates (actually the bid consisted of bribes, for which
Fall was sent to prison). Today's so-called "competitive lease sales" of federal
coal tracts in the Powder River Basin often attract just one bidder, and it is
not surprising that it's usually the company that nominated the parcel for
lease.[11]

With time, this expanse of thirsty grasses and leathery sagebrush came to fuel the state economy—not just government corruption. While oil has flowed for a century, a coal boom started in the 1970s. Today, the basin hosts the eight largest mines in the country, accounting for 40 percent of the country's coal, which is shipped to power stations in seventeen states from Washington to Massachusetts and Minnesota to Louisiana. Until the recent glut of natural gas, the Powder River Basin's 26,000 square miles (about three times the area of Vermont) of Tertiary deposits had generated 20 percent of the nation's energy and 14 percent of our greenhouse gas emissions. The most productive of the eight counties in the basin produces nearly $4.5 billion worth of taxable minerals.[12]

Mining companies had long known that methane was trapped in all that coal, but there was no efficient way of extracting the natural gas used to heat homes and businesses. The late 1980s heralded a method for drawing out the highly flammable gas, creating an economic boom. Statewide there was $140 billion in coalbed methane just waiting for extraction—and Wyoming planned to reap more than $20 billion through taxes and royalties.[13] By drilling into a coalbed and rapidly pumping out the water, the gas is depressurized and rushes to the surface. Then, it's just a matter of sending the gas to consumers with the help of jet engine–powered compressor stations, the noise of which can drive people to take extreme actions.[14] For example, when a homeowner in the Powder River Basin received no help from the county commission, the sheriff, or the Wyoming Department of Environmental Quality in doing something about the continuous drone of a compressor, he took matters into his own hands. He shot at the damnable thing—which he described as "an airplane continually hovering above your home, circling but never landing"—with a hunting rifle. During his arrest for reckless endangerment, he told the deputy that the company should be charged with disturbing the peace. They weren't, and they continued to ignore the problem.[15]

Even worse than noise was what to do with all the groundwater that was pumped out at a rate of up to one hundred gallons a minute. The total water production from the state's coalbed methane was sufficient to fill the Great Salt Lake. In fact, most often the water was saline, but it could be dumped into waterways—at least until downstream users complained. In these cases, the water could be held in evaporation ponds, where there were fewer people to ask uncomfortable questions about the fate of the twenty tons of salt that a typical well produced per year.[16] And drowning out the voices of the 160,856 people in the Powder River Basin wasn't difficult considering that outside of the towns there are fewer than two people per square mile. If the water is of high quality, it can be discharged into otherwise dry stream-beds, which tend to erode dramatically as a result. In addition, people whose wells run dry can be obstreperous. In the arid West, wasting fresh water to extract methane has been described as throwing away the gold to get to the silver.

With newfound access to coalbed methane, a new gold rush played out in the Powder River Basin as wildcatters, major energy companies, and everyone in between began drilling. In 2000 the US Department of the Interior's Bureau of Land Management office in Buffalo, Wyoming, handled 900 drilling permits—a manageable workload. But by 2005 the office was inundated with 2,580 applications and managed to process about half of these. The next year, nearly 4,000 applications were received, and the feds somehow evaluated and approved a third of these.[17] With federal and state lands open for business, private landowners discovered that they were living on split estates. They owned the surface but not the minerals under their land—these were owned by the federal government and sold to energy companies.[18]

Throughout much of the western United States, owning land means that a person has control over only the surface rights—the mineral rights are held by the federal government. In Wyoming, this situation prevails across private lands equal in area to the entire states of Vermont and New Hampshire. Split estates are the legacy of the Stock Raising Homestead Act of 1916, when the federal government wanted to encourage settlement of the West but saw the value of the region's minerals. So when the government, specifically the US Department of the Interior's Bureau of Land Management, decides to make some money by selling its mineral under someone's land, nothing can stop the company that buys the rights from drilling.

Many westerners are more familiar with the General Mining Act of 1872 (30 USC §§ 22–42) and might reasonably presume that this law opened the door to the fossil fuel industry. However, the act did not include oil, gas, or coal. Indeed, a later amendment, the Mineral Leasing Act of 1920,[19] excluded certain nonmetallic minerals, such as petroleum and oil shale, from claim staking. So to access fossil fuels, the energy companies must work through the government.

When state legislators convened in Cheyenne, the industry's lobbyists ensured that the Wyoming government did little to protect the land and water. Under the governorship of Jim Geringer, the infamous "Go Blue" memo (an allusion to the color of state lands on ownership maps) from the Office of State Lands invited developers to drill with abandon.[20] Wyoming's Department of Environmental Quality was facing enormous pressure from elected officials who wanted the agency to remove impediments to the flow of gas and taxes. Geringer's successor, Governor Dave Freudenthal, argued that if Wyoming impeded the industry, the industry would pull up stakes and head to less regulated pastures.[21] The energy industry convinced the state engineer to issue an Orwellian judgment that "pumping water out of a coal seam and dumping it on the ground was a viable use of the water,"[22] and the federal government played along. For the Bureau of Land Management, neither the exhaustion of aquifers nor the saline contamination of fresh water sources constituted a significant environmental impact.[23]

By 2007 the Powder River Basin was producing 442 billion cubic feet of gas annually (enough to fill a balloon five-and-half miles in circumference). With more than 24,000 wells pockmarking the land (the number was predicted to quintuple by 2027), Wyoming was producing 20 percent of the nation's domestic coalbed methane.[24] Other states were in the game by this time—and discovered that although the losers varied, the winner was inevitably the energy industry.

Wasted and polluted water is bad enough, but a blowout of a gas well creates the possibility of a devastating explosion. When a well blew in the Powder River Basin and released two million cubic feet of natural gas into the countryside a few miles from Douglas, Wyoming (the county seat and home of the state fair), fifty people were driven from their homes. The well was capped after three days and the company was found to have acted recklessly, but Wyoming imposed no sanctions.[25]

The photographic exhibit that drove Wyoming's energy bosses to demand that the state's most prominent museum censor the arts emerged from an ironic setting.[26] The Ranch at Ucross is an expanse of twenty-two thousand acres tucked between the scoria-dotted hills of the Powder River Basin and the snow-covered peaks of the Big Horn Mountains. As well as being a working cattle ranch, Ucross is an internationally renowned artists' retreat. Since 1981 the land has been owned and operated by the Ucross Foundation—the brainchild of Raymond Plank, the billionaire owner of Apache Corporation, an oil and gas company.

Like most other landowners, the Ucross Foundation didn't hold subsurface mineral rights to much of the ranch. Plank tried to dissuade his fellow industrialists, but for all his money he couldn't do anything to stop the wildcatters from sinking wells. Plank might not have objected if there'd been a reason to drill, but from his decades of experience he suspected that there wasn't enough gas to make the exploration financially worthwhile. And he was entirely correct—none of the fifty wells that sprang up on his property during the CBM boom in the early 2000s produced anything but water.[27]

Sharon Dynak, president of the Ucross Foundation, lacked Plank's expertise and money, so it would be easy to underestimate her. She doesn't look formidable, but she possesses "grace in the midst of a tornado" and is a "rock solid"[28] manager of (often difficult) people. But even this and her experience as a consummate handler of crises could not turn back the tide of drillers; Dynak said, "it was upsetting to see all of the development when you know there's nothing coming of it . . . a lot of it was a scam."[29] She got it half-right—and half-wrong.

Dynak described the venture as a "giant shell game" of rigs and workers that Everest Energy had sold to investors (including Detroit's Wayne County Employee Retirement System, the Detroit General Retirement System, and the Detroit Policemen and Firemen Retirement System) who poured $57 million into Everest Energy. This "sure thing" became Wyoming's contribution to Detroit's downfall, which culminated with the city's bankruptcy in 2013. That the company came into existence less than two weeks before meeting with pensioners and demanding a bloated management fee did not set off any alarms. The sales pitch turned out to be the only hot air produced by the company, which never sold a cubic foot of gas from the Powder River Basin.[30]

What Dynak got wrong was that nothing came of all that drilling. Ucross tried hard to be a good neighbor. As drilling proceeded at breakneck pace and folks began to worry about their water, Ucross hooked up with the Powder River Basin Resource Council (PRBRC—an environmental protection organization founded in 1973) to monitor the condition of Clear Creek, a tributary of the Powder River and a valuable natural resource for the abundant wildlife and dispersed ranches in the region.

As Ucross and PRBRC collaborated to protect the creek, they started talking about what else might be done to draw attention to the changes and catalyze discussion. The organizations made strange bedfellows. The PRBRC, if not itching for a fight, was not known for backing down, while the Ucross Foundation, if not conflict averse, was not an organization looking for trouble.

The Ucross Foundation decided to invite some of the region's most talented photographers to their residency program to create an exhibit: *The New Gold Rush: Images of Coalbed Methane*.[31] Although no gas had been found on the property, there was an abundance of fuel for perceptive artists—and a great deal came of their work, which documented the devastating changes wrought throughout the Powder River Basin.

After the photographs had hung at the Ucross gallery, which was twenty miles from the nearest town, the show was scheduled for exhibition at the Nicolaysen Museum in Casper, which had agreed to host the exhibit.[32] Dynak insisted that "our intent was not political. . . . I work closely with people in the energy business and they've been generous." In defense of the exhibit, she reassuringly observed, "I'm sure people have strong feelings about it, but really it's just a documentation of land in change, not so much a pro and con statement. . . . It may be a great thing to schedule another exhibition in 10 years [2016] because everything will look different then."[33] Reassuring but overly optimistic. With the fossil fuel rush shifting north to the Bakken Shale of North Dakota, companies abandoned some three thousand wells in the Powder River Basin after dumping nearly a gallon of water for every US citizen onto Wyoming's landscape. The time frame for cleanup is at least another ten years,[34] and reclamation bonds paid by the industry covered less than 10 percent of the costs that would be incurred by the state.[35]

To make matters worse, the collapse of the coal industry was on the horizon, taking with it any hope of restoring the land. A provision of the Surface Mining Control and Reclamation Act of 1977 allows companies to "self-bond" as a means to ensure cleanup costs of reclamation. Wyoming accounts for 83 percent of the self-bonding in the western United States.[36] In principle, corporations with sufficient assets are legally bound to pay for reclamation but gain an enormous financial benefit because they avoid tying up their money in surety bonds. But bankruptcy changes everything.

The major coal companies in the Powder River Basin began to claim that they couldn't pay their creditors. Alpha Natural Resources was obligated to provide $411 million to reclaim its two mines in the Powder River Basin, but when the company declared bankruptcy, the Wyoming Department of

Environmental Quality reached an agreement that the state would get first priority in court for a measly $61 million in reclamation costs, leaving the public with a $350 million unpaid bill.[37] When Arch Coal declared bankruptcy, a similar deal was struck in which Wyoming secured just $92 million on the company's $485 million reclamation bonding obligation.[38] The day before declaring bankruptcy, Arch Coal paid its top executives more than $8 million in bonuses and allowed company insiders—including Wyoming's former governor Dave Freudenthal—to convert more than $70,000 in phantom stocks (a type of financial derivative whose value is linked to the performance of real shares).[39] Alpha Natural Resources had modeled this appalling practice by paying its top officials $12 million in bonuses just prior to declaring bankruptcy, and Peabody Coal was the next domino to file for Chapter 11.[40]

But in 2006 few saw this coming, and the Ucross leadership sought to smooth ruffled feathers among energy executives who were sensitive to how their industry was portrayed, never imagining that the goose laying the golden egg for Wyoming would be plucked clean in a decade. Even the PRBRC tried to pacify the companies. Their chairman wrote in the exhibit guide for *The New Gold Rush*: "[We] recognize the importance of coalbed methane development to our state but these images prompt us to wonder, 'What will our legacy be?'"[41]

It's too bad that the Nicolaysen Museum didn't ask the same question when it folded under pressure from the energy industry and canceled the exhibit a month later.

The 25,000 square-foot building that houses the Nicolaysen Art Museum (the Nic) is owned by the city of Casper, but the museum's operations are supported by private donors. And in Wyoming, that means energy. Casper is not only in the middle of Wyoming, it is the centerpiece of the energy industry—and the home of some of its wealthiest and most powerful players.

In 1890 drillers struck oil in Casper, and within five years the city hosted its first refinery.[42] The inaugural boom came after World War I as the country thirsted for petroleum. Forty years later, Casper underwent a cultural renaissance when the big oil companies built regional offices in the city. Many professionals had their first posting in the boondocks of Wyoming before heading to major cities in the United States or abroad. After cosmopolitan careers, some of these executives came back to the peace and quiet of Casper, which they missed, and began to generously support the arts.[43]

By 2000 the major companies had moved their regional offices and the financial fate of the arts had fallen into fewer and fewer hands. According to a long-time Casperite, "Now we have people with a narrow view of the world. They don't get it."[44] Perhaps what they get is that they pay no state income tax thanks to energy revenues, and their county's income is dependent on oil, gas, and coal.[45]

Ben Mitchell was hired in 2003 as the Nicolaysen Art Museum's director of exhibits and programs. Had it not been for *The New Gold Rush* exhibit, he might have retired in Casper. Although he could pass as an English professor, Mitchell is intimately familiar with fossil fuels. He grew up in a gritty, mid-century coal town in West Virginia along the Ohio River, working in his father's store, where he saw "men terribly broken from mine accidents . . . with skin the color of ash, wheezing, coughing, fighting for breath." He listened to the grownups whisper about snipers hired by the companies to shoot at the miners' picket lines from distant ridges, and he bore witness to "resource exploitation, environmental degradation, and ravaged landscapes." Mitchell beat the odds and became a teacher and then earned an MFA on his way to becoming an art curator. He escaped from the oppression of West Virginia, only to find himself in Wyoming.[46]

Mitchell has no qualms about sharing his commitments and faults. He believes deeply in "the fundamentally positive and necessary role and humanizing force that the arts and humanities play in a healthy community." Harkening back to his Appalachian youth and the horrific treatment of people and land by the coal companies that has been captured in film, stories, and songs, he insists that "you *always* have the potential to learn something new from a painting, photograph, poem, dance, or string quartet that authentically speaks to the times we live in." And equally important to what transpired at the Nic, he admits to not suffering fools and cowards gladly.[47]

Given his experience with the arts, Mitchell proposed that he would oversee exhibits and programs and Holly Turner, the executive director, would take the lead in development and board management. The shared authority worked well for three years, until the tension between fundraising and freedom created an explosive mix around *The New Gold Rush* exhibit.

When he booked the photographic exhibit, Mitchell had big plans for engaging the community with educational and outreach activities. But neither he nor Turner had experience with the inflammatory potential of public art. A former board chair of the Nic described how things had worked until

Roughnecks punch a drill bit into the coal formations of the Powder River Basin, Wyoming, in midwinter. The extraction of fossil fuels does not make for a pretty picture, either literally or figuratively. Between 2000 and 2010, Wyoming had the worst, or among the worst, workplace fatality rate in the nation, with many of the deaths occurring in the oil and gas industry (photo by Ted Wood).

then: "As for funding and the energy folks, you censor yourself before things get started. Boards get scared about money, so they avoid controversy." After a reflective pause, he added, "Sometimes it's even hard to notice that it's happening."[48] But it is easy to notice when self-censorship isn't happening.

When the word was out that a photographic exhibit showing at the Ucross gallery and scheduled for the Nic "made the energy field look bad," Turner and a contingent of her board members drove two hours north to see for themselves.[49] The visitors from Casper found a series of photographs that depicted the grim landscapes, machinery, and people associated with coalbed methane.

The Ucross board hadn't been fazed by the images, but they were a much more cosmopolitan group.[50] Perhaps most important, unlike the Nic's bene-factors, the Ucross ranch hadn't fared well under the split-estate conditions that allowed the flurry of drilling. But once the Nic's board and executive director saw that the industry was not portrayed positively as bringing jobs and revenues to the backwaters of Wyoming through a fossil-fueled Manifest Destiny, a fuse was lit. And when the flame reached Casper's energy leaders, all hell broke loose.

"The feedback I received was petulant and angry," recalls Mitchell, who believed that "enormous, powerful influence was brought to bear on the board and the director."[51] The first call he received was from state senator Kit Jennings,[52] the self-serving Casper Republican we met in chapter 4.[53] Succinctly described as "a bully" by the then executive director of the Wyoming State Equality Center (a broad-based coalition for political accountability) and others,[54] Jennings had previously demanded that a visiting artist at the University of Wyoming be fired for her criticisms of the energy industry.[55] During the invective-laced diatribe with Mitchell, Jennings warned that if the exhibit wasn't canceled, support for the Nic would be yanked. Then came an onslaught of thuggish calls from Anadarko Petroleum Corporation and other energy companies, along with icy silence from sullen, purse-lipped board members of the Nic.[56]

The ranks closed with alarming speed. Although Mitchell never felt physically threatened, he experienced a gut-wrenching fear "for our basic rights, for our intellectual freedoms, for the Nic's and our community's health and vitality as a positive and safe place for dialogue, for the free exchange of ideas."[57] However, Mitchell might have been well advised to worry about his well-being.

The McMurrys have had a long history of using psychological, legal, and physical intimidation to silence their enemies, which includes anyone with environmental concerns that impede mineral extraction. Vickie Goodwin, who worked for years with the Powder River Basin Resource Council, recalls "several meetings where the McMurrys tried to intimidate people." Neal McMurry (Mick's father and the family patriarch) would arrive early at public hearings, flanked by burly roustabouts, position himself in the front row, and stare down the speakers. Individuals who showed up planning to testify would decide to remain silent, knowing that Neal's implicit threat was backed up by a demonstrable willingness to use a SLAPP (strategic lawsuit against public participation) to financially punish those who spoke out.[58]

In one memorable case, Vickie met with state and federal agencies regarding the environmental damage of a mining project that McMurry was planning. The day after a Bureau of Land Management employee shared her concerns with Neal, the agency representative called Vickie to alert her to danger. He didn't tell her exactly what McMurry had said, but in a deeply concerned voice he warned, "I'd be careful if I were you." Mick McMurry continued the family legacy of silencing opponents through intimidation.

When a well starts to blow, a roughneck can identify his real friends by seeing who has his back. When Mitchell looked around, he was all by himself in the middle of a political firestorm. He was hauled into a meeting of the board to explain himself. Or so he thought.

Mitchell began his explanation at the meeting by observing that "none of us go to our banker for trustworthy dental work, none of us go to our insurance agent to get our car's carburetor fixed. Museum curators are trained art professionals who work with art and ideas all day long."[59] But it was clear that his defense was falling on deaf ears. The rest of his presentation to the museum's star chamber was no more persuasive, but one has to admire his chutzpah. Mitchell noted that *The New Gold Rush: Images of Coalbed Methane* was artistically compelling and culturally important to the people of Wyoming. He spoke eloquently about the long and vital tradition of documentary photography as a means of exploring social, economic and political issues: "I reminded the group of Jacob Riis's photographs of abject poverty and human degradation in late 19th century New York City, documented in his *How the Other Half Lives* and published in 1890. I also provided an overview of the 1936 WPA-era research the writer James Agee and photographer Walker Evans did about the inhumane and grinding poverty of white southern sharecroppers."[60] He recounted how Riis's art was pilloried by New York's elite and that Agee and Evans's contract was canceled, only for their work to be published five years later as *Let Us Now Praise Famous Men*, which became a journalistic classic infused with iconic images that are housed in the Library of Congress. With a deep belief that *The New Gold Rush* could make a seminal contribution to the social history of the High Plains, he argued that the pushback was exactly why the museum should exhibit the work and host community education programs.

Mitchell's denouement was incisive. He reminded his board that Raymond Plank, the owner of a multinational oil and gas corporation with proven reserves equivalent to nearly three billion barrels of oil, had established the Ucross Foundation with these words: "Shouldn't extraction companies and individuals put something back? Could the environment, open lands and natural beauty be preserved and enhanced through stewardship?"[61] The board's icy rejoinder was framed as another rhetorical question: "Who do you think supports the Nic in this town?" This was to become the museum's variant of Wyoming's mantra: "Who do you think pays for our schools and roads?"

In 2006 the board had three people with connections to the energy industry: the area manager for a company that made gas compression systems, the chief operating officer of GasTech, and the public relations officer for NERD Gas.[62] Although these three board members provided a vivid reminder that Casper was a company town, today's board is even more connected to the energy industry. This domination lets the museum's administration know that there's to be no art that depicts coal, oil, or gas in negative (or even starkly neutral) terms.

Mitchell was called into the executive director's office for a meeting with Turner and told to sign an agreement, which he did with grave reservations, stating that she and the board would approve all exhibits and shows. While Mitchell is rather angular with a Clint Eastwood squint and distinguished gray at the temples, Turner has a kind of aging plumpness and a wide smile. But there was nothing soft or smiling that day. The executive director wanted no part of art getting in the way of the museum's finances.

Turner's own connection to energy was evident. Her husband was the director of the Rocky Mountain Oilfield Testing Center, which was embedded in the infamous federal Naval Petroleum Reserve No. 3, best known as the site of the Teapot Dome scandal. Today, the oil field is being put up for sale, and speculation has it that Anadarko Petroleum Corporation is interested given that they own the nearby Salt Creek field.[63] And, of course, this time the private company will surely pay fair market value.

The censorship of *The New Gold Rush: Images of Coalbed Methane* would seem to reflect a lack of courage and integrity on the part of the museum's director and board, but it's important to understand the nature of the socioeconomic pressure that was brought to bear on these citizens. In a sense, they were bit players in a tragedy. The power and wealth that ultimately dictated what work could be shown in Wyoming's flagship museum of contemporary art never stepped onto the stage. But there's no doubt as to who was lurking in the wings.

CHAPTER 9

Give Us Liberty or Give Us Oil

Ben Mitchell, the former curator of Casper's Nicolaysen Museum, observed, "The energy industry touches upon and strongly shapes *all* aspects of Wyoming's political, economic, and social structures . . . the exercise of their reach, power, and influence is immense."[1] In less eloquent but perhaps more incisive terms, a source close to the Nic remarked, "We all play the game . . . It's not going to change."[2] At least not until we figure out the players and the rules.

Casper's syndicate of wealth and power, which one wag referred to as the H-oily Trinity, consists of the Wolds, Trues, and McMurrys. The Wold family's prosperity is grounded in oil, gas, and uranium. Their statewide influence is formidable: they have provided an endowed Chair of Energy to the University of Wyoming and underwritten the Wold Physical Science Building at Casper College (not to mention a $20 million donation to the patriarch's New York alma mater, Union College).[3] The family patriarch, John Wold, launched the Wyoming Heritage Foundation, a right-wing organization that takes exception to anthropogenic climate change, renewable energy, and policies to reduce carbon emissions.[4] GasTech, the company whose executive was a Nicolaysen museum board member is also a Wold company.

The True companies had their beginning in 1948 when wildcatter H. A. True moved to Casper with a single drilling rig, which spawned True Drilling and True Oil. These grew into a petrochemical conglomerate of forty Casper-based companies—along with a bank, a trucking company, feed lots, and four hundred square miles of ranchland. The rags-to-riches trope is played to the hilt by the patriarch's three sons and daughter who count among their "causes" the Rocky Mountain Oil and Gas Association.[5] Family members have held various roles, such as a chairman of the Independent Petroleum Association of America and the Wyoming Republican Party, a Wyoming state legislator for twenty years (including a stint as the Senate president), the director of the Hilltop National Bank and the National Petroleum Council, and two trustees at the University of Wyoming.[6] Although a few malcontents ask what the Trues have done with their $100 million empire to help build a

The Jonah Field was the goose that laid the golden, gassy egg for W. M. "Neil" McMurry, along with his son, Neil "Mick" McMurry. In a period of eight years, the number of wells grew from 3 to 1,347. The field has a productive area of about thirty-three square miles, but within this relatively small area lies perhaps 1.3 percent of the entire natural gas resource in the lower forty-eight states (photo by Ted Wood).

community in Casper, there's no doubt that the family has enormous influence.[7] The Hilltop Bank and True Foundation are major donors to the Nic, and the current president of the museum's board of directors is Jennifer True, whose husband is steeped in the oil industry.

While the Wold and True families do their part to make Wyoming's energy mafia look like a benevolent creator of jobs and a generous payer of taxes, they can't hold a candle (or flaring gas well) to the McMurrys. And nobody knows this better than the board of the Nic. When Holly Turner was hired, the state's flagship art museum was $190,000 in debt with an annual operating budget pushing a million dollars.[8] But Turner had the conservative credibility and interpersonal skills needed to endear herself to the McMurrys. According to a source close to the Nic, Turner was a devoted conservative whose right-hand assistant had a screensaver that alternated between images of George Bush and Jesus.[9] Mick McMurry and his wife contributed $350,000 to the museum over three years, which constituted the largest single donation in the museum's history and got their man on the board (remember the guy from NERD Gas—that's a McMurry company). The money bought their name over the main gallery—along with the privilege of censoring art that didn't fit their sociopolitical values.[10] But how did Mick McMurry become the godfather of Wyoming energy with the clout to order a hit on *The New Gold Rush*?[11]

The McMurry family history tracks the story of energy in Wyoming.[12] Mick's grandfather worked for the Standard Oil Refinery in Casper. Mick's father made his initial wealth in construction, profiting from the cash cow of the federal highway system that was being built in the 1960s. Mirroring their father, Mick and his brother started their own highway construction business, but they overreached and the company failed in 1988, so Mick joined his father in the fledgling McMurry Oil Company.

In 1992 a Denver oil company was selling its Jonah Gulch leases near Pinedale, Wyoming. The McMurrys bought the venture on a hunch, knowing that a state-subsidized pipeline was being laid nearby. Their breakthrough came courtesy of a savvy consultant who developed an innovative fracking method. Realizing the staggering potential of their investment in what is now called the Jonah Field, the McMurrys quietly amassed federal leases. Applying the Bush-Cheney policy of obliging industry, the Bureau of Land Management decided that there would be no significant impact from wholesale development of the gas field (since then, declines in the area's wildlife and air quality suggest that the feds were badly mistaken).[13] In four years, the McMurrys had sewn up nearly two hundred square miles of leases and were producing eighty million cubic feet of gas per day. After surreptitiously bidding up leases at auctions to inflate the value of their holdings, the McMurry Oil Company cashed out.[14] In 2000 they sold their interests to Alberta Energy Company (which became Encana) for $1.1 billion, and a dynasty was born.[15] The crown jewel of the family holdings is arguably the Jonah Bank, which specializes in lending to oil and gas ventures.[16]

Mick McMurry and his wife also pursued philanthropic ventures. When they started, donations from their foundation were made quietly, if not anonymously. But that changed; Casperites perceived self-aggrandizement and implicit power as being the McMurrys' modus operandi. Perhaps their most illustrative contribution was a $5 million donation to the University of Wyoming, and the petroleum-based, artificial turf at the football field was appropriately named the Jonah Field[17]—which now also features towering pipes that flare gas to celebrate a touchdown and remind the crowd who's in charge.[18] While their foundation has dispersed almost $50 million over the course of fifteen years, the giving appears more grudging than selfless.[19] A source inside the world of nonprofits recounts a meeting at which McMurry was lauded for his generosity, to which he replied, "It's either give it to the government [in taxes] or give it to charity"—a view echoed in an interview with the local paper.[20]

But McMurry's money hasn't been merely given away. It's bought the subservience and loyalty of those who receive personal gifts and lucrative jobs—such as their company's public relations officer, a childhood friend of Mick's who sat on the Nic's board, traveled to Ucross, and sounded the alarm when *The New Gold Rush* was on its way to Casper.[21] Although fracking was the McMurrys' meal ticket, not drilling coalbeds, within Wyoming's carbon-based syndicate the bosses watched out for one another. As a person affiliated with the Nic (who understandably wished to remain anonymous) observed, "People do not buck the McMurrys."[22]

Once the decision was made to whack *The New Gold Rush*, the energy bosses needed someone to take the fall. Holly Turner was the perfect mark. She was smart and articulate, but what was most important, they knew she'd be loyal. The news broke in early February 2006, with a headline in the *Casper Star-Tribune*, the state's largest newspaper: "Nicolaysen Blocks Methane Exhibit."[23] Turner stepped forward as the sole perpetrator so that the energy families and the politicians beholden to the industry, such as Kit Jennings (he served along with McMurry on the Wyoming Business Alliance and received a generous campaign contribution from the True family), wouldn't take the heat.[24] Turner told reporters that "she alone had decided to cancel the exhibit [saying that] there was no pressure from the museum's supporters in the oil and gas industry." And when asked about coercion from industry supporters, she refused to rat out the politicians, saying, "That's definitely not the case." The article quoted the Powder River Basin Resource Council chairman as saying, "[The Nic] got leaned on very hard. It tells me some in the industry are not too proud of what they're doing."[25] Ben Mitchell, the Nic's curator at the time, later observed, "The idea that in the state of Wyoming a controversy like the one that blew up around *The New Gold Rush* exhibit would *not* generate direct communication to a museum director and a museum's board members from powerful bureaucrats in the energy industry is preposterous." Although he can't produce the smoking gun, he has no doubt that Turner was "overwhelmed by negative feedback from McMurry, True, Anadarko, and a state legislator."[26]

A source close to the McMurrys said that the industrialists accused Ted Wood of outright deception in the purportedly before-and-after photographs.[27] They noted that paired images were not of the same places and called foul. It would've been unfair had there actually been any before-and-after images. In reality, the exhibit included some photos by Wood showing both pristine and impacted landscapes, and "the images were not presented at all as 'this is what it used to look like and this is what it looks like now.' They were presented to show what the landscape looks like with and without development."[28] His explanation is reinforced in the gallery guide, which makes clear that these are not then-and-now pairings.[29]

The next move was for Turner to offer up an alibi, however implausible. She told the press that the exhibit "was not in keeping with the organization's mission statement."[30] However, the museum's stated mission was to provide "a place to educate, stimulate, and promote the understanding of art so that people can meet, view, study, create and enjoy contemporary art of the Rocky Mountain Region."[31] Perhaps what Turner meant was that hosting *The New Gold Rush* was contrary to this mission in that offending the energy mafiosos could result in there being no place for people to enjoy the arts.

When Turner's story began to crumble, she turned the tables and asserted that the censorship was justified because *The New Gold Rush* had "political overtones" (as if censorship had none).[32] She seemed to be implying that the Nic hadn't been squeezed; rather, those activist photographers were dragging controversy into a museum that should be filled with apolitical art. Mitchell finds this ridiculous, arguing that having a point of view "can *never* be used as an excuse to silence an artist's voice, or to stifle open, free, and complex dialogue."[33] After an eloquent disquisition on the history of art in shaping society's understanding of labor, poverty, and war, Mitchell concluded, "Let's also remember an awfully simple thing: The works in *The New Gold Rush* were straightforward documentary photography. The oil and gas industry created the scenes that the artists recorded."[34]

Soon, Turner was grasping at straws. She told her board and the press that she'd been surprised to learn that *The New Gold Rush* was scheduled for the Nic. Mitchell insists that he'd told her well in advance and that she had the date marked on her calendar.[35] There's no way to resolve the he said, she said

Above: Ted Wood's photographs of the impacts of coalbed methane extraction, such as these images of CBM wastewater ponds, were part of the show *The New Gold Rush*. The documentation of the environmental legacy of this frenzied race to extract natural gas incensed the energy industry, and powerful interests pressured the Nicolaysen Art Museum to cancel the exhibit (photos by Ted Wood).

Left: One of the objections raised about Ted Wood's images of coalbed methane extraction was that his paired images misrepresented before-and-after contrasts. However, photographs such as these, which were slated for *The New Gold Rush*, show unaffected and impacted landscapes of the Powder River Basin that could not reasonably be mistaken for such comparisons of the same locale (photos by Ted Wood).

argument, but exactly when Turner found out about the show isn't terribly relevant. Had there been photographs showing pronghorns munching placidly in front of drill rigs and ducks swimming happily in coalbed methane evaporation ponds, it's hard to believe that the museum's executive director would've killed the exhibit just to show the curator who was boss.

At the time, Mitchell struggled with whether to speak up publicly. He chose to let Turner control the message because he believed that revealing the role of the energy industry risked the life of the museum: "Oil and gas interests were so supremely powerful and vindictive that they could kill the Nic."[36] Shortly after the cancelation of *The New Gold Rush*, Mitchell resigned. He admits to having underestimated the willingness of "industry to undermine the roots of democracy" and overestimated the principled courage of an art museum in a company town. Today, he regrets having allowed money to buy his silence, believing that self-censorship "left a weakened institution and a weakened cultural community in Wyoming."[37] Mitchell sees the destruction of *Carbon Sink* on the University of Wyoming campus as the Nic's legacy: "The extraction industry must have felt emboldened by the ease with which they influenced and changed a major cultural institution's independent programming."[38]

The good people of Casper were mostly silent after the story broke, knowing that many of the city's amenities and services were funded by energy money. One resident nearly convinced the community college to host the exhibit, but all sorts of problems arose, such as providing security—an issue that had never previously impeded the display of artwork on campus. Even a downtown coffee shop with liberal leanings and art-covered walls shied away. Perhaps the most eloquent public response came in a letter to the editor published by the *Casper Star-Tribune*:

I feel so very sad about the Nicolaysen Art Museum's recent decision to cancel the exhibition presenting various views of the mineral development of our state. I feel sad for the people who made the decision. What must it be like to operate under pressure so intense as to separate them from their mission? I feel sad for the people who influenced the decision. What must it be like to fear that if other people saw what they are doing, some would think they should be ashamed? I feel sad for the artists. What must it be like to have dared to affirm your vision, and to endure the gatekeepers' rejection of that vision before it can reach its audience?[39]

But the most incisive critique came from a reader who simply concluded, "*Res ipsa loquitur*"—the thing speaks for itself.[40]

The blowout of a gas well means that something went wrong—and a responsible company learns from its mistakes (even if state regulators look the other way).[41] The political blowout of *The New Gold Rush* suggests that there were lessons to be learned. And at least some of those involved have gained insights about Wyoming and the nation.

Sharon Dynak, the Ucross Foundation president who is the devoted peacekeeper and optimist, believes that whatever was said leading up to the exhibit, the Nic's executive director and board were surprised. She maintains that if there had been diplomatic conversations and advanced planning, *The New Gold Rush* might have passed the censors.[42] At least it seems possible that the energy bosses and politicians would have had a less heavy-handed response.

Ted Wood, the outdoorsy photographer whose landscape images evoked such ire inside the McMurry circle, figured that by quashing the exhibit the industry would draw attention to the photographs. He was counting on the attraction of the forbidden fruit; if art was too controversial for public display, then who could resist seeing what was so dangerous? And Wood was right—the show was booked throughout the Rockies and in demand on the coasts.

Ben Mitchell, the Nic's curator, bridges the Appalachian mining of his childhood and Wyoming drilling of his adulthood in extracting a lesson that he hopes the energy companies will heed:

> The industry is short-sighted, self-important, arrogant, and zealously powerful; that's my reading of the past and the present. And I think that the severance taxes and their combined charitable giving in Wyoming is what they believe is their "pass." . . . No amount of charitable work—helping universities build football stadiums, underwriting museums' galleries, writing checks to the Boys and Girls Club—allows any company or individual any immunity from reasonable criticism, respectful challenge, tough questions, and the ordinary expectation that our industries be good neighbors and keep a clean nest.[43]

The Nic's board and directors continued to allow socioeconomic pressures to limit artistic discourse (Turner left in 2010 to become the executive director of the National Historic Trails Center Foundation in Casper). Marta Amundson is a quilt maker whose work includes allegorical references to global affairs, feminism, endangered species, and health care. An exhibit of her work was planned for the Nic in 2012, but a few of the quilts included uncomplimentary allusions to Dick Cheney, who grew up in Casper and has a high school football stadium and a federal building named in his honor. One of the Nic's board members with close ties to Cheney objected, and Amundson was given the choice of canceling the show or pulling the offensive quilts. She chose the latter.[44] A few of the quilts that alluded to environmental issues passed by the censors, probably because they were sufficiently subtle. However, the curator's plan to have Amundson's quilts shown along with Edward Burtynsky's ironically beautiful photographs of industry-ravaged landscapes was nixed.[45]

Corporate control of the arts is not just restricted to the conservative backwaters of the West. In an interesting convergence of work and life, shortly before his residency at Ucross, Ted Wood photographed Subhankar Banerjee—the photographer whose depictions of the Arctic National Wildlife Refuge were to appear in the main hall of the Smithsonian's Natural History Museum in 2003. Under political pressure, the show was moved to a back corridor, which, when the word got out, assured that crowds flocked to the images.[46] Indeed, the silencing of artists, curators, and exhibitions is a global phenomenon with extensively documented cases of censorship in London, including the influence of BP on the world-renowned Tate museum.[47]

In the end, the power of Wyoming's industrialists and politicians was brought to bear on an art museum that was planning to show a bunch of photographs that perhaps a few hundred people might have seen. The response seemed staggeringly disproportional to the threat. Even the real mafia doesn't take out a contract on a downtown gallery that shows unflattering images of the drug trade or prostitution. Metaphors aside, Casper's censors weren't criminals. In fact, they were law-abiding conservatives who claimed to defend constitutional freedoms. So why did art lead upstanding citizens and politicians to threaten a curator, bully a museum director, and ultimately repress free speech?

Dynak's view cuts to the heart of the issue: "Art is a power."[48] She knows that supporting artists through Ucross's famed residency program has risks: "The reason people make art is it has a powerful impact. It can be intellectual, emotional and aesthetic—and all those things at the same time."[49] The leadership of the Powder River Basin Resource Council takes this explanation one step further, maintaining that while the energy industry knows how to lobby against a bill, reply to expert testimony, and rebut a newspaper editorial, they are struck dumb by art. Their only reply to a photograph that portrayed the grim reality of CBM extraction was to "destroy it."[50] Although it would have been shrewd to have simply not responded to *The New Gold Rush*, "they are incapable of ignoring art, because it gets them inside somewhere."[51]

Ted Wood thinks that art disturbed those in power because, in the classical tradition of photojournalism, the images gave "voice to the voiceless . . . the people who are living out in the Powder River Basin are some of the most forgotten people on the planet." And he counsels Wyoming that, "If no one's watching what's happening in a critical way, then really all you have is an energy colony in the US."[52] But if you're the colonialist or becoming rich by collaborating with the empire, then Wood's dystopian community is your bread and butter.

The idealist Ben Mitchell continues to believe in the value of art, beauty, and intellectual freedom despite "the social and economic inequalities that are poured down upon working Americans and kept firmly in place by the capitalistic oligarchy." But he worries that "[corporations'] increasingly nefarious control over our political process today has nearly fatally damaged our democracy." He was deeply shaken by "how such an enormous, successful, powerful, wealthy industry remains so thin-skinned to even the smallest criticism or challenge, so petulant and angry when questioned." He doubts that the McMurrys or others acted out of a sense of shame for their environmental damage. Based on his years of experience in shattered communities in Appalachia and ravaged lands in Wyoming, he's concluded that "the industry sees itself as our benevolent provider, the ones doing the hard and dirty work so that we can all live in material bliss." For Mitchell, this vainglorious mindset does not abrogate the people's right to ask, "Why continue to do the work so sloppily, so badly?"[53]

The coal-town kid turned erudite curator puts what happened in stark terms that reach far beyond the bleak hills of West Virginia or the pockmarked plains of Wyoming. We are in deep trouble when leaders in a self-romanticizing culture prone to sociopolitical conservatism and suspicion of intellectualism feel justified in suppressing difficult or controversial programming to protect the comfortable status quo. With his passion for an America that seems to be fading, Mitchell says, "All of us who love and are engaged in art, culture, inquiry, learning—in the potential that art and science offer us for discovery—should be frightened by the steady erosion of one of our greatest contributions to human history: the free and safe expression of speech, ideas, and imaginative invention."[54]

While the citizens of Casper were being denied the opportunity to learn how their landscape was being transformed into a wasteland, two hundred miles to the southwest in the mountain town of Pinedale, Wyoming, the residents were discovering what happens when natural gas effluent was transformed into ozone. As the bloody battle over freedom of speech was being fought at the Nicolaysen Art Museum, the people living downwind from one of the nation's largest natural gas fields were trying to stanch their bleeding noses. When the big guns of fossil fuels—Encana, Shell, BP—encountered miserable and angry citizens who could no longer see the pristine peaks above Pinedale through the smog, the corporations had to choose between reducing pollution or suppressing speech. And the choice was not difficult.

The Case of
an Atmosphere of Fear and Silence

*Surely by now there can be few here who still believe the purpose
of government is to protect us from the destructive activities of corporations.
At last most of us must understand that the opposite is true: that the primary
purpose of government is to protect those who run the economy
from the outrage of injured citizens.*

—DERRICK JENSEN, *ENDGAME*

Where the Skies Are Smoggy All Day

The people of Wyoming—like most Americans—are torn between environmental quality and individual liberty. On the one hand, Wyomingites take great pride in their crystal-clear air. On the other hand, they are staunch defenders of self-determination, which means, among other things, the right to smoke.

Only eight towns in the state have adopted ordinances that even partially protect people from secondhand tobacco smoke.[1] Pinedale is not one of these. Although some of the bars and restaurants along the main street in this town of two thousand people have smoke-free seating, folks have no problem finding a place where a cigarette, steak, and whiskey go together. Tourists on their way to the glitz of Jackson Hole, an hour up the road, might want to have a smoke before getting to Wyoming's bastion of liberalism. So when secondhand haze from the natural gas fields above Pinedale began filling the lungs of the residents and blurring the view for the visitors, the locals were initially predisposed to let the corporations light up their gas flares and exhale the vaporous by-products.

It was a tough call, given that the Upper Green River Valley that cradles Pinedale was said, at one time, to have the cleanest air in the nation, rivaling the atmospheric purity of the remote Tibetan Plateau.[2] But just as Texans describe the stench of refineries as the smell of money, the people of Pinedale figured that eye-burning ozone was the price to pay for lucrative employment. At least for a while.

The geography around Pinedale reflects the sociopolitical tension. To the north rise the spectacular Wind River Mountains with a thousand square miles of wilderness, and to the south are the Pinedale Anticline and Jonah Field—two of the largest natural gas fields in North America. This energy vault is 80 percent owned by the federal government, which transfers the mineral rights to the highest bidder.[3] These were the lands that yielded riches for the McMurry family (see chapter 9). Multinational energy corporations have leased three hundred square miles of sagebrush sprinkled over a vast, gently sloping ridge of folded rock that geologists call an anticline.

The gas fields outside of Pinedale, Wyoming, with the picturesque, if somewhat hazy, Wyoming Range in the background. The Pinedale Anticline encompasses three hundred square miles, and the forty trillion cubic feet of gas reserves would serve the nation's entire natural gas demand for nearly two years (photo by Wendy Shattil/Bob Rozinski—International League of Conservation Photographers; Creative Commons).

Beneath this expanse of land lies thirty-five trillion cubic feet of gas,[4] enough to inflate five million Hindenburgs—which would cover the states of Vermont and New Hampshire in zeppelins. There's a good reason that this area has been called the Saudi Arabia of natural gas.

The stakes were high for the companies pumping out gas and for the people of the valley breathing in the industrial by-products. But the energy companies had a model for keeping the populace quiet and the politicians at bay—big tobacco. Philip Morris and RJ Reynolds had shown how to silence, obfuscate, confuse, and delay government responses to imminent health threats.[5] So the energy industry manufactured doubt, created controversy, and laid a political smokescreen to assure that while noses bled, lungs hacked, and eyes burned, the government would dither with endless analyses and hearings.

To understand how the fossil fuel industry silenced opposition, it's necessary to grasp the geochemical, socioeconomic, and political events that transformed the Upper Green River Valley. This region was a microcosm of what was unfolding in the American West under the Bush-Cheney administration. In 2004 the White House asked cabinet officers to "identify ways your agency could expedite the review of permits [and] accelerate the completion of such projects."[6] After the energy industry provided about $140 million in federal campaign contributions, the number of drilling permits on public land tripled.[7] Sometimes you really do get what you pay for.[8]

In Wyoming, where drilling had been going on for several years, a major change came in 2000, when the US Department of the Interior's Bureau of Land Management (BLM) lifted restrictions on wintertime drilling to allow the energy companies to extract gas year-round.[9] During the long nights, Pinedale residents began to notice an ominous glow on the southern horizon, as excess gas and fracking effluents were flared until the pressure in a new well became manageable (Wyoming statutes exempt vented and flared gas from taxation, costing the state millions of dollars).[10] The companies incinerated at night so that the smoke would dissipate and slumbering people would not readily associate flaring with the thickening haze in the valley. But the real danger was invisible.

The emissions were ripe with nitrogen oxides and volatile organic compounds, including methane, which is a major contributor to global warming, although Wyoming's concern did not extend beyond its borders in this case. Intense exposure to sunlight coming from above and being reflected from snow drives a photochemical reaction that generates ozone from these precursors.[11] Although ground-level ozone from photochemical reactions was familiar in cities during the summer, winter production was unknown until gas development came to Wyoming.[12]

Ozone consists of three oxygen atoms that readily degrade into O_2 and a highly reactive, single oxygen atom. This free radical damages mucous membranes, triggers asthma and bronchitis, and causes chronic cardiovascular illness.[13] Tobacco smoke is likewise laced with free radicals. While people could avoid smoke-filled bars, there was no escaping industry's toxins when inversions trapped colorless miasmas of ozone that slid into the neighborhoods, parks, and streets of Pinedale. On a bad day, breathing the air was equivalent to smoking a pack of cigarettes.[14]

While ozone was—and continues to be—the focus, more recent studies have revealed other air quality problems associated with gas and oil operations. Air samples taken in thirteen of fifteen sites in western Wyoming had concentrations of benzene, xylene, toluene, and other toxic chemicals that exceeded federal standards. Seven samples contained hydrogen sulfide in concentrations from 2 to 660 times the level considered immediately danger-ous to human life, and another seven samples contained high levels of hexane (a neurotoxic chemical), with one location measured at 7,000 times OSHA's minimum risk level. Air sampled from one site contained formaldehyde at a concentration exceeding the EPA's "most hazardous cancer level." Such a cocktail of chemicals could only have made breathing more difficult for the people of Pinedale.[15]

In 2003 an enormous fireball erupted from the anticline when a pulse of gas caught a fracking operator by surprise. As the black mushroom cloud dissipated, the haze spread across 1,200 square miles.[16] The Wyoming Department of Environmental Quality (DEQ), which had been studiously avoiding air quality problems in the region, could no longer turn a blind eye to the burning eyes in Pinedale.

The agency responded to growing discontent by initiating cursory moni-toring and requiring "green completion" of all new wells to recover, rather than burn, the toxic cocktail of fracking chemicals.[17] But the state's regula-tions included various exemptions, such as not requiring green completion if the company did not have the necessary equipment readily available.[18] It was like requiring a smoker to go outside for a cigarette, unless the door was inconveniently far away.

Meanwhile, the Bush-Cheney administration was making sure that the federal agencies were serving industry. A White House memorandum all but required BLM state directors to issue leases on demand to the oil and gas industry.[19] Drilling approvals on western lands increased by 62 percent in 2004 to encompass an area equal to the state of Florida.[20]

The BLM shifted personnel from tracking airborne pollutants to process-ing (the euphemism for approving) drilling applications.[21] If a regional office fell behind in issuing permits, the operators could contact the Task Force on Energy Project Streamlining, a Washington-based office that the Bush White House had created to function as a complaint desk. The task force could pressure the local directors, who then hired industry consultants as "hosted workers" to expedite permitting.[22]

Eventually the murk in Pinedale couldn't be ignored and DEQ established a systematic monitoring program using 2005 as the baseline for air quality,[23] which was tantamount using the Marlboro cowboy's lungs as the standard for health. Even though the nitrogen oxide emissions from the gas field exceeded by five-fold the value set by the BLM, the agency worked with companies to expand production.[24] While drilling was increasing, mule deer and sage grouse populations were declining by half—and the Bush administration began referring to wildlife protections as "impediments" to the gas industry.[25]

In 2007 the BLM revised its environmental impact statement to permit another 4,400 wells, along with an additional twenty square miles of surface disturbance, and explicitly allowed further declines of wildlife populations.[26] And if the companies were still feeling squeezed, they could request exemptions that were approved 98 percent of the time.[27] The state director of the BLM defended the new guidelines as representing "a delicate compromise"[28]—much like designating one stool at the bar as nonsmoking.

The next winter saw DEQ warn residents five times to stay inside as ozone levels reached 122 ppb (the EPA's eight-hour exposure limit being 75 ppb).[29] The governor and others implausibly attributed the pollution to the interstate highway 80 miles south of Pinedale, dirty air drifting 250 miles from Salt Lake City, and automobile exhaust from the residents of Sublette County (population density, two people per square mile).[30]

The citizens pressured the governor until he recommended in 2009 that the US Environmental Protection Agency (EPA) consider whether the afflicted region was in "non-attainment" (meaning a failure to meet regulatory standards), which could preclude further development.[31] The correlation between air quality and human health in Pinedale was unmistakable; clinic visits for respiratory problems increased by 3 percent for every 10 ppb increase in ground-level ozone.[32]

Despite efforts to reduce emissions, the winter of 2011 saw thirteen ozone alerts, with levels higher than the worst smog day in Los Angeles during that year.[33] Nevertheless, the BLM entertained a proposal to further expand gas production in the Jonah Field.[34] The industry was happy to seek out new sites for drilling, but they were not pleased with studies refuting the claim that distant highways and cities were the source of the ozone. Over the next two years, the Pinedale Anticline Project Office, which financed virtually all monitoring and mitigation work, steadfastly refused to support university research designed to map major emissions plumes and pinpoint problem facilities.[35]

Although ozone levels decreased, probably due in part to the companies reducing emissions (there was also less snow cover and hence less photochemical conversion of precursors into ozone),[36] the decline was close but no cigar. In 2013 the EPA issued a declaration of "marginal non-attainment," which triggered a three-year clock.[37] If the state and industry didn't bring the region into compliance, the EPA could impose strict limitations on further gas development. Encana and BP were planning another 13,288 wells in the next decade, so something had to be done.[38] Well, maybe. Even if the goal of breathable air wasn't reached, the EPA could decide that there was enough progress to keep the industry puffing away. Indeed, Encana sold its holdings on the Jonah Field for $1.8 billion, reportedly so the company could focus on oil production, although one has to wonder whether the air quality violations and potential EPA sanctions were also a consideration.[39]

The plan that emerged in 2013 was something like a one-pack-a-day smoker upping consumption to three packs a day and hoping that switching to filtered cigarettes will stave off lung cancer. The state adopted putatively tougher standards, such as requiring operators to use the best available technology to reduce emissions—except for older facilities that were grandfathered.[40] Proposed regulations included just 1 percent of storage tanks. Even though 97 percent of wells would be exempted from quarterly tests, requiring only annual monitoring, the industry vehemently protested the requirements—and Wyoming senator John Barrasso (R) repeated a phrase used in an industry study, calling the standards "the most expensive regulation ever."[41] The physician turned politician argued that the health impacts of unemployment (which he maintained would result from raising air quality standards, although he provided no supporting evidence) outweighed the benefits of cleaner air.

If it seemed unlikely that the air quality criteria would be met, it was even more improbable that some of the world's most powerful corporations would be required to snuff out their leaky operations by 2016.[42] So nobody was surprised that as the winter of 2014 arrived, the state decided to delay implementation of air quality standards until 2017.[43]

How did it happen that for more than a decade the energy industry has been allowed to inflict such a serious health risk on the people? At first, many citizens in Pinedale and the tiny outlying communities tolerated the "secondhand smoke" from the gas fields, but increasing numbers soon tried to speak out. The story of how their voices were silenced through corporate and governmental duplicity stands as a warning to any community where industrial and political powers stand to gain—and the people stand to lose.

Climate change is a global risk, but the hazards of fossil fuel extraction are also intensely local. The people of Pinedale (pop. 2,030) were exposed to ozone originating in the gas fields above town at levels higher than those found on the worst day in US cities. Roughnecks can make twenty dollars an hour or more, but their injury and death rates are among the highest in the nation (photo by Ted Wood).

Of the dozens of residents who tried to protect their quality of life and air, Perry Walker was a particularly fine exemplar of a citizen activist. His slight build and boyish countenance were more reminiscent of a gracefully aging schoolteacher than a retired US Air Force major. But Walker spent his career in military intelligence, nuclear testing, infrared research, Reagan's Star Wars program, and the Airborne Warning and Control System (AWACS).

Walker grew up in Green River, Wyoming, eighty miles south of Pinedale, and earned a bachelor's in physics and a master's in nuclear reactor engineering. After a distinguished military career, he settled into a hilltop home twenty miles west of Pinedale in the hamlet of Daniel (population 150), where the local bar and library share a building. Walker grimly watched the ineluctable deterioration of air quality in his beloved valley while state and federal agencies did nothing. So, he bought an optical spectrometer and starting documenting the changes. But the corporations declared war and outmaneuvered the former air force officer on the political battlefield.

And "war" is not a contrived metaphor. Richard Berman, whose consulting firm solicited $3 million from the oil and gas industry to finance an advertising and public relations campaign, met with the Western Energy Alliance in Colorado Springs in June of 2014. In a secretly recorded speech to industry executives from companies including Devon Energy, Halliburton, and Anadarko Petroleum, Berman said, "Think of this as an endless war." And war is hell, so he told those gathered not to worry about offending the general public because "you can either win ugly or lose pretty."[44]

On the Pinedale front, the industry-government alliance employed diversionary tactics, directing their enemy away from the battle. The DEQ relied on an air quality model because without adequate field monitoring, mathematical simulations had to constitute regulatory reality.[45] The model was predicated on the wind always blowing away from Pinedale, in defiance of meteorological data. The agency's computer program had been developed by a fellow paid by the energy industry who successfully diverted public attention from worrying about rasping lungs to debating modeling assumptions.

When Walker's data revealed that lithium was part of the spectrum coming from the fires in the gas field, Encana officials replied that they were unaware of any such chemical in their flared emissions.[46] The company most certainly knew that fracking fluids often contained lithium (as well as sodium and potassium, which also were prevalent in the emissions), but a savvy general keeps the enemy guessing. Feigning ignorance diverted public time and energy into digging for information that the industry kept secret with the blessing of the government.[47]

The DEQ took a more direct approach to Walker's ozone measurements, which were taken using EPA-approved equipment and protocols. Confronted with a wartime atrocity, a crafty commander can resort to simple denial. When the director of the DEQ met with Walker, the agency head chuckled and said, "If I were to ever to take anybody's data yours would be it, but I will never accept your ozone measurements."[48]

Camouflage can also divert the enemy's attention. To hide the obvious cause of a sharp decline in mule deer populations on the anticline, a Questar executive blamed drought. When attention focused on the role of drilling, the company cloaked the impacts of extraction beneath a claim that the deer had successfully adapted by moving into new areas.[49] It was, however, a bit harder to hide the 25 percent decline in the number of sage grouse on the gas fields outside of Pinedale.[50]

The most disingenuous effort to shift public attention was to blame distant cities and highways. The governor insisted that the source of ozone was an open question long after the gas fields were known to be the origin.[51] And the Sublette County commission, whose coffers were being filled by the energy industry, hired a consultant to link the ozone problem to smog in Salt Lake City (urban centers being well-known sources for air pollution). Walker saw through the political smokescreen and pointed out the consultant's fatally flawed methods, to no avail.[52]

The outcome of a battle can be decided by a weapon that only one side possesses—repeating rifles, chlorine gas, atomic bombs. And in the battle to silence public resistance to natural gas exploitation, industry's government lackeys could stifle outspoken citizens with bureaucracy.

The BLM chartered the Pinedale Anticline Working Group (PAWG) in 2004 to represent public, industry, and government perspectives on air quality.[53] For PAWG to effectively sap the time and energy of concerned citizens, the bureau had to assure that the group could not accomplish anything substantive. Along with various procedural impediments, such as requiring consensus before making any recommendation, the bureaucrats prohibited the group from discussing any drilling project over which BLM had yet to rule.[54] As Walker wrote in a letter to the editor of the state's largest newspaper, "[The agency's] assertion is that we have no jurisdiction over 'pre-decisional' issues. This is asinine in a practical sense because once a BLM decision is made, any 'discussion' is doomed to become nothing more than talk radio without the radio."[55]

Despite the government's best efforts to stifle discourse, PAWG issued a report to the Pinedale office of the BLM. A year passed without a response, so the group sent an updated report and asked what had become of their first submission. Eventually, the director admitted that he had never read the initial report. The rules specified that the BLM was under no obligation to accept (or apparently even read) any of PAWG's recommendations. After another six months, the agency offered a patronizing response to the second report.[56]

The bureaucratic shield was also wielded when citizens became fractious and insisted on being heard. In November 2005 the BLM hosted a public meeting regarding the Shell-Ultra-Anschutz winter drilling proposal.[57] The agency's moderator told the crowd of more than fifty Pinedale residents that each person was to approach the staff stationed around the perimeter of the room to obtain individual answers. When the people objected to this divide-and-conquer approach and insisted that the agency answer questions publicly, the BLM official shushed the unruly crowd and disdainfully explained that brief comments should be written on approved forms that would be used to develop the agenda for another meeting in six months. Instead, the citizens crafted a petition expressing their disgust with the bureaucratic obstructions to civic discourse. Perry Walker sent the petition to the governor's office. There was no response.

When facing the possibility of defeat, a commander may resort to extreme tactics. Truman contemplated dropping atomic bombs to prevent a North Korean victory, and the energy-government alliance in Wyoming resorted to their own nuclear option. If the people didn't retreat into obsequious silence, the industry could vaporize businesses. They might even opt for mutually assured destruction, pulling up stakes, abandoning profits, and leaving behind ghost towns. Or so the people were led to believe.

In the dark days of the recession, Wyoming enjoyed low unemployment rates and billion-dollar budget surpluses. Sublette County's tax valuation increased from $379 million in 1999 to more than $2 billion in 2005. With $121 million in tax revenue, the seven thousand residents were treated to a remodeled courthouse, a fancy ice arena, a newfangled senior center, and a lively discussion about artificial turf for the high school.[58]

Sure, the influx of gas-field workers stretched the health-care infrastructure and the courts wallowed in DUIs, battery charges, and drug-related arrests (methamphetamine being useful when working twelve-hour shifts for two straight weeks). But who was going to complain about making $35 an hour for unskilled work (other than local businesses who couldn't match these wages)? To a guy driving a truck, that's good income—and to the company, that's cheap hush money.

A love-it-or-leave-it sentiment developed as townsfolk employed in the gas fields blamed "the Greenpeace people" for instigating unrest that could drive the companies away.[59] Meanwhile, the industry was trying out tactical nuclear arms to silence obstreperous voices on the battlefield. For example, a gas-field manager stopped by the Ford dealership to tell the owner that it would be good for business (the energy industry bought lots of vehicles) if the fellow would quiet down his father, an irascible legislator who sometimes spoke ill of the industry. Walker also knew several other owners of small businesses in Pinedale who didn't dare to speak up because the gas companies were paying top dollar for their services.[60]

Apocalyptic threats notwithstanding, gas production is anticipated to continue on the Pinedale Anticline for seventy-five years, with reclamation of damaged ecosystems continuing for more than a century.[61] This is a war of attrition. In modern society, the most reliable tactic for dragging out decisions and muffling discourse is driving your enemy into the no-man's-land of the committee.

The Wyoming media described the twenty-six members of PAWG as a "crazy quilt of different, sometimes conflicting, interests: local residents, environmentalists, natural gas industry representatives and local, state and federal government officials."[62] When a sense of futility inevitably killed the PAWG in 2012, another task force was formed by the former director of the DEQ. The University of Wyoming facilitated the gathering and declared victory for collaborative decision making, not unlike successfully resolving the shape of the table during the negotiations to end the Vietnam War. The task force eventually forwarded recommendations to the current director of the DEQ so the agency could begin "an analysis to determine if they can be implemented."[63]

Time is money, and a potent weapon in the war of attrition was cash. In 2006 Wyoming's governor Dave Freudenthal accepted $36 million from the natural gas companies to pay for environmental mitigation—fixing, reversing, or otherwise undoing the damage.[64] The operators agreed to pay out the money as long as they could produce gas (and ozone) year-round. So, in reality the industry bought years of regulatory silence. Various projects were funded, but the results were never quite sufficient to convince regulators to alter the industry's practices. As Walker puts it, "This was a classic tactic practiced by both BLM and DEQ to hold the public off by claiming that they're engaged in a study. That study being one that never ends, never comes up with findings."[65]

In Vietnam, as in other far-flung conflicts, those battling an overseas enemy realized that they didn't need to win the war—they only needed to not lose. If the insurgents could avoid a decisive battle, the Americans would eventually become dispirited and go away. The same strategy worked for the industry-BLM alliance. The revision of the environmental impact statement drew citizens into spending thousands of hours over three excruciating years. The BLM buried the public in massive, jargon-filled documents, allowing just thirty to sixty days (and sometimes as few as ten) to respond.[66] Walker and others provided detailed technical critiques that generated canned responses ("Thank you for your comment, we believe we've done all the necessary research").[67] The BLM summarily dismissed more than sixty-eight thousand public comments as being "unsubstantial, negative statements against the plan with no suggestion of alternatives"[68]—effectively scolding: don't bring us your problems unless you also provide us with solutions.

When Walker challenged the DEQ's authority to implement a cap-and-trade system allowing companies to exchange reductions in one ozone pre-cursor for increases in another (even when their contributions to the problem differed), the agency took three months to figure out how to avoid a decisive battle. Their guerilla tactic was to claim that they were adopting an interim policy—and temporary protocols were not subject to public challenge. Six years later, the system remained in effect and Walker's question of when "interim" becomes "permanent" was never answered by the agency[69]—sort of like asking how long George W. Bush's "swift punishment" of US enemies in Afghanistan will last.

After a decade of trying to pin down the industry and agencies, Walker was exhausted. He grew despondent when the Wyoming Oil and Gas Conservation Commission started revising their records from three and four years earlier, so that all of his meticulous analyses of production and leakage were negated. With something between melancholy and bitterness, he reflected on how those with power and money drew out the conflict: "They had the advan-tage of scores of employees paid to crank out data while environmentally minded citizens were lone individuals, often with real day jobs, who could be so overwhelmed with information that they could not use it in any timely or useful fashion."[70] Perry Walker has five gigabytes of official correspondence, agency records, legal documents, production spreadsheets, raw data, emissions graphs, and meteorological tables. But he also has the ability to distill his years of experience and mounds of information into an incisive summary: "[Their] localized and focused approach included stonewalling of citizen efforts to elicit corrective actions from industry, cleverly targeting donations of minor monetary sums to local projects, hosting of 'listening' forums to ostensibly take feedback from concerned citizens, and automatic denunciation of any science-based findings that might reveal environmental damage which could threaten gas developers' ability to conduct their business as usual."[71]

It was this last element, the stifling of science, that seems so reprehensible. In sociopolitical struggles, those who can create clever diversions, wear down opponents, and bend the rules might be darkly admirable. But suppressing the investigation of the nature and sources of harm to fellow humans is antithetical to the long struggle of Western culture—the pursuit of truth about the world and the sharing of knowledge.[72]

Government and industry conspire to sustain profits and ignorance at a grim cost to the people of Pinedale, as in many other communities across the nation where the corporatocracy also decided that fossil fuels trump human health. Consider the neighborhoods in Pennsylvania where fracking contaminated water supplies and caused grave illnesses, the towns in West Virginia where coal mine accidents have crushed, suffocated, and immolated workers for decades, and the community of Lac-Mégantic, Canada, where the town center was decimated and forty-seven residents killed when railroad tank cars filled with crude oil derailed and exploded. So we turn now to parallel tales of silencing science. The grim story of how Wyoming's hegemonic alliance quashed research into ozone in the Upper Green River Valley has another chapter in which those in power censored scientific discourse about the role of carbon dioxide in the state's changing climate.

CHAPTER 11

The Calculated Absence of Evidence

D r. Robert Field was a highly regarded air quality expert looking for a change in his life when he met a woman traveling in the United Kingdom. A British scientist might not seem to have much in common with an American painter, but love at first sight defies explanation. Six weeks later, Field was in Laramie, where his wife-to-be was on the art faculty at the University of Wyoming. After finding work teaching courses in environmental science and policy for the university, he returned to his research roots. Field was hired by the European Commission to conduct a complex, multinational air quality project. As that contract was ending in 2006, he became intrigued by an air pollution problem unlike those of urban and urbane Europe—ozone in the Upper Green River Valley.[1] He was certainly aware that environmental regulation could be controversial, but he didn't fathom how politically charged a rural landscape could be.

Perry Walker, the rabble-rousing citizen scientist, was excited to have a high-powered expert visiting Pinedale, but he warned Field, "What you're planning will not be allowed. The Department of Environmental Quality will not let you reveal unfavorable information in the eyes of the industry." Field, an intense fellow with more than a passing resemblance to Johnny Depp, bristled. He insisted that he would not let politics pervert his science. The environmentally battle-hardened Walker sighed, "I hope you can stick to that."[2]

The university was pressing companies to fund the new School of Energy Resources, whose interim director was studiously avoiding Walker.[3] It was not long before Walker learned that Field, whose university position and salary depended on grant support that required the Wyoming Department of Environmental Quality's (DEQ) blessing, didn't dare let the agency know that the two men were talking about ozone. Meanwhile, the University's leadership told their School and Institute of Environment and Natural Resources, where Field had taught for several years, not to pursue research that could upset the energy industry in Sublette County.[4] The school had been chastised by the governor and industry for a report on the mismanagement of water from coalbed methane production,[5] and the administrators didn't want another scientific critique of industry.

In fact, Field was the scientist who discovered that ozone was being produced from methane leaks in the gas fields. But as long as the entire gas field was only vaguely responsible, regulators could look no further. The idea was to diffuse responsibility in a political formulation of the old adage: dilution is the solution to pollution. However, Field's next line of investigation violated the "see no evil" dictum—and then he had the gall to speak evil.

In 2012 Field presented his findings at a citizens' ozone forum in Pinedale. There, he explained how he'd met all of DEQ's data requirements—and then had taken the first steps to link methane emissions to particular sites. Field thought that he was solving, not creating, a problem.[6] Without eventually pinpointing the sources of precursors, how could anyone hope to reduce ozone levels? But his rationale presumed that less ozone, rather than more gas, was the goal.

Later that year, Field's next research proposal, which included precise mapping of emissions plumes using a mobile monitoring station, was rejected by the state. The ostensible reason provided by the Pinedale Anticline Project Office, the interagency body tasked with dispersing the industry's mitigation fund, was that Field's project didn't fit their funding schedule.[7] What they didn't say was that conforming to their calendar made wintertime sampling impossible—a happy coincidence for the energy industry.

When the DEQ's own Air Quality Citizens Advisory Task Force criticized the funding decision, the agency changed its explanation. The regulators contended that Field's $128,000 proposal (which represented 0.4 percent of the industry fund) did not directly mitigate impacts.[8] True enough, but this was like arguing that frantically applying splints to an accident victim is more important than figuring out what's broken.

Pressed further, officials resorted to absurd excuses—anything other than admitting that gas-field operators would not tolerate being exposed. The Anticline Project Office claimed that driving around to measure methane levels would stress wildlife populations,[9] as if drilling rigs, massive trucks, compressor stations, and gas clouds were soothing. State regulators maintained that Field's work was experimental, so they couldn't use the data for regulatory purposes, although no rules prohibited them from doing so.[10]

In an effort to appease the industry's minions, Field revised his proposal the next year. The Project Office funded six out of the seven projects based

Among the thousands of gas drilling rigs on the Jonah Field and Pinedale Anticline, the majority of toxic emissions probably come from a small proportion of the facilities. However, when scientists sought to pinpoint the sources of ozone precursors using a mobile monitoring station, the project was rejected by state regulators over citizens' objections (photo by Ted Wood).

on DEQ's rankings. Field's research was the loser. Unlike a program to feed mule deer, Field's work was deemed to be research rather than mitigation.[11] Once again, there was money to stock up on splints, but no interest in buying an X-ray machine to diagnose the problem. Having rejected Field, DEQ paid a consultant to collect data using a specific protocol. Field said, "I could design a study to say whatever they want to hear, but I won't position monitors to get a result that someone wants."[12]

In the end, Perry Walker was right and Rob Field was forced by funding attrition to abandon his work on the Pinedale Anticline. To survive as a grant-funded atmospheric scientist in Wyoming, there are certain lines of inquiry that are untouchable. This lesson came too late to another scientist at the university. Local ozone production is a serious concern, but methane is an extremely potent greenhouse gas—and global climate change is beyond the pale in conservative politics.

Dr. Steve Gray, the state climatologist, made no friends at a public forum on

Wyoming lands and people in September 2008.[13] Although he had the healthy and trim look that conveyed a sense of clear thinking, his audience wasn't keen on hearing about a future climate with increasingly severe droughts. Like a far-flung, codependent family of 532,000 people, Wyoming was committed to denying the existence of the oily, gassy, coal-dusted elephant in the room and its contributions to global warming. With alcoholism rates and drunk driving deaths far above the national average, Wyomingites were well practiced at denial in the face of overwhelming evidence.[14]

Gray grew up in Oklahoma, where Boy Scout hikes and family camping trips fed his fascination with natural history and weather. As an undergraduate, he participated in a project using pollen records to reconstruct long-term weather patterns, which convinced him that his passions for biology and climatology could be melded. In his master's thesis at the University of Oklahoma, Gray used the expansion of red cedar to study the effects of drought. From there, he earned a doctorate at the University of Wyoming by applying paleoclimatology to contemporary water management challenges. He then traveled from Montana to Arizona, developing climate monitoring systems for the national parks and studying the ancient hydrology of the Colorado River, but he yearned for the sublime landscapes of Wyoming.[15] So when a position opened up at the university for a state climatologist and director of the Water Resources Data System in 2005, Gray brought his young family "home."

Gray couldn't have imagined that he'd be the last state climatologist in Wyoming. However, he knew he was coming to the state with the largest percentage of climate change skeptics; 53 percent of the people were in denial (versus 16 percent nationwide).[16] So when Gray spoke about the ongoing drought as "evidence pointing toward the climate changing,"[17] you'd think that the state's committed denialists would have sent him packing.

However, the Wyoming household recognized that something should be done—as long as nobody talked about what caused the turmoil. Folks could see the rangeland drying up, hay prices going through the roof, and municipal water supplies disappearing. In discussing drought, Gray found that he could allude to climate change because people rationalized that nature was always in flux. But specifying *anthropogenic* climate change was like a family acknowledging that the mess in the living room was due the alcoholic passed out in the garage.

Gray characterized his interactions in the state as "surprisingly positive."[18] Wyomingites were hard-nosed, if short-sighted, pragmatists who wanted to solve problems without worrying about their causes. So he didn't draw the connection between the fossil fuel industry and the drought that was crippling agriculture, recreation, and towns. Gray was well aware of what had happened a few years earlier to the unit that preceded his own, when science and politics had collided.[19]

The Wyoming Water Research (later, Resources) Center existed for a tumultuous eleven years, beginning in 1987. With time, the research became increasingly academic, until the legislature declared that the center no longer met the water management needs of the state. For "water buffaloes"—the political kingpins who called the shots—water was like coal, a resource to be extracted and used for economic gain. In the ensuing standoff, the director defended basic science and defied ornery politicians. Bad move. The legislature yanked its funding, and from the ashes of the Water Resources Center arose two government-funded programs with profoundly different views of the world: the Office of Water Programs and the Water Resources Data System.

Science—or what passes for science—doesn't get much more conservative than that practiced by the Office of Water Programs.[20] This university venture was funded through the powerful Wyoming Water Development Office, overseen by a commission appointed by the governor. The Office received about $150 million per year through severance taxes and mineral royalties. To remind everyone who is in charge, the Water Development Office trumpeted the "sound philosophy of utilizing a portion of the income the state receives from the development and use of its non-renewable resources, such as coal, oil and gas, to develop and manage a renewable resource, water."[21] Discussions of the linkages between fossil fuels and drought are simply not welcome—much like a family chatting about the connection between drinking and domestic violence.

To assure silence, the university's Office of Water Programs was headed by a committed climate change denier. Greg Kerr, an agricultural engineer, dismissed the findings of the Intergovernmental Panel on Climate Change (IPCC)—made up of the world's leading experts—by saying, "All these climate change models look like a bunch of spaghetti."[22] As for the decline in Wyoming's glaciers, which are vital to the state's water supply, he wrongly asserted that temperatures had declined over the last fifty years.[23] And he defended the fossil fuel industry by asking, as if this were a serious question, "Are we going to stop energy production and starve to death?"[24]

Kerr distributed $300,000 a year—a paltry sum in terms of research—to various projects on campus that "provide data and factual information."[25] Given the cost of the Office of Water Programs to the university, which approached the amount of funding that it brought in, one has to wonder why the institution supported such a marginal venture.

The best explanation is fear. Nobody wanted a repeat of the fiasco that shut down the original Water Research Center. Kerr convinced the university's Office of Research that any mention of climate change would generate an epic blowup.[26] The vice president of research wanted to keep money and research overhead flowing, and if that meant quashing mention of the elephant in the room, so be it.

To get a sense of the politics within the Office of Research (later Research and Economic Development, which says a great deal), consider the former entrepreneur who ran the Office of Research's small business grant program. Eugene Watson was involved in the funding of scientific and technological enterprises while continuously and publicly pronouncing ludicrous views of climate change (and declaring his doubt that HIV causes AIDS):

> Gov. Matt Mead has the courage of convictions in disclosing that he hasn't partaken of the Al Gore junk-science Kool Aid propaganda with respect to human-caused global climate change (warming). . . . there is absolutely no empirical scientific evidence that humans have any detectable impact on global climate; zero, zilch, zip, nada, none. Ask any of the faculty at the UW School of Energy Research—they aren't able to produce any scientific evidence in support of Gore's self-serving speculations. Atmosphere carbon dioxide is a nutrient, not a pollutant, without which there would be no terrestrial food chain, thus no humans.[27]

So the state climatologist found himself in a rather difficult position. Gray's responsibilities included directing the other major water program on campus, the Water Resources Data System, which was also funded through the state's Water Development Office. Gray's staff provided hydrological and climatological data to public agencies. This might seem a rather mundane task, but when water is involved, controversy isn't far behind. Gray recalled, "Providing climate and water data services is not, in the end, a very fun business. For example, the data could result in cattle being pulled off a lease. . . . There were many no-win situations." He paused and then completed the picture:

Politicians struggle to understand how anthropogenic carbon dioxide could be altering the climate. Meanwhile, the venting and flaring of natural gas is allowed across the nation, with 260 billion cubic feet wasted every year. Wyoming accounts for 13 percent of this total, which is more than the amount consumed by all natural gas–powered vehicles in the country (photo by Ted Wood).

"And this was made all the worse by those who wanted to further complicate the problem with political spin."[28]

Gray tactfully spoke about climate change to Rotary Clubs, bankers, and town councils, "where there wasn't a liberal hair in the room," but he never sensed the sort of animosity that he encountered on campus. When his educational ventures were discovered by the administration, "I'd be called to task in [the vice president's] office with Kerr leading the charge to take me to the woodshed. There was constant resistance on the university side to climate change via the Office of Water Programs in combination with the state Water Development Office."[29] And these organizations had some potent allies at the state and national level.

The Wyoming legislature is chronically about 85 percent Republican.[30] Although they are not a monolithic group, it's a safe bet that Jerry Paxton (the representative from Carbon County who we met in chapter 6) is pretty typical in noting, "I have problems really understanding or thinking that what the United States is doing, especially in the use of coal, is having any significant effect."[31] It is hard to grasp the size of the earth—but it's also hard to imagine that Wyoming mined its ten billionth ton of coal in May 2013 (that's about a ton of coal for every human who has been alive since 1900).[32]

Wyoming's current governor, Matt Mead, is also a climate change skeptic who is convinced that burning coal is good for his state but remains "unconvinced that climate change is man-made."[33] Like an unwavering creationist, he insists that the science "is still under debate." Mead, like his predecessors, insists that there's no connection between global climate change and the state's drought.[34] In front of the 2015 legislature, Governor Mead vowed to "work with bulldogged determination" to promote the coal industry.[35] Not wanting the other fossil fuels to feel left out, he added, "We fight for coal as we will fight for oil and gas and other resources if they are targeted by oppressive federal regulations."[36]

Back in Washington, Wyoming's delegation was united in denial. Cynthia Lummis, the state's sole representative, struck the standard disingenuous pose of the deniers, saying, "The jury's still out."[37] Among other extremist positions, she voted to open the Outer Continental Shelf to drilling and to bar the EPA from regulating greenhouse gases.[38]

The standard bearer for the fossil fuel industry is Senator John Barrasso, who offered this combination of indisputability and implausibility: "Climates continue to change, and the role of man in that is completely unknown."[39] He denied the expertise of the United Nation's IPCC, while deriving his position from television meteorologists and oil-industry funded think tanks. Barrasso sat on two key committees—Energy and Natural Resources and Environment and Public Works—to feed the industry that dumped nearly $200,000 into the his campaign fund.[40] Barrasso's position was that the United States' reducing emissions won't matter without Russia, India, and China falling in line.[41] The senator contended that we didn't need to act ethically unless others did as well, which is the sort of moral reasoning one might expect of a child caught shoplifting along with a group of other delinquents.

Wyoming Senator Mike Enzi joined Barrasso in signing on to a bill repealing the law phasing out incandescent bulbs in favor of the energy-saving compact fluorescent lamps, saying, "I'm from Wyoming. Our approach is, leave us alone."[42] Enzi, who figures that a Wyoming snowstorm in May refutes global climate change,[43] is less reactionary than his colleague in terms of climate change rhetoric, suggesting that carbon sequestration could provide economic opportunities. Of course, he introduced the Carbon Storage Stewardship Trust Fund Act while his son was employed by North American Power Group Ltd.—a company positioned to profit handsomely from the legislation.[44] The younger Enzi, who holds a journalism degree, had his time billed to the federal government at eighty dollars per hour for working on a facility to "recycle" low-quality coal by burning it in what would otherwise be called a power plant—a thinly veiled scam that made so little substantive progress that the IRS yanked the tax-exempt status for its industrial revenue bonds.[45]

The people of Wyoming have been warmly complicit with the climate change denials of their elected officials. Barrasso and Enzi have enjoyed the highest approval rates of any US senators. Congress might have had an 11 percent approval rating, but Wyoming's denier duo enjoyed 69 and 63 percent approval among constituents.[46] You can pick up empty beer cans while everyone refuses to confront the alcoholic for only so long. At some point, you can no longer enable the pathology. For Gray, it became clear that the university and the Water Development Office were not going to allow him to address the ongoing drought in terms of the state's codependency with the energy industry.

The final straw came when the Water Development Office pulled the plug on Gray's hiring a much needed data analyst because the funding was coming from the National Oceanic and Atmospheric Administration—and the "water buffaloes" figured that outsiders brought trouble. Gray realized that "there was no chance to expand the program to better meet the State's needs."[47] And so, worn down and beat up, Gray left Wyoming for the US Geological Survey's Climate Science Center in Alaska, where, he says, "It's not hard for people to see the relevance of climate change when your village is falling into a river as the permafrost melts."[48]

So, Steve Gray had the dual distinction of becoming the first permanent director of the Alaskan center and the last state climatologist of Wyoming (only two other states lack this expertise).[49] The university and state didn't fire Gray, but in codependent relationships, passive-aggressive behavior is a common way to express power. The then director of the Water Development Commission is coy about what happened: "There were Wyoming Development commissioners and legislators that were not very enamored with the results of some of the climate change research being conducted by Mr. Gray. In addition, Governor Mead was seeking agency budget cuts. Therefore, the funds for the State Climatologist were struck from our budget. Apparently, UW chose not the fund the position."[50]

Kerr echoed this classic approach to starving undesirable science by removing funding and then denying any role in the resulting death of research. He defended the commission: "If somebody else wants a state climatologist and they want to pay for it, fine. But why should Water Development do it?"[51] Maybe because Wyoming is the fifth-driest state and is in the early stages of recovering from a decade-long drought?[52] But this might mean coming to terms with how we pamper, resent, and depend upon the gas-belching, oil-soaked, coal-dusted elephant in the room.

Interestingly, Gray's departure foreshadowed what has become a mass exodus of scientists and other scholars from the University of Wyoming. In the words of Randy Lewis, formerly one of the institution's research superstars, "What I saw happening at Wyoming, which dampened my enthusiasm to stay, was I felt a very large overemphasis on energy-related research."[53] Lewis is now at Utah State University, advancing his work on biomaterials and contributing to the economic diversification of the Cache Valley. One way of silencing dissonant voices at an institution is to drive dissenters away.

Gray's successor in the role of Water Resources Data System director was a smart fellow, with no background in climatology. Chris Nicholson has a master's degree in archeology along with a keen sense of how not to dig up trouble. He was originally hired by Gray because of his skills in geographic information systems and experience in land and water-use planning.[54]

So it was that Nicholson found himself in a situation strikingly similar to that of Rob Field, the atmospheric researcher who discovered the source of Pinedale's ozone. The former fellow had to censor himself when speaking about global climate change and the latter when talking about local air quality, but both knew that professional survival demanded that they master three essential tactics of self-censorship.

We might call the first approach "Speak no evil." Across Wyoming, when a public meeting is about water, people show up. And drought—like empty bottles and broken furniture—is the focus of attention: "They discuss planning for less water and improving efficiency," says Nicholson, "but nobody talks about the *causes* of there being less water."[55] Climate change has been deemed unspeakable, so Nicholson uses a euphemism: weather variability—sort of like the family who alludes to dad's moodiness rather than talking about his drinking.

Field has learned that when it comes to talking about the detrimental effects of natural gas drilling, "The louder you are, the more comes back. So I've been very quiet."[56] Although he censors himself in Wyoming, he recently found a safe house—Field presented his work on Pinedale's ozone at an environmental science conference in Belgium[57] and has begun to publish his research in peer-reviewed journals where politics are muted if not absent.[58]

Even the University of Wyoming's School of Environment and Natural Resources, where Field taught for a while, got the message. Its former director Harold Bergman observed, "The capstone courses have been eviscerated." These classes, in which advanced undergraduate students take on extensive research into environmental issues have been toned down: "We used to do controversial things, like the consequences of climate change on the Colorado River Watershed," but now the projects focus on far less contentious issues.[59]

The next tactic can be called "Just the facts" after Sergeant Joe Friday's classic line in *Dragnet*. Nicholson sticks assiduously to reporting data.[60] This approach works as long as the facts themselves don't aggravate the energy industry or their political allies. Reference to the facts of climate change appeared in the unit's newsletter when Gray was the director,[61] but this phrase is now conspicuously absent from their material. This silence is reminiscent of the disappearance of "climate change" and "global warming" in any communications from the Florida Department of Environmental Protection in accordance with an unwritten, but eminently clear, policy that arose after Rick Scott, a Republican, was elected governor.[62]

Since 2012 links to the IPCC reports have been stricken from Wyoming's Water Resources Data System's website.[63] Field maintains that sticking to peer-reviewed science will keep him from getting trampled by the elephant. And when asked if he could explain DEQ's motives in blocking his project to pinpoint sources of ozone precursors, Field refused to speculate on the record.[64]

The pressure on researchers to function as if science were merely the process of taking measurements and tabulating data without providing explanations is not unique to Wyoming. When a geologist with the Arkansas Geological Survey and a seismologist from the University of Memphis teamed up to study the relationship between fracking and earthquakes, the governor of Arkansas, Mike Beebe, forced the geologist to remove his name from the pending publication in a leading scholarly journal. The state's leader explained, "The (Geological) Survey is in the business of data collection, not interpreting that data and reaching conclusions."[65]

The United States is not alone in silencing science. Canadian government scientists labor under egregious forms of censorship in which political ideology is used by officials to constrain what climate change researchers may say or publish.[66] In a scientifically literate world, perhaps we could let "data speak for itself," but environmental studies generate complex findings and the energy industry's political lackeys want to make sure that scientists don't translate the data into anything meaningful—or dangerous.

The final tactic of self-censorship is "Hold the hemlock" (named for the poison that Socrates took upon being convicted of impiety and corrupting the youth of Athens). The Wyoming scientists sense the dilemma of being paid by the public but unable to deliver information that is crucial to social well-being. Nicholson acknowledges that his unit has been effectively silenced when it comes to climate change: "You have to be an authority on a topic if you're going to provide information, and we don't have that expertise." As Nicholson puts it, if the Water Development Commission decides to pull funding, "we all go away."[67]

Field refuses to structure his research to "please a regulator or the industry," and believes that his "responsibility is to the citizens," but he draws the line at professional suicide.[68] He has determined that asking certain scientific questions of grave importance to the public incites political retribution. Field's paycheck depends on grant funding and, as he put it, "I'm not into hari-kari." In a state dependent on the energy industry, the absence of tenure can be key to assuring self-censorship: "If you're a tenured professor, then you have certain job security. I made some big tactical mistakes early on with being too bold because I'd forgotten where I was. I didn't properly understand the sensitivities or the political climate."[69]

From Wyoming to the World
The Future of Censorship

Once a government is committed to the principle of silencing the voice of opposition, it has only one way to go, and that is down the path of increasingly repressive measures, until it becomes a source of terror to all its citizens and creates a country where everyone lives in fear.

—HARRY S. TRUMAN

CHAPTER 12

The Death of Free Speech
Finding the Killer

In my conversations with an attorney working for DKRW—the coal-to-gas grifters in Carbon County—I suggested that the Wyoming Department of Environmental Quality was chummy with the energy industry. The lawyer frostily challenged me to produce "a smoking gun." I explained to her that in my experience, powerful people rarely make it easy to trace corruption and censorship back to the source. The lawyer scoffed and insinuated that I was on the verge of insulting some very important individuals, which could have adverse consequences. Evidently, she figured that taking aim in my direction was good enough—no need to pull the trigger.

The *Carbon Sink* fiasco notwithstanding, most energy executives and government officials are smart enough to cover their tracks or to get others to do their dirty work. Although the evidence of malfeasance is not often explicit, it can be as compelling as gunshot residue.

Prosecutors understand that circumstantial and physical evidence can be much more reliable than eyewitness testimony. And so discerning the role of the energy industry in censorship often is a matter of finding a modus operandi—a pattern of action from which one can draw reasonable conclusions. Could I be mistaken about what lies behind any particular case in Wyoming? Absolutely. But could I be wrong in connecting the abundant dots and drawing a picture of how industry and government have conspired to censor science, art, and education? Almost certainly no. Like a juror, my task has been to make an inference to the best explanation, drawing conclusions that most reasonably fit the evidence.

In the prosecution of a defendant, the common sense formulation of the legal standard of guilt is motive, means, and opportunity. Did the accused have a reason, an ability, and a chance to break the law—even if there were no smoking gun?

Profit and power are compelling *motives*. Beginning in the late 1960s, the tobacco industry initiated a wickedly effective strategy for quashing dissent. Motivated by anticipated restrictions on their products and profits, cigarette companies turned to sowing disinformation and fostering doubt. With the help of well-compensated scientific consultants who often had no biomedical expertise, the industry mounted a campaign to deceive the public and confuse policy makers. An internal memo of the Brown and Williamson Tobacco Company made their position explicit: "Doubt is our product."[1] Industry-funded conservative think tanks drowned out the voices of credible researchers. However, the companies were not beyond directly censoring scientists who spoke out.

For example, when Dr. Victor DeNoble's experiments established the addictive properties of nicotine in the course of trying to develop a safer cigarette for Philip Morris, his employer saw the imminent danger to their profits. The company realized that DeNoble had evidence that cigarettes were effectively drug delivery systems, and if that information got out, there was going to be big trouble. So in 1983 they fired DeNoble and made him agree to never discuss his work in order to receive severance pay.[2]

A decade later, under congressional pressure, Philip Morris released the scientist from the coerced agreement. DeNoble testified that the company knew that nicotine was addictive and sought to enhance its effects. Not even the for-hire "experts" could save the tobacco industry from a massive lawsuit that led to a $209 billion settlement.[3] But the dangers of tobacco had been obscured and suppressed for years, so the model of confuse-and-censor could surely work for other industries.

When acid rain became a national issue in the 1980s, the coal companies contracted with the "merchants of doubt." The same firms, with many of the same players who distorted research for the tobacco companies, took up the cause of deceiving the public and lawmakers about acid rain. And they successfully delayed environmental legislation for a decade.[4]

The motivation to confuse thought and censor speech in order to sustain power and profit is evident today with climate change. But now the stakes involve the entire planet and the players include the wealthiest industries in history. So we might expect corporations to crush dissonant voices as they have in the past. However, this time they have an accomplice who is packing more muscle than ever before.

Industrialized nations have come to accept, even celebrate, the business-political alliances that foster the emergence of corporatocracies that provide the *means* for corporations to turn governments into their censors.[5] When political conservatives dismissed the relevance of President Obama's cabinet because few members had business experience, the liberal reply was to reanalyze the data and defend the president as having more than three-quarters of his appointees with private-sector backgrounds.[6] Nobody questioned whether having such corporate connections, perspectives, or allegiances was a good thing for a democracy. Just like in Wyoming, where nobody seemed perturbed that the state treasurer had worked for Apache Corporation (a fossil fuel company) or that the senate vice president was a drilling contractor for the oil and gas industry.[7]

The flow of power operates in both directions, with elected officials taking lucrative positions in the industries that they formerly regulated. This movement to and from the public and private sectors has been called "the revolving door." For example, Linda Fisher was an administrator in the US Environmental Protection Agency (EPA) before becoming a vice president for DuPont—the world's third-largest chemical company and fourth-greatest polluter of US waterways.[8] Likewise, Dick Gephart parlayed his fourteen terms in the US House of Representatives into a multimillion-dollar lobbying firm for corporations such as Goldman Sachs, Boeing, and Visa.[9] Just like in Wyoming, where the former state auditor is the vice president of Rocky Mountain Power and the ex-governor cashed in his political chips for a lucrative seat on the board of Arch Coal.[10]

In today's politics, winning an election often means raising more money than your opponent. In recent years, candidates for the US House of Representatives who spent less than $700,000 on their campaigns had about a 1 percent chance of election.[11] Candidates' need for money and corporations' desire for political advantage provide the raw materials for corporatocratic collusion. This quid pro quo is sanctioned by the judicial branch; the US Supreme Court infamously ruled in *Citizens United* that corporations had a right to free speech—and insofar as contributing money was a form of speech, corporations were to be unlimited in funding political campaigns.[12]

Corporate leaders know that access to politicians is a function of money. Lobbyists understand that there is a price for admission—and campaign donations are the ticket to offices in state capitals and Washington.

If corporations have the motive to censor and governments have the means, we're left with the question of *opportunity*. Does the accused appear in the places and times where and when voices are silenced in America? A great deal of incisive research has focused on cases in which companies manipulated the political process through prevarication, deception, and distraction.[13] The well-funded think tanks and their scientists-for-hire have been adept at manufacturing doubt by creating echo chambers to recycle fatuous claims in a shockingly successful version of "proof by repetitive assertion."

Perhaps no other case of censorship more powerfully illustrates how energy corporations have exploited opportunities to control public discourse than the story of climate change. In 1965 the President's Science Advisory Committee asked the director of the Scripps Institution for Oceanography to assess and summarize the dangers of carbon dioxide–induced atmospheric warming, and the industry began plotting.[14]

Not ten years later, just as the evidence was mounting, Nixon dissolved the President's Science Advisory Committee—and both nature and politics abhor a vacuum.[15] The empty niche in America's power structure was quickly filled by corporate think tanks, which adapted the tactics that they'd developed to undercut the scientific community on the risks of smoking in service to the tobacco industry. The Heritage Foundation was established in 1973 and spawned a cadre of lucrative firms devoted to environmental skepticism.[16] The assault on science was underway and an assassination of the First Amendment was in the works. Despite the corporations' best efforts, in 1977 the National Research Council managed to sound the alarm of runaway climate change.[17]

The 1980s were a tough time for free speech. Religious conservatives drew in their political allies to attack publicly funded art such as Robert Mapplethorpe's homoerotic photographs and Andre Serrano's infamous "Piss Christ." President Reagan's call for ever more research on acid rain delayed environmental action and revealed that the merchants of doubt had done their job.[18] Encouraged by the conservative political climate, corporations seized the opportunity for state-sanctioned censorship. For example, a West Virginia coal company filed a libel suit to silence activists who had criticized the company in the environmental group's newsletter. The state's Supreme Court rejected the industry's claim, saying, "We shudder to think of the chill our ruling would have on the exercise of the freedom of speech and the right to petition were we to allow this lawsuit to proceed."[19]

Having lost in the courts, energy corporations pressed on with their use of think tanks. Knowing that the EPA had called for an immediate reduction in coal burning, the Marshall Institute—having already denied the harmful effects of tobacco, the existence of acid rain, and the role of chlorofluorocarbons (CFCs) in creating the ozone hole—dismissed anthropogenic climate change and blamed the sun for rising temperatures.[20]

After the first report by the Intergovernmental Panel on Climate Change (IPCC) in 1990, the denial machine shifted into high gear.[21] Reports, articles, and news releases created a reverberating network of skepticism. This echo chamber grew to enormous proportions with Internet bloggers drowning out peer-reviewed science. But the energy industry didn't team up with the government and impose censorship of federal agencies—at least initially.

When the IPCC's second report in 1995 concluded that there was "a discernible human influence on global climate," Republican legislators hosted a "scientific integrity" hearing to criticize the use of computer models.[22] Leading scientists pushed back with a letter in the *Wall Street Journal* that was edited to weaken the scientific argument, and the paper ran a series of dissembling rebuttals.[23]

With newspapers and magazines becoming increasingly dependent on advertising revenues, companies capable of delivering big checks effectively bought editorial control. As energy companies came to own public discourse, they shaped American thought—and confusion. The American Petroleum Institute's "Global Climate Science Communication Action Plan" made clear that the goal was to spread uncertainty.[24]

Journalists were bamboozled into believing that balanced reporting meant giving the skeptics equal time, which fostered the illusion that there was a scientific controversy. And it worked. In 1991, 35 percent of people believed that global warming was a serious problem; five years later that number dropped to 22 percent despite mounting scientific evidence.[25]

As President George W. Bush and Dick Cheney were taking office in 2001, the IPCC was concluding that "most of the warming observed over the last 50 years is attributable to human activities."[26] With this as the motive and his office as the means, Cheney seized the opportunity to arm the coal and oil industries by allowing them to write the nation's energy policy.[27] This signaled the energy corporations that the White House was a willing partner in silencing science.

In short order, the administration's Council on Environmental Quality tried to strike references to studies of anthropogenic climate change from the

EPA's report on the state of the environment, but the EPA refused to submit to censorship. The agency dropped the section on climate change rather than promulgate industry propaganda, and the EPA administrator resigned.[28]

A modus operandi emerged as the Bush administration continued to support the energy industry by censoring federal agencies. According to a senior official in the US Climate Change Science Program, the president's lackeys "were adding and deleting in such a way as to systematically—paragraph after paragraph, page after page—introduce the idea that there was some sort of fundamental scientific uncertainty that still needed to be debated."[29] When it came to light that the censor was the chief of staff for the White House Council on Environmental Quality, he submitted his resignation and took a position with ExxonMobil.[30]

The energy corporations shaped the 2012 presidential election by assuring that neither of the major candidates discussed climate change. And the same silence is characterizing the 2016 election. Ever since Congress had been briefed on the emerging crisis a quarter century earlier, presidential aspirants had confronted the issue during their campaigns, even if to deny there was a problem. But now, with disappearing ice, temperature records, and a devastating drought, the politicians are silent.[31]

And so, if the politicians are gagged, what happens when the people speak up concerning climate change? Wyoming provides an answer that reflects the national condition. When a group of local citizens proposed reforms to the state's policies regarding the flaring of natural gas from oil wells that pumped tons of carbon dioxide into the air without pumping any revenues into the public coffers, the governor told reporters, "My view is changes in rules and regulations should be driven by the commission (Wyoming Oil and Gas Conservation Commission), or by this office."[32] In other words, the public should shut up.

To further assure that lawmakers wouldn't be bothered by pesky citizens, in 2015 the legislature moved its operations to the Jonah Business Center (another part of the McMurry business empire) in Cheyenne until 2018 while the capitol building was being renovated. In conducting the state's business on private property, the government decreed that the public couldn't fully exercise its First Amendment rights because such gatherings could inconvenience the other tenants. When the weather was inclement (i.e., most of the time during winter in Cheyenne), the state would restrict the number of people allowed in the building—and even during decent conditions, protestors

An environmental "smoking gun." One of the massive cooling towers at the Naughton Power Plant in Wyoming, which was commissioned in 1963. The plant can burns 2.8 million tons of coal per year (equivalent to unloading a coal car every twenty minutes, twenty-four hours a day, 365 days a year). The coal is mined by Chevron Mining and delivered on a 4,200-foot conveyer belt and burned in a twenty-story-high boiler (photo by Scott Kane).

were restricted to a grassy area on a side of the building that virtually assured invisibility to legislators. As Wyoming's political pundit Kerry Drake noted, "There's no mention in the Constitution about abridging this right if it would upset private businesses, or if space is limited."[33]

The corporatocracy has the motive and the means to censor speech, and they've taken advantage of repeated opportunities to silence dissent. In *Censoring Science*, Mark Bowen makes clear that the leaders of government and industry have no alibi. He puts the political-economic situation into moral terms:

The [climate change] contrarians will be remembered as court jesters. There is no point to joust with court jesters. They will always be present. . . . The real deal is this: the "royalty" controlling the court, the ones with the power, the ones with the ability to make a differences, with the ability to change our course, the ones who will live in infamy if we pass the tipping points, are the captains of industry, CEOs in fossil fuel companies such as ExxonMobil, automobile manufacturers, utilities, all the leaders who have placed short-term profits above the fate of the planet and the well-being of our children.[34]

There's one last element of a case that must be established, along with motive, means, and opportunity—the corpus delicti. In the killing of free speech, we can ask, "Where is the body?" In Wyoming perhaps the most disturbing victim is the university, where censorship is arguably most devastating to a functioning democracy.

Colleges and universities have historically done the bidding of local, state, and national governments. But the contemporary American university is increasingly coming to resemble a company town, with corporations determining and enforcing what can be researched, taught, written, and spoken.[35] Those who violate the new standards can be dismissed, academic freedom and tenure be damned. This practice first emerged among private institutions, but it is now clear that censorship is becoming normalized in public universities.

The role of the energy industry as educational censor is painfully evident in Wyoming, where the past (Democratic) governor endorsed the current (Republican) governor's efforts to shape research and teaching: "Support Governor Mead in what he is doing. We need to have a university that matches our economy."[36] The view that education is the servant of industry now has bipartisan support and this might be cause for deep concern among the citizenry—if only the implications of life in corporatocracy were salient to the public. But that would require an educational system in which raising such issues was viewed as a civic responsibility, and therein lies the insidious problem.

As the former director of the University of Wyoming's School and Institute of Environment and Natural Resources (ENR) observed, "After the coalbed methane water report, the energy industry wanted ENR silenced. . . . And if pitiable funding was not enough to muzzle environmental researchers, the leash has been pulled tight on course content in recent years."[37] But again, Wyoming is only a lens into a larger social phenomenon unfolding across America.

Consider that in 2010 the South Dakota state legislature passed a bill that "urge[d]" the state's public schools to teach students "that global warming is a scientific theory rather than a proven fact"[38] (echoing the scientific illiteracy of the creationists). Educators are encouraged to convey that there is a so-called debate on global warming when there is, in fact, none among climate scientists. And to get a sense of the legislature's grasp of science, the bill also urges teachers to instruct students "that there are a variety of climatological, meteorological, astrological [presumably they meant "astronomical" rather than suggesting that the signs of the zodiac were relevant], thermological [a new word, probably meaning something about the physics of heat], cosmological [probably an allusion to the defunct theory that the sun, rather than anthropogenic carbon dioxide, is responsible], and ecological dynamics that can effect [sic] world weather phenomena and that the significance and interrelativity of these factors is largely speculative."[39] Censoring education is particularly appalling when combined with bad writing and bad thinking.

Censorship of educators is not the exclusive purview of western states. The attorney general of Virginia called for an investigation of the University of Virginia to determine if a faculty member had violated the state's Fraud against Taxpayers Act, a law intended to prosecute people who had obtained government funds based on false claims.[40] The attorney general's target was Dr. Michael Mann, who had the gall to use public funds to investigate climate change and publish his findings in leading scientific journals on his way to becoming honored as a fellow of both the American Geophysical Union and the American Meteorological Society.[41] The goal of the legal action was to send a chilling message and intimidate professors into silence.

The energy companies are not limited to educational institutions in the United States when it comes to shaping public discourse. University endowments in the United Kingdom have invested $8.4 billion into fossil fuel corporations and are busily cutting deals with companies to underwrite positions, buildings, and conferences. The industry has effectively bought its way onto British campuses and purchased access to students through sponsored lectures.[42] And to the north, the Canada Imperial Oil and the Canadian Association of Petroleum Producers attempted to remove exhibits from the Canada Science and Technology Museum because the industry perceived itself as having been unsympathetically portrayed.[43]

All of this goes to the heart of why I wrote this book. Ray Bradley, a climatologist and University Distinguished Professor at the University Massachusetts who became a target of political attacks for his research on climate change, notes with grim melancholy, "Alas, my experience of the last few years has shown me how fragile that concept [academic freedom] is when the political and financial stakes are high."[44] Likewise, I worry about the future of public discourse not only within our universities but, perhaps even more importantly, between scholars and the public.

Being a tenured professor at a public university carries with it a moral duty. I contend that faculty have an obligation to act in accordance with what we genuinely understand to be the best interests of society. After all, it is only through the consent of my fellow citizens that I have been provided with the protection of tenure, and if I am unwilling to say what is both true and dangerous, then I am merely enjoying a kind of elite privilege. So there is, in my mind, a social contract in which the public has agreed that my job is secure in exchange for my responsibly exploring and honestly exposing aspects of the world that others—who are subject to the retribution of those in positions of privilege, power, and wealth—would need great courage to pursue. To what end is tenure, if not to protect the capacity to speak truth to power?

CHAPTER 13

For Sale
Free Speech

Censorship is nothing new in America, but what seems to be changing is our acceptance of its various guises. Maybe this complacency is related to our new relationship with information and privacy. This could be why it seems unremarkable that public workers are fired for speaking to the press, that artworks are removed because companies are offended, or that teachers are prohibited from telling their students about climate change. But the more troubling explanation is the emergence of a government that is no longer "for the people." In an Islamic theocracy such as Iran, citizens don't question that the government requires religious observances and punishes heretics. And in a corporate plutocracy on its way to becoming a thoroughgoing corporatocracy such as the United States, people take it to be normal that most everything is treated as a commodity—including speech.

The commodification of public and private life took root as the Cold War was ending. Industrial societies bought into the metaphor of society as business.[1] In 1962 Milton Friedman argued that free markets warranted the same protections as religion or speech.[2] Despite a few economic bumps along the way, "the era of market fundamentalism" arrived in the early 1980s. Ronald Reagan and Margaret Thatcher unabashedly declared that market forces, not government programs, would assure national prosperity and social flourishing.[3] We would all be better off when citizen-consumers could choose via their purchasing power among educational, medical, and transportation opportunities. We would be safer if for-profit institutions imprisoned criminals, private security guards patrolled the streets, and contracted soldiers fought our wars.

By the turn of the millennium, individuals could rent wombs ($70,000 in the United States, but just $12,000 in India—"for all your baby needs at warehouse prices"[4]), companies could buy the right to pollute, and cities could sell the names of museums, stadiums, and virtually any other civic space.[5] And in the frenzied marketplace, the energy industry purchased academic positions, scientific questions, and classroom curricula, as well as the power to censor public art, dismiss university researchers, and silence educators. Today, you can pay to upgrade your prison cell, shoot an endangered species, or immigrate to the United States—and you can get paid to advertise on your body, lose weight, or serve as a guinea pig in a pharmaceutical trial.[6] And, of course, you can pay to have your view broadcast to the nation—or to silence the voice of others.

In *What Money Can't Buy*, philosopher Michael Sandel argues that a core tenet of market faith is that commercialization does not change the character of whatever is being bought or sold. But the problem is that markets crowd out moral judgments. If speech is commodified, then its value and function in a democracy are profoundly altered. In the starkest sense, what was once "free" speech—an activity in which every individual had a right to engage— becomes the property of those who purchase it. And just as allowing sex or parenting to be purchased changes how we understand these activities and ourselves, so it is with speech in all of its varied forms.

Sandel's objections to markets come down to concerns about fairness and corruption. When speech can be bought and sold, economic inequality assures that only the rich can speak in ways that are heard (the top 10 percent of Americans now control at least 75 percent of the wealth, with Senator Bernie Sanders asserting that the top 0.1 percent have nearly as much wealth as the bottom 90 percent[7]). As speech becomes purchased in a world where communication is tantamount to power, buying into the conversation becomes prohibitively expensive. In effect, commodification may be the most potent tool of censorship in corporatocracies and throughout the industrial world.

Outside my office window is a plaza in front of the University of Wyoming Student Union. When the weather is decent, fundamentalist preachers and political ideologues perch themselves on a box or bench and pronounce their beliefs. I can hear them through my window, but they soon blend into a kind of white noise. That is, until passing students decide to engage their would-be saviors. The shouting and arguing becomes a cacophonous shambles, except that—if one listens attentively—each voice is responding to another. They're all being heard at some level, even if few minds are changed.

Democracies are noisy and inefficient, but they allow the formation of communities in which ideas can be presented, challenged, and accepted or dismissed on their merits, rather than their price tags. But with the concentration of wealth comes the consolidation of speech. As the media scholar Sue Curry

Jansen contends in *Censorship: The Knot That Binds Power and Knowledge*, "I believe we are now witnessing removal of the last vestiges of social pluralism and the emergence of a monolithic society in which the *market is the measure of all things*. That is, America is at last fulfilling Adam Smith's vision of a society in which the rules of the marketplace become the rules of civil society."[8] Nicholas Stern, the former chief economist of the World Bank, called climate change "the greatest and widest-ranging market failure ever seen."[9] Despite the disastrous implications of framing our society in terms of corporate structures and our lives in terms of commodities, we persist in using these conceptual models.

Thinking of the world as a marketplace allows the energy industry and its customers to sidestep moral obligations. For example, buying carbon offsets justifies the comfortable habits and blasé attitudes that continue to underwrite anthropogenic climate change. Likewise, allowing industries to purchase the right to emit carbon means that pollution—and its harm to humans and other species—is merely a cost of business.[10]

Americans were outraged to learn that during the 1970s the Ford Motor Company used a cost-benefit analysis to determine that it was more economical to allow 180 fiery deaths per year than it was to make an $11 upgrade to the Pinto.[11] But today we celebrate the cleverness of economic models that allow corporatocracies to trade carbon credits. As Michael Sandel argues, "We should try to strengthen, not weaken the moral stigma attached to despoiling the environment . . . if rich countries could buy their way out of the duty to reduce their own emissions, we would undermine the sense of shared sacrifice necessary to future global cooperation on the environment."[12]

Sandel's concerns echo voices raised in the later years of the Industrial Revolution, when perceptive folks began to see the implicit deal that had been struck between humanity and business. In 1806 William Wordsworth poetically warned:

> The world is too much with us; late and soon,
> Getting and spending, we lay waste our powers:
> Little we see in Nature that is ours;
> We have given our hearts away, a sordid boon![13]

Today we have exchanged our liberty for the sordid boon of fossil fuels, and nowhere is this more evident than in Wyoming, a harbinger of what is coming to a nation with banks that are too big to fail and industries that write our laws.[14] But perhaps there's hope. Prompted by years of legislative meddling, journalists have seen what the commodification of speech means for our fundamental freedoms—and they've begun to raise their voices. The editorial board of the *Wyoming Tribune Eagle*, which is published in the state's capital, finally had enough in the fall of 2014 and put the situation into stark terms: "What is the value of academic freedom? That's the question all Wyomingites should be asking themselves. To state lawmakers, it is a commodity that can be bought and sold, like coal or oil. . . . What was once non-negotiable at UW now has a price tag on it. Lawmakers have sold the school to the highest bidder—the energy industry."[15] The writers also recognized that the capacity to silence dissident voices has become an instrument of wealth and power. The newspaper incisively portrayed the insidious nature of self-censorship: "In fact, several members of UW's faculty refused to be interviewed for the article, fearing repercussions. And can you blame them? When lawmakers like state Rep. Tom Lubnau, R-Gillette [the legislator who led the effort to have Chris Drury's *Carbon Sink* removed], threaten to cut funding to UW for allowing a sculpture on campus critical of the energy industry, the faculty gets the message: Speak up and it could be you next time."[16] Maybe it will be me, or the department of philosophy or the creative writing program. But my colleagues have been adamant that they will take what comes, rather than asking me to be quiet. Living behind a carbon curtain of silence is too high a price to pay.

Mike Sullivan described Wyoming as "a small town with very long streets." As the governor from 1987 to 1995, he was considered a moderate (the only way for a Democrat to be, and stay, elected). Even so, his connections to the energy industry ran deep—and still do. Sullivan earned a bachelor's in petroleum engineering and a law degree from the University of Wyoming. And in his post-gubernatorial career, he served on the board of directors of Cimarex Energy, a multibillion-dollar oil and gas exploration and production company trading on the New York Stock Exchange.[17] In 2013 he signed onto a letter calling for the Obama administration to accelerate, rather than impede, coal production and utilization.[18] It seems that Mike Sullivan was almost right about his home state. Wyoming is a small *company* town with very long streets.

This book has told the stories of artists, scientists, and educators censored by the energy industry in collusion with the government. Perhaps some readers will be unsurprised, but I hope that many are disturbed, even

The coal company town of Red Ash, Virginia, in 1929. In this classic image,
the railroad through the valley is flanked by miners' homes. Symbolizing the
socioeconomic order, the mine superintendent's home is up the hill (upper left). The
road through town is made of "red dog" or slag, a byproduct of the smelting process
(photo by Jack Corn; US National Archives Identifier 556331).

outraged. If I've succeeded, these people will be wondering what's next.
What can anyone in a small town or a large state or a massive nation do
about the silencing of voices?

Let me start by saying I don't know. I'm not a social scientist or political
activist. But from the stories in this book, it would appear that there are two
structural defects that foster censorship in Wyoming. First, the hegemony of
the energy industry is undoubtedly a contributing factor. A diversified economy would mitigate this concentration of power, but exactly how Wyoming
can achieve this outcome is a decades-old puzzle that economists and political scientists with far greater mastery of such matters than my own understanding have yet to solve.

The second defect pertains to the connection between political elections
and corporate money. And this is a challenge to our democratic government
and capitalistic economy that is also beyond my realm of legitimate expertise—not to mention that it would be the subject of another book altogether.
Social scientists might be able to find ways of disconnecting politics and

business, but I suspect that the solutions will require great insight and nuance.

So what about the rest of us? I believe that grassroots resistance to the abuse of power complements higher-order structural corrections. The mechanisms of change are not an either-or proposition (national structures or local movements). Consider how protests in Ferguson, Missouri, and elsewhere are fueling national changes in policies. And at least in terms of local action I have some relevant experience.

In addition to my efforts on behalf of academic freedom at the University of Wyoming, I worked closely with the Laramie community following the murder of Matthew Shepard (a University of Wyoming student who was beaten to death in 1998 because he was gay). I collaborated in developing a bias crime ordinance, testifying to the city council, managing a memorial fund, writing letters to the newspaper, and organizing events. I was the chair of the board of the Unitarian Universalist Fellowship, which received a national award for its efforts to foster social justice.

Perhaps some of this experience provides relevant insight to addressing the injustice of censorship. I don't claim to know how movements arise and why they succeed. I suspect that such phenomena are much easier to explain after the fact than to predict in advance. That said, three elements of social action are worth considering. These insights may lack radical originality, but sometimes novelty is overrated.

First, with regard to free speech, nothing is likely to change—except for the worse—if we don't recognize that there is censorship. Those in power do not willingly give up their capacity to control material and social resources; the rich get richer in terms of money and influence, so share this book with friends and neighbors. But share your own story as well. I suspect that the practice of censorship is among the most challenging injustices to address. How do we raise our voices when the problem is that people are being silenced? If a person fears retribution, then speaking out is not an easy task. But it is incumbent on us to object in some way to whoever we think might listen. Maybe it is at the dinner table or during a coffee break or after Sunday service or in a Rotary Club meeting or through a letter to the editor. Say something.

Second, we should heed the wisdom of Margaret Mead, who said, "Never doubt that a small group of thoughtful, committed citizens can change the world. Indeed, it is the only thing that ever has." Massive protests on the mall of Washington, DC, are great, but big changes often arise through the accumulation of small actions (hence, the notion of a tipping point in complex systems).[19] I don't know if we can fix censorship in Wyoming without national legislation to stop corporations from effectively purchasing election results. But then, had the people of Ferguson, Missouri, waited for Black Lives Matter to become a national movement, they'd still be sitting quietly in their homes. We must begin to solve problems for which the solutions are yet to be imagined.

Third, as a university professor I'm ineluctably drawn to the power of education. I worry that young people don't grasp the nature or importance of free speech. Surveys by the First Amendment Center have been profoundly revealing—and worrying.[20]

Although 47 percent of Americans name freedom of speech as the most important liberty (freedom of religion is next at 10 percent), 36 percent could not identify this or any other right as being guaranteed by the First Amendment. And in terms of the need for education, young people tend to more strongly agree that the Constitution goes too far with freedoms. While 47 percent of people eighteen to thirty years old agree that the First Amendment overreaches in the rights it guarantees, just 24 percent of those forty-six to sixty years old agree.

And when Americans are afraid, their tolerance of First Amendment rights declines even further. After the Boston Marathon bombing, there was sharp jump in the proportion of people who thought the First Amendment excessively protected our freedom. And after the September 11 attacks, about 40 percent favored restrictions on the academic freedom of professors to criticize government military policy during war.

Today, 63 percent of Americans rate the educational system as doing only a fair to poor job in teaching students about the First Amendment. Perhaps people are right. Knowledge that the US Constitution guarantees freedom of speech is trending downward.[21] As the country becomes more diverse, free speech may erode further. African Americans and Hispanics are more likely to say that the First Amendment overreaches. Fifty-two percent of African Americans and 50 percent of Hispanics agree, while only 29 percent of whites agree that the First Amendment goes too far.[22]

The task of educators is daunting. Perhaps students who read this book will be unperturbed: "What can you expect when you bite the hand that feeds you?" But I also worry that students will just be perplexed: "Don't private and public employers have the right to decide what their employees can say and write?" Maybe I'm being uncharitable, but remember the effect of fear on our tolerance for oppression. The fear of foreign attacks trumps our defense of free speech, and one has to imagine that economic fears—particularly given the misery of the Great Recession for young people seeking work—will have a corresponding effect. If we do not defend freedom in our classrooms, we may well lose liberty in our town, states, and nation.

There are three caveats for those wanting to take action in response to corporate-sponsored censorship by politicians and government agencies. First, be careful. No viable ethical system requires self-destruction. My job is secure, but this is not the case for most people, who are at-will employees. Heed the admonition of General George Patton to US troops in 1944: "No bastard ever won a war by dying for his country. He won it by making the other poor dumb bastard die for his country."[23]

Second, be courageous. It is also true that no action is morally praiseworthy if one stands to lose nothing. Justice entails struggle, while remaining silent is safe. Of course, for some people, perhaps many, other demands on their lives make the risks of social action untenable. As Socrates recognized centuries ago, courage is profoundly contextual. Each person must decide what free speech is worth compared to the costs of speaking out. But as Marianne Williamson wrote, "Our deepest fear is not that we are inadequate. Our deepest fear is that we are powerful beyond measure."[24]

My third caveat concerns the nature of commitment. In working toward a more just world, we often yearn for the completion of our task. We pin our hopes on success, on seeing the fruits of our labor. We aspire to make our town or state or nation into a place where people can express themselves without fear of retribution. But the work of social justice will never be done. That is the curse and the blessing of being human. It's a curse in that there is no completion of our labors, a blessing in that there shall always be meaningful work.

To know what we can do, to understand what the world needs of us, we must hear the muted voices of our neighbors, read the accounts of destroyed art and suppressed science, and listen for what can't be said in classrooms. But to sustain our work, we must look inside ourselves. There we shall find the understanding that world-making is self-making, that the endless labor of life is about repairing our own dignity. It is good to cultivate freedom, whether or not it fixes a broken democracy.

The research for this book began in 2011, and the final approval of the text was given by University of New Mexico Press in 2016. That's a rather extended period during which the role of the energy industry and those who censor science, art, and education on its behalf have had to adapt to changing social, political, and economic conditions. Given that there's nearly a year between the submission of the manuscript and the book that you're now holding, there surely will be a number of developments that would have warranted consideration.

I can be fairly confident that efforts to shape public discourse—crossing the line into censorship—will continue across Wyoming. In March 2016 Governor Matt Mead issued his plan for the future of the state's energy, environment, and economy. The document was titled "Leading the Charge"[1] but might've been more appropriately called "Deepening the Trenches." He described his strategy as "doubling down on coal" while making "a very good start" on renewable energy.[2]

The governor called for every state agency to "align itself such that every employee understands that his or her job is related to a vision of balanced energy production and environmental stewardship."[3] But there can be no doubt that this vision is myopically focused on fossil fuels. Mead recently wrote, "What I hope more can agree upon is that regardless of one's beliefs on the causes of climate change—no serious discussion can ignore coal as a plentiful resource and its benefits to our country."[4]

With regard to science, Mead wants the University of Wyoming to push "carbon innovation" and clean coal technologies.[5] He's planning to pump tens of millions of dollars of public monies into fossil fuel technology and encourage corporations to infuse more cash into shaping the course of research at the state's sole university. The image of scientists frantically modeling how to best arrange the deck chairs on the *Titanic* comes to mind. Mead's dream appears to be one of "building an industry around carbon."[6]

As for education, the governor proudly noted that through his last plan, the state "established a task force that looked at the best ways to integrate energy literacy into K–12 education programs." The new strategy will "showcase how energy resources are produced and used, as well as the reclamation that occurs in lockstep" (presumably setting aside the deepening problems with coal companies declaring bankruptcy and defaulting on their reclamation bonds, which is hardly "lockstep"). The plan also includes an interactive energy education center at the university along with tours for school groups to be organized "with assistance from private industries."[7]

In the realm of aesthetics, the University of Wyoming Art Museum appears to be taking its role seriously as a purveyor of critical thinking and provocative engagement. So don't be surprised to learn about political fallout from an exhibit by Brandon Ballengée—a biologist/artist and environmental activist whose earlier works include an unflattering installation and disturbing images concerning the impacts of the BP *Deepwater Horizon* oil spill.[8]

Last-minute (or month) updates are not a reality in book publishing, but I'd like to address a major change in the national context of fossil fuels that had begun when this manuscript went to press. This dynamic is almost certain to have continued in the past year. That change is the precipitous decline in the value of oil, gas, and coal. March 31, 2016, was called "Black Thursday" when two of the nation's largest coal companies cut 465 miners from their Wyoming payrolls (corporate executives paid themselves millions of dollars in bonuses just days earlier).[9] Consider that in the state's most energy rich counties, between January 2015 and January 2016, unemployment increased by 40 percent, topping 7 percent in Natrona County.[10] Statewide unemployment rose from 3.8 to 4.7 percent, and the state's population declined as jobs evaporated.[11] This socioeconomic instability is likely to have consequences for free speech in Wyoming and elsewhere.

One might expect that coal's collapse would mean that the industry would wield less political influence.[12] But oddly, weakness has empowered the failing corporations. Remember, Wyoming's governor is calling for the state to "double down" on coal. When a company town is faced with the prospect of losing its industry, the civic leaders panic. They'll do virtually anything to sustain the unsustainable venture that anchors the economy. Mead has insisted that "we will continue to fight for coal. These companies and the coal energy they provide fuel our way of life."[13]

And so when I sought collaborators for a symposium to feature the new book, *Fracture: Essays, Poems, and Stories on Fracking in America* (2016), which included a powerful essay by one of the creative writing faculty at the University of Wyoming, I found few takers across campus. The request didn't even require monetary support from other departments—only a willingness to sign on as a cosponsor of the public discourse. By reading between the lines of some replies, it was clear that this was perceived as the wrong time to risk offending the energy industry and the institutional administration that will be doling out cuts as the state's revenues decline. Smart politics, savvy leadership, or self-censorship?

NOTES

Note: Some of the websites cited below are no longer active, but the author is in possession of the original content referenced.

Preface

1. Fred Wertheimer and Susan W. Manes, "Campaign Finance Reform: A Key to Restoring the Health of Our Democracy," *Columbia Law Review* 94 (1994): 1126–59; Richard Briffault, "Public Funding and Democratic Elections," *University of Pennsylvania Law Review* 148 (1999): 563–90; Gerald Sussman, *Global Electioneering: Campaign Consulting, Communications, and Corporate Financing* (New York: Rowman and Littlefield, 2005); Evan Osborne, *The Rise of the Anti-Corporate Movement: Corporations and the People Who Hate Them* (Santa Barbara, CA: Praeger, 2007); Lloyd H. Mayer, "Breaching a Leaking Dam? Corporate Money and Elections," *Notre Dame Legal Studies Paper*, no. 09-36 (2009); Sheldon S. Wolin, *Democracy Incorporated: Managed Democracy and the Specter of Inverted Totalitarianism* (Princeton, NJ: Princeton University Press, 2010); Jeffrey D. Clements, *Corporations Are Not People: Reclaiming Democracy from Big Money and Global Corporations* (Oakland, CA: Berrett-Koehler, 2014); Conor M. Dowling and Michael G. Miller, *Super PAC!: Money, Elections, and Voters after Citizens United* (New York: Routledge, 2014); Timothy Kuhner, *Capitalism v. Democracy: Money in Politics and the Free Market Constitution* (Redwood City, CA: Stanford Law Books, 2014); Yasmin Dawood, "Campaign Finance and American Democracy," *Annual Review of Political Science* (forthcoming), accessed July 5, 2016, http://papers.ssrn.com/sol3/Papers.cfm?abstract_id=2528587; Lee Drutman, *The Business of America Is Lobbying: How Corporations Became Politicized and Politics Became More Corporate* (New York: Oxford University Press, 2015); Suzanne Robbins, *Campaign Finance and Electoral Competition: The New World of Outside Money* (New York: Routledge, 2015).

2. David F. Noble, *America by Design: Science, Technology, and the Rise of Corporate Capitalism* (New York: Oxford University Press, 1979); David F. Noble, *Forces of Production: A Social History of Industrial Automation* (New York: Oxford University Press, 1986); Michael A. Dennis, "Accounting for Research: New Histories of Corporate Laboratories and the Social History of American Science," *Social Studies of Science* 17 (1987): 479–518; David A. Hounshell and John Kenly Smith Jr., *Science and Corporate Strategy: Du Pont R and D, 1902–1980* (New York: Cambridge

University Press, 1988); Robert Bell, *Impure Science: Fraud, Compromise and Political Influence in Scientific Research* (New York: Wiley, 1992); David F. Noble, *Progress without People: New Technology, Unemployment, and the Message of Resistance* (Toronto: Between the Lines, 1995); Leo Marx, *The Machine in the Garden: Technology and the Pastoral Ideal in America* (New York: Oxford University Press, 2000); Daniel Lee Kleinman, *Impure Cultures: University Biology and the World of Commerce* (Madison: University of Wisconsin Press, 2003); David S. Egilman and Susanna R. Bohme, "Over a Barrel: Corporate Corruption of Science and Its Effects on Workers and the Environment," *International Journal of Occupational and Environmental Health* 11 (2005): 331–37; David Michaels, *Doubt Is Their Product: How Industry's Assault on Science Threatens Your Health* (New York: Oxford University Press, 2008); Raymond S. Bradley, *Global Warming and Political Intimidation: How Politicians Cracked Down on Scientists as the Earth Heated Up* (Amherst: University of Massachusetts Press, 2011); Naomi Oreskes and Erik M. Conway, *Merchants of Doubt: How a Handful of Scientists Obscured the Truth on Issues from Tobacco Smoke to Global Warming* (New York: Bloomsbury Press, 2011); Thomas O. McGarity and Wendy E. Wagner, *Bending Science: How Special Interests Corrupt Public Health Research* (Cambridge, MA: Harvard University Press, 2012).

3. William Roberts, *Corporate and Commercial Free Speech: First Amendment Protection of Expression in Business* (Santa Barbara, CA: Praeger, 1985); Sue Curry Jansen, *Censorship: The Knot That Binds Power and Knowledge* (New York: Oxford University Press, 1991); Lisa B. Bingham, "Employee Free Speech in the Workplace: Using the First Amendment as Public Policy for Wrongful Discharge Actions," *Ohio State Law Journal* (1994): 341–91; Cynthia L. Estlund, "Free Speech and Due Process in the Workplace," *Indiana Law Journal* 71 (1995): 101–51; David C. Yamada, "Voices from the Cubicle: Protecting and eEncouraging Private Employee Speech in the Post-Industrial Workplace," *Berkeley Journal of Employment and Labor Law* 19 (1998): 1–59; Lawrence Soley, *Censorship Inc.: The Corporate Threat to Free Speech in the United States* (New York: Monthly Review Press, 2002); Sue C. Jansen and Brian Martin, "Making Censorship Backfire," *Counterpoise* 7 (2003): 5–15; Jack M. Balkin, "Free Speech and Hostile Environments," *Columbia Law Review* (1999): 2295–320; Joel Bakan, *The Corporation: The Pathological Pursuit of Profit and Power* (Washington, DC: Free Press, 2005); William. A. Wines and Terrance J. Lau, "Can You Hear Me Now—Corporate Censorship and Its Troubling Implications for the First Amendment," *DePaul Law Review* 55 (2005): 119–58; Bruce Barry, *Speechless: The Erosion of Free Expression in the American Workplace* (Oakland, CA: Berrett-Koehler, 2007); Surya Deva, "Corporate Complicity in Internet Censorship in China: Who Cares for the Global Compact or the Global Online Freedom Act?," *George Washington International Law Review* 39 (2007): 255–319; Lewis Maltby, *Can They Do That? Retaking Our Fundamental Rights in the Workplace* (New York: Portfolio,

2009); James A. Gross, *A Shameful Business: The Case for Human Rights in the American Workplace* (Ithaca, NY: Cornell University / ILR Press, 2010); Jeffrey Kassing, *Dissent in Organizations* (Somerset, NJ: Polity, 2011); Eric Jensen, *Mediating Social Change in Authoritarian and Democratic States: Irony, Hybridity, and Corporate Censorship* (Charlotte, NC: Information Age, 2012); Michael J. Sandel, *What Money Can't Buy: The Moral Limits of Markets* (New York: Farrar, Straus and Giroux, 2012); Joel Simon, *The New Censorship: Inside the Global Battle for Media Freedom* (New York: Columbia University Press, 2014).

4. Nicholas A. Ashford, "A Framework for Examining the Effects of Industrial Funding on Academic Freedom and the Integrity of the University," *Science, Technology, and Human Values* (1983): 16–23; Victoria D. Alexander, "From Philanthropy to Funding: The Effects of Corporate and Public Support on American Art Museums," *Poetics* 24 (1996): 87–129; David C. Mowery and Bhaven N. Sampat, "Patenting and Licensing University Inventions: Lessons from the History of the Research Corporation," *Industrial and Corporate Change* 10 (2001): 317–55; Henry A. Giroux, "Neoliberalism, Corporate Culture, and the Promise of Higher Education: The University as a Democratic Public Sphere," *Harvard Educational Review* 72 (2002): 425–64; Magnus Gulbrandsen and Jens-Christian Smeby, "Industry Funding and University Professors' Research Performance," *Research Policy* 34 (2005): 932–50; Jennifer Washburn, *University, Inc.: The Corporate Corruption of Higher Education* (New York: Basic, 2006); Mark Bowen, *Censoring Science: Inside the Political Attack on Dr. James Hansen and the Truth of Global Warming* (New York: Dutton, 2007); Frank Donoghue, *The Last Professors: The Corporate University and the Fate of the Humanities* (Bronx, NY: Fordham University Press, 2008); Kathryn Mohrman, Wanhua Ma, and David Baker, "The Research University in Transition: The Emerging Global Model," *Higher Education Policy* 21 (2008): 5–27; Gaye Tuchman, *Wannabe U: Inside the Corporate University* (Chicago: University of Chicago Press, 2009); Ellen Schrecker, *The Lost Soul of Higher Education: Corporatization, the Assault on Academic Freedom, and the End of the American University* (New York: The New Press, 2010); Jonathan Levy, *Freaks of Fortune: The Emerging World of Capitalism and Risk in America* (Cambridge, MA: Harvard University Press, 2012); Robert E. Wright, *Corporation Nation* (Philadelphia: University of Pennsylvania Press, 2013); Mangala Subramaniam, Robert Perrucci, and David Whitlock, "Intellectual Closure: A Theoretical Framework Linking Knowledge, Power, and the Corporate University," *Critical Sociology* 40 (2014): 411–30; Zephyr Teachout, *Corruption in America: From Benjamin Franklin's Snuff Box to Citizens United* (Cambridge, MA: Harvard University Press, 2014).

5. Richard Kearney, *On Stories* (New York: Routledge, 2002), 3.

6. Ramit Plushnick-Masti, "EPA's Water Contamination Investigation Halted

in Texas after Range Resources Protest," *Huffington Post*, accessed December 9, 2013, http://www.huffingtonpost.com/2013/01/16/epa-water-contamination-investigation-fracking_n_2484568.html; Mike Soraghan, "Barnett Shale: Homeowners Renew Complaints about Water Near Range Wells," EnergyWire website, accessed December 9, 2013, http://www.eenews.net/energywire/stories/1059987422.

7. On discrediting the faculty member, see Robert W. Howarth, Renee Santoro, and Anthony Ingraffea, "Methane and Greenhouse-Gas Footprint of Natural Gas from Shale Formations," *Climate Change* (2011) (DOI 10.1007/s10584-011-0061-5); Anthony Ingraffea, "Gangplank to a Warm Future," *New York Times*, July 28, 2013, accessed December 9, 2013, http://www.nytimes.com/2013/07/29/opinion/gangplank-to-a-warm-future.html?_r=0; "Does the Natural Gas Industry Need a New Messenger?," *CBC News*, accessed December 9, 2013, http://www.cbc.ca/news/canada/new-brunswick/does-the-natural-gas-industry-need-a-new-messenger-1.1002634; Steve Horn, "Smeared but Still Fighting, Cornell's Tony Ingraffea Debunks Gas Industry Myths," Desmogblog.com, accessed December 9, 2013, http://www.desmogblog.com/smeared-still-fighting-cornell-s-tony-ingraffea-debunks-gas-industry-myths. On misrepresenting university officials and the School of Mines researcher, see Joe Massaro, "Professor Ingraffea: The Next Monster under the Bed," *Energy in Depth*, accessed December 9, 2013, http://energyindepth.org/marcellus/professor-ingraffea-the-next-monster-under-the-bed.

8. Y. C. Wang, "The Dangerous Silence of Academic Researchers," *Chronicle of Higher Education*, February 23, 2015, accessed June 2, 2015, http://chronicle.com/article/The-Dangerous-Silence-of/190251.

9. Deborah Sontag, "Where Oil and Politics Mix," *New York Times*, November 24, 2014, A1, 16–17.

Introduction

1. Sean Walker, "Pussy Riot's Tour of Sochi: Arrests, Protests—and Whipping by Cossacks," *Guardian*, February 20, 2014, accessed December 15, 2015, http://www.theguardian.com/music/2014/feb/20/pussy-riot-tour-of-sochi-protest-winter-olympics; Jeffrey T. Richelson and Michael L. Evans, "Tiananmen Square, 1989: The Declassified History," National Security Archive, George Washington University, accessed October 15, 2014, http://www2.gwu.edu/~nsarchiv/NSAEBB/NSAEBB16; Zhao Ziyang, *Prisoner of the State: The Secret Journal of Premier Zhao Ziyang* (New York: Simon and Schuster, 2010).

2. Suzanne Goldenberg, "US Presidential Debates' Great Unmentionable: Cli-

mate Change," *Guardian*, October 23, 2012, accessed October 15, 2014, http://www.guardian.co.uk/environment/2012/oct/23/us-president-debates-climate-change.

3. Ahmed Rashid, "After 1,700 Years, Buddhas Fall to Taliban Dynamite," *Telegraph*, March 12, 2001, accessed December 15, 2015, http://www.telegraph.co.uk/news/worldnews/asia/afghanistan/1326063/After-1700-years-Buddhas-fall-to-Taliban-dynamite.html; Kevin Sieff, "Florida Pastor Terry Jones's Koran Burning Has Far-Reaching Effect," *Washington Post*, April 2, 2011, accessed October 15, 2014, http://www.washingtonpost.com/local/education/florida-pastor-terry-joness-koran-burning-has-far-reaching-effect/2011/04/02/AFpiFoQC_story.html.

4. "The Universal Declaration of Human Rights," United Nations, accessed November 25, 2014, http://www.un.org/en/documents/udhr.

5. Michael J. Sandel, *What Money Can't Buy* (New York: Farrar, Straus and Giroux, 2012).

6. "Book Burning," *Wikipedia*, accessed October 15, 2014, http://en.wikipedia.org/wiki/Bookburning; Jeremy Fugleberg, "Emails: University of Wyoming Officials Sped Up, Touted Removal of Anti-Coal Sculpture," *Casper Star-Tribune*, October 14, 2012, accessed October 15, 2014, http://trib.com/business/energy/emails-university-of-wyoming-officials-sped-up-touted-removal-of/article_4f9332ee-d83c-5d58-a38b-19e913ba739d.html.

7. Soley, *Censorship Inc.*

8. Samuel Western, *Pushed Off the Mountain, Sold Down the River: Wyoming's Search for Its Soul* (Moose, WY: Homestead, 2002).

9. Ibid., 105.

10. Ibid., 10.

11. Ibid.

12. Ibid.

13. Laura Hancock, "Methane-Farming Co. May Owe Wyoming, Campbell County $739K in Back Taxes," *Casper Star-Tribune*, October 14, 2013, accessed October 20, 2014, http://trib.com/business/energy/ methane-farming-co-may-owe-wyoming-campbell-county-k-in/article_8865f74f-45a0–53ec-a79d-ecc475be02cc.html; "Wyoming: State Profiles and Energy Estimates," US Energy Information Administration, August 21, 2014, accessed October 20, 2014, http://www.eia.gov/state/analysis.cfm?sid=WY.

14. "Wyoming State Profile and Energy Estimates," US Energy Information

Administration, accessed December 15, 2015, http://www.eia.gov/state/?sid=
WY#tabs-3; Eve Newman, "Official: Coal Industry Needs to Diversify," *Laramie
Boomerang*, January 22, 2013, A3; "Countries Worldwide Propose to Build 1,200
New Coal Plants," Institute for Energy Research, accessed October 15, 2014,
http://instituteforenergyresearch.org/analysis/countries-worldwide-propose-
to-build-1200-new-coal-plants.

15. "Water Production from Coalbed Methane Development in Wyoming: A
Summary of Quantity, Quality and Management Options," Ruckelshaus Institute of
Environment and Natural Resources, University of Wyoming, December 2005,
accessed December 15, 2015, http://www.uwyo.edu/haub/ruckelshaus-institute/
publications/reports-and-proceedings.html; "Wyoming State Profile and Energy
Estimates," US Energy Information Administration, accessed October 15, 2014,
http://www.eia.gov/state/?sid=WY#tabs-3.

16. Dustin Bleizeffer, "Drillers on Pace to Continue 500 Wells per Year in
Southern Powder River Basin Oil Play," WyoFile, January 21, 2014, accessed July 5,
2016, http://wyofile.com/dustin/drillers-pace-continue-500-wells-per-year-southern-
powder-river-basin-oil-play/#sthash.bjjL22wo.dpuf; "Wyoming State Profile and
Energy Estimates," US Energy Information Administration, accessed October 15,
2014, http://www.eia.gov/state/?sid=WY#tabs-3; Dustin Bleizeffer, "Wyoming Produced More Oil and Coal, but Less Gas in '14," WyoFile, February 17, 2015,
accessed June 2, 2015, http://www.wyofile.com/blog/wyoming-produced-oil-coal-
less-gas-14.

17. Bleizeffer, "Wyoming Produced More."

18. "Uranium," Wyoming State Geological Survey, accessed October 15, 2014,
http://www.wsgs.uwyo.edu/Research/Energy/Uranium.aspx; "Wyoming State Profile and Energy Estimates," US Energy Information Administration, accessed October 15, 2014, http://www.eia.gov/state/?sid=WY#tabs-3.

19. "Installed Wind Capacity," US Department of Energy, accessed October 15,
2014, http://apps2.eere.energy.gov/wind/windexchange/wind_installed_capacity.
asp; "Wyoming Wind Energy," American Wind Energy Association, accessed October 15, 2014, http://awea.rd.net/Resources/state.aspx?ItemNumber=5096.

20. Dustin Bleizeffer, "Gov. Mead Begs for Coal's Rescue While Denying
Man's Role in Climate Crisis," WyoFile, May 16, 2014, accessed July 5, 2016, http://
wyofile.com/dustin/gov-mead-begs-for-coals-rescue-while-denying-mans-role-in-
climate-crisis/#sthash.3Rk2BVBZ.dpuf; Stephanie Joyce and Willow Belden, "Wyoming Public Media's 2014 Forum on Coal," Wyoming Public Media, February 29,
2014, accessed July 5, 2016, http://wyomingpublicmedia.org/post/wyoming-public-
medias-2014-forum-coal-open-spaces; Eli Bebout and Steve Harshman, "Planning

for Wyoming's Future," WyoFile, February 18, 2014, http://wyofile.com/wyofile-2/
planning-wyomings-future-budget; "Wyoming State Government Revenue Forecast:
Fiscal Year 2014–Fiscal Year 2018," Consensus Review Estimating Group, October
2013, accessed October 15, 2014, http://eadiv.state.wy.us/creg/GreenCREG_Oct13.
pdf.

21. "Wyoming," US Census Bureau, accessed October 15, 2014, http://
quickfacts.census.gov/qfd/states/56000.html; "Wyoming—Largest Cities,"
Geonames, accessed July 5, 2016, http://www.geonames.org/US/WY/largest-
cities-in-wyoming.html.

22. Bill McCarthy, "Wyoming: The Story behind the Score," StateIntegrity.org,
accessed October 15, 2014, http://www.stateintegrity.org/wyoming_story_
subpage1.

23. Joyce and Belden, "Wyoming Public Media"; Gregory Nickerson, "Wyoming
Mining Association Conference Paints Picture of Challenges and Opportunities,"
WyoFile, June 29, 2013, accessed October 15, 2014, http://wyofile.com/gregory_
nickerson/wyoming-mining-association-conference/#sthash.oPb8QSRo.dpuf.

24. Philip Roberts, Department of History, University of Wyoming, e-mail to
author, August 28, 2014.

25. Julian Petley, *Censorship: A Beginner's Guide* (Oxford: Oneworld, 2009), 2.

26. Zachariah Chafee Jr., *Free Speech in the United States* (Cambridge, MA: Har-
vard University Press, 1948); Alan H. Goldman, "Ethical Issues in Proprietary
Restrictions on Research Results," *Science, Technology, and Human Values* 12 (1987):
22–30; P. Sherwill-Navarro, "Internet in the Workplace: Censorship, Liability, and
Freedom of Speech," *Medical Reference Services Quarterly* 17 (1998): 77–84; Bernard S.
Black, "Disclosure, Not Censorship: The Case for Proxy Reform," *Journal of Corporate
Law* 17 (1991): 49–86; Carl Jensen, *Censored—The News that Didn't Make the News*
(New York: Seven Stories Press, 1996); A. D. Lowe, "The Price of Speaking Out,"
American Bar Association Journal 82 (September 1996): 48–53; George Pring and
Penelope Canan, *SLAPPs: Getting Sued for Speaking Out* (Philadelphia: Temple Uni-
versity Press, 1996); Solveig M. Singleton, "Privacy as Censorship: A Skeptical View
of Proposals to Regulate Privacy in the Private Sector," available at *Social Science
Research Network 1600253* (1998), accessed December 15, 2015, http://www.ssrn.
com/en; Eveline Lubbers, ed., *Battling Big Business: Countering Greenwash, Infiltration,
and Other Forms of Corporate Bullying* (Cambridge: Green Books, 2002); Lawrence
Soley, *Censorship Inc.: The Corporate Threat to Free Speech in the United States* (New
York: Monthly Review Press, 2002); J. Richter, "Public-Private Partnerships for
Health: A Trend with No Alternatives?," *Development* 47 (2004): 43–48; William. A.
Wines and Terrance. J. Lau, "Can You Hear Me Now—Corporate Censorship and Its

Troubling Implications for the First Amendment," *DePaul Law Review* 55 (2005): 119–68; Rosemary Coombe, "Commodity Culture, Private Censorship, Branded Environments, and Global Trade Politics: Intellectual Property as a Topic of Law and Society Research," in *The Blackwell Companion to Law and Society*, ed. Austin Sarat, 369–91 (Malden, MA: Basil Blackwell, 2004); Gary E. Dann and Neil Haddow, "Just Doing Business or Doing Just Business: Google, Microsoft, Yahoo! and the Business of Censoring China's Internet," *Journal of Business Ethics* 79 (2008): 219–34; Gary C. Gray and Victoria B. Kendzia, "Organizational Self-Censorship: Corporate Sponsorship, Nonprofit Funding, and the Educational Experience," *Canadian Review of Sociology* 46 (2009): 161–77.

27.   Melville B. Nimmer, "The Constitutionality of Official Censorship of Motion Pictures," *University of Chicago Law Review* 25 (1958): 625–57; Leonard Levy, *Legacy of Suppression* (Cambridge, MA: Belknap Press, 1960); B. A. Roy, "Movie Censorship: A Public and Private Concern," *Louis University Law Journal* 15 (1970): 156; Thomas L. Tedford, *Freedom of Speech in the United States* (New York: Random House, 1985); C. Berry and D. Wolin, "Regulating Rock Lyrics: A New Wave of Censorship," *Harvard Journal on Legislation* 23 (1986): 595–619; Annabel Patterson, "Censorship," in *Encyclopedia of Literature and Criticism*, ed. Martin Coyle et al. (Detroit: Gale Research, 1991); Rae Langton, "Speech Acts and Unspeakable Acts," *Philosophy and Public Affairs* 22 (1993): 293–330; Susan Dwyer, ed., *The Problem of Pornography* (Belmont, CA: Wadsworth, 1995); Daniel Jacobson, "Freedom of Speech Acts? A Response to Langton," *Philosophy and Public Affairs* 24 (1995): 64–79; Geoff Kemp, ed., *Censorship Moments: Reading Texts in the History of Censorship and Freedom of Expression* (New York: Bloomsbury, 2014); Emily Knox, "'The Books Will Still Be in the Library': Narrow Definitions of Censorship in the Discourse of Challengers," *Library Trends* 62 (2014): 740–49.

28.   Michel Foucault, *Power/Knowledge: Selected Interviews and Other Writings*, ed. and trans. Colin Gordon (New York: Pantheon, 1980); Richard Burt, ed., *The Administration of Aesthetics: Censorship, Political Criticism, and the Public Sphere* (Minneapolis: University of Minnesota Press, 1994); Jacob Septimus, "The MPAA Ratings System: A Regime of Private Censorship and Cultural Manipulation," *Columbia VLA Journal of Law and Arts* 21 (1996): 69–84; Wendy Brown, "Freedom's Silences," in *Censoring and Silencing*, ed. Robert C. Post, 313–27 (Los Angeles: Getty Research Institute for the History of Art and the Humanities, 1998); George E. Marcus, "Censorship in the Hart of Difference: Cultural Property, Indigenous Peoples' Movements, and Challenges to Western Liberal Thought," in Post, *Censoring and Silencing*, 221–46; Mario Biagioli, "From Book Censorship to Academic Peer Review," *Emergences: Journal for the Study of Media and Composite Cultures* 12 (2002): 11–45; Endre Dányi, "Xerox Project: Photocopy Machines as a Metaphor for an 'Open Society,'" *Information Society* 22 (2006): 111–15; Ramaswami

Balasubramaniam, "The Rhetoric of Multiculturalism," *New Perspectives in Literature, Film and the Arts* (2008): 31–42; Kirsten Bell and Danielle Elliott, "Censorship in the Name of Ethics: Critical Public Health Research in the Age of Human Subjects Regulation," *Critical Public Health* 24 (2014): 385–91; Petley, *Censorship*, ix; B. F. Jackson, "Censorship and Freedom of Expression in the Age of Facebook," *New Mexico Law Review* 44 (2014): 121–67; Marua Pramaggiore, "Privatization Is the New Black," in *The Routledge Companion to Global Popular Culture*, ed. Toby Miller, 187–96 (New York: Routledge, 2014); Gopal K. Sahu, "Reconceptualising News and Redefining Its Values: Postmodern Perspective," *Journal of Exclusion Studies* 4 (2014): 165–82.

29. Frederick Schauer, "The Ontology of Censorship," in Post, *Censoring and Silencing*, 162.

30. John B. Bury, *A History of the Freedom of Thought* (New York: Oxford University Press, 1913); Sidney S. Grant and S. E. Angoff, "Recent Developments in Censorship," *Boston University Law Review* 10 (1930): 488–509; S. N. Siegel, "Radio Censorship and the Federal Communications Commission," *Columbia Law Review* 7 (1936): 447–69; Nimmer, "Constitutionality of Official Censorship," 625–57; Levy, *Legacy of Suppression*; Roy, "Movie Censorship," 156; Paul S. Boyer, *Purity in Print: The Vice-Society Movement and Book Censorship in America* (London: Gollancz, 1975); H. A. Linde, "Courts and Censorship," *Minnesota Law Review* 66 (1981): 171; New York Public Library, *Censorship: 500 Years of Conflict* (New York: Oxford University Press, 1984); Tedford, *Freedom of Speech*; Berry and Wolin, "Regulating Rock Lyrics," 595–619; Patterson, "Censorship"; Langton, "Speech Acts," 293–330; Dwyer, *Problem of Pornography*; Jacobson, "Freedom of Speech Acts?," 64–79; Richard Burt, "(Un)censoring in Detail: The Fetish of Censorship in the Early Modern Past and the Postmodern Present," in Post, *Censoring and Silencing*, 17–42; Debora Shuger, "Civility and Censorship in Early Modern England," in Post, *Censoring and Silencing*, 89–110; Kenji Yoshino, "The Eclectic Model of Censorship," *California Law Review* 88 (2000): 1635–55; Kemp, *Censorship Moments*; Knox, "Books Still in Library," 740–49; Adam Parkes, "Obscene Modernism: Literary Censorship and Experiment, 1900–1940 / Prudes on the Prowl: Fiction and Obscenity in England, 1850 to the Present Day," *Textual Practice* 28 (2014): 1145–53.

31. Donald Thomas, *A Long Time Burning: The History of Literary Censorship in England* (New York: Praeger, 1969); Mark W. Hopkins, "The Meaning of Censorship and Libel in the Soviet Union," *Journalism and Mass Communication Quarterly* 47 (1970): 118–41; O. O. Oreh, "The Beginnings of Self-Censorship in Nigeria's Press and the Media," *International Communication Gazette* 22 (1976): 150–55; Marvin Alisky, *Latin American Media: Guidance and Censorship* (New York: Wiley-Blackwell, 1981); S. Blixen, "Uruguay: TV Owners, Videos and the Military," *Index on*

Censorship 19 (1990): 16–17; Lawrence Douglas, "Policing the Past: Holocaust Denial and the Law," in Post, *Censoring and Silencing*, 67–88; Barbara R. Johnston and Terence Turner, "Censorship, Denial of Informed Participation, and Human Rights Abuses Associated with Dam Development in Chile," *Professional Ethics Report* 11 (1998): 6–8; U. Siriyuvasak, "Regulation, Reform and the Question of Democratising the Broadcast Media in Thailand," *Javnost—The Public* 8 (2001): 89–108; C. Stevenson, "Breaching the Great Firewall: China's Internet Censorship and the Quest for Freedom of Expression in a Connected World," *Boston College International and Comparative Law Review* 30 (2007): 531–58; Rebecca MacKinnon, "Flatter World and Thicker Walls?: Blogs, Censorship and Civic Discourse in China," *Public Choice* 134 (2008): 31–46; Emily Anderson, "Containing Voices in the Wilderness: Censorship and Religious Dissent in the Japanese Countryside," *Church History* 83 (2014): 398–421; Ásta G. Helgadóttir, "The Icelandic Initiative for Pornography Censorship," *Porn Studies* 1 (2014): 285–98; B. Yesil, "Press Censorship in Turkey: Networks of State Power, Commercial Pressures, and Self-Censorship," *Communication, Culture and Critique* 7 (2014): 154–73.

32. Donna A. Demac, *Liberty Denied: The Current Rise of Censorship in America* (New Brunswick, NJ: Rutgers University Press, 1990); Catharine A. MacKinnon, *Only Words* (Cambridge, MA: Harvard University Press, 1993); Beth Orsoff, "Government Speech as Government Censorship," *Southern California Law Review* 67 (1993): 229; K. M. Sullivan, "Free Speech Wars," *Southern Methodist University Law Review* 48 (1994): 203; Robert Paul Wolff, Barrington Moore Jr., and Herbert Marcuse, *A Critique of Pure Tolerance* (Boston: Beacon Press, 1965); Owen M. Fiss, *Liberalism Divided: Freedom of Speech and the Many Uses of State Power* (Boulder, CO: Westview Press, 1996); Ruth Gavison, "Incitement and the Limits of Law," Sanford Levinson, "The Tutelary State: 'Censorship,' 'Silencing,' and the 'Practices of Cultural Regulation,'" and David Wasserman, "Public Funding for Science and Art: Censorship, Social Harm, and the Case of Genetic Research into Crime and Violence," all in Post, *Censoring and Silencing*, 169–94; Sana Ahmed, "Censorship and Surveillance in the Global Information Age: Are Telecommunications Companies Agents of Suppression or Revolution," *Case Western Reserve University Journal of Law, Technology and the Internet* 4 (2012): 503; Seth F. Kreimer, "Censorship by Proxy: The First Amendment, Internet Intermediaries, and the Problem of the Weakest Link," *University of Pennsylvania Law Review* 154 (2006): 11–101; Jeffrey Toppe, "Big Brother's Little Brother: Privatizing First Amendment Violations through Government-Encouraged Censorship," *Holy Cross Journal of Law and Public Policy* 18 (2014): 49.

33. Post, "Censorship and Silencing," 1.

34. Soley, *Censorship Inc.*, ix.

35. "Excerpts from Aristotle's Nicomachean Ethics," Carnegie Mellon University, Online Guide to Ethics and Morality, accessed October 15, 2014, http://caae. phil.cmu.edu/Cavalier/80130/part1/sect1/texts/NE.html.

36. Paul Freilberger and Daniel McNeill, *Fuzzy Logic* (New York: Simon and Schuster, 1993).

37. Sue Curry Jansen, *Censorship: The Knot That Binds Power and Knowledge* (New York: Oxford University Press, 1991), 4.

38. Daniel Flynn, *Why the Left Hates America* (New York: Crown Forum, 2004).

39. George F. Will, "American Higher Education Is a House Divided," *Washington Post*, December 28, 2015, accessed December 29, 2015, https://www. washingtonpost.com/opinions/higher-education-is-a-house-divided/2015/12/ 18/1a54f548-a4f4-11e5-9c4e-be37f66848bb_story.html.

40. Petley, *Censorship*; "Iconoclasm," *Wikipedia*, accessed October 15, 2014, http://en.wikipedia.org/wiki/Iconoclasm.

41. "Burning the Koran?," *Patriot Post*, September 10, 2010, accessed October 15, 2014, http://patriotpost.us/articles/7218.

42. Rashid, "After 1,700 Years."

43. Petley, *Censorship*, 14.

44. "1989: Ayatollah Sentences Author to Death," BBC's "On This Day," accessed October 15, 2014, http://news.bbc.co.uk/onthisday/hi/dates/stories/ february/14/newsid_2541000/2541149.stm.

45. Walker, "Pussy Riot's Tour."

46. Soley, *Censorship Inc.*

47. Ibid.; Vickie Goodwin, former employee at Powder River Basin Resource Council, interview with the author, November 10, 2014; Cathy Killean, *To Save a Mountain* (Casper, WY: Bessemer Bend, 1998), 88–93.

48. Petley, *Censorship*, 145.

49. Judith Butler, "Rule Out: Vocabularies of the Censor," in Post, *Censoring and Silencing*, 247–60.

50. Jansen, *Censorship*.

51. Petley, *Censorship*.

52. Anthony M. Orum and John G. Dale, *Political Sociology: Power and Participation in the Modern World* (New York: Oxford University Press, 2009).

53. John P. R. French Jr. and Bertram Raven, "The Bases of Social Power," in *Group Dynamics*, ed. D. Cartwright and A. Zander, 150–67 (New York: Harper and Row, 1960); Bertram H. Raven, "Social Influence and Iower," in *Current Studies in Social Psychology*, ed. I. D. Steiner and M. Fishbein, 371–82 (New York: Holt, Rinehart and Winston, 1965).

54. Joseph S. Nye Jr., *The Future of Power* (New York: Perseus, 2011).

55. Michael Mann, *Power in the 21st Century* (Malden, MA: Polity, 2011).

56. C. Wright Mills, *The Power Elite* (New York: Oxford, 2000).

57. Orum and Dale, *Political Sociology*.

58. Nye, *Future of Power*.

59. Ulrich Beck, *Power in the Global Age* (Malden, MA: Polity, 2005).

60. Ibid.

61. Timothy Mitchell, *Carbon Democracy: Political Power in the Age of Oil* (New York: Verso, 2011).

62. Chad Parker, "Aramco's Frontier Story," in *Oil Culture*, ed. R. Barrett and D. Worden, 171–88 (Minneapolis: University of Minnesota Press, 2014).

63. Michael Watts, "Oil Frontiers: The Niger Delta and the Gulf of Mexico," in Barrett and Worden, *Oil Culture*, 198.

64. Ibid.; Jennifer Wenzel, "Petro-Magic-Realism Revisited: Unimagining and Reimagining the Niger Delta," in Barrett and Worden, *Oil Culture*, 211–25; Matthew T. Huber, "Refined Politics: Petroleum Products, Neoliberalism, and the Ecology of Entrepreneurial Life," in Barrett and Worden, *Oil Culture*, 226–43.

65. Christopher F. Jones, *Routes of Power: Energy and Modern America* (Cambridge, MA: Harvard University Press, 2014); Steve Coll, *Private Empire: Exxon Mobil and American Power* (New York: Penguin, 2012).

66. Stephanie LeMenager, *Living Oil: Petroleum Culture in the American Century* (New York: Oxford University Press, 2014).

67. Mitchell, *Carbon Democracy*.

68. Ken Silverstein, *The Secret World of Oil* (New York: Verso, 2014).

69. "Franklin D. Roosevelt's 'Four Freedoms' Speech: Annual Message to

Congress on the State of the Union, 01/06/1941," accessed October 15, 2014, http://www.fdrlibrary.marist.edu/pdfs/fftext.pdf.

70. Ibid., 7.

Chapter 1

1. Robert R. Kuehn, "Shooting the Messenger: The Ethics of Attacks on Environmental Representation," *Harvard Environmental Law Review* 26 (2002): 417–58.

2. Ibid.

3. University of Wyoming Foundation, "Annual Report on Giving: 2001–2002," accessed March 7, 2014, http://www.uwyo.edu/foundation/resources-and-publications/annual-report1.html. http://www.uwyo.edu/foundation/_files/docs/annualreport2002.pdf]

4. Associated Press, "UW Fundraising Campaign Raises $200 Million," *Casper Star-Tribune*, August 15, 2005, accessed May 22, 2014, http://trib.com/news/state-and-regional/uw-fundraising-campaign-raises-million/article_62360c9c-45f4-5627-87ce-ebd7ff538e9b.html.

5. Ruckelshaus Institute of Environment and Natural Resources, "Water Production from Coalbed Methane Development in Wyoming: A Summary of Quantity, Quality and Management Options," University of Wyoming, Laramie, December 2005, accessed March 7, 2014, http://www.uwyo.edu/haub/ruckelshaus-institute/_files/docs/publications/2005-cbm-water-final-report.pdf.

6. "Compensation of University of Wyoming Fundraisers Criticized," *Philanthropy News Digest*, April 2, 2006, accessed May 22, 2014, http://www.philanthropynewsdigest.org/news/compensation-of-university-of-wyoming-fundraisers-criticized.

7. Bob Moen, "William Ayers Wyoming Speech Concludes without Incident," *Huffpost College*, April 29, 2010, accessed April 7, 2014, http://www.huffingtonpost.com/2010/04/29/william-ayers-wyoming-spe_n_556881.html; Bob Moen, "University of Wyo. Cancel[s] William Ayers Speech," *Denver Post*, March 31, 2010, accessed April 7, 2014, http://www.denverpost.com/news/ci_14792297.

8. Bill Ayers, "Doublespeak at the University of Wyoming," *Huffpost College*, April 7, 2010, accessed April 7, 2014, http://www.huffingtonpost.com/bill-ayers/doublespeak-at-the-univer_b_527223.html.

9. Rone Tempest, Anne MacKinnon, and Philip White, "First Amendment: A

Document for All Seasons" WyoFile, April 29, 2010, accessed May 22, 2014, http://wyofile.com/wyofile-2/federal-judge-orders-uw-to-let-ayers-speak.

10.   Jeremy Pelzer, "Emails Show UW Faced Pressure," *Casper Star-Tribune*, April 29, 2010, accessed May 22, 2014, http://trib.com/news/state-and-regional/e-mails-show-uw-faced-pressure/article_66361c75-d8a9-5eba-b8e2-50dc24c15202.html.

11.   Tempest, MacKinnon, and White, "Free Speech at UW."

12.   Ayers, "Doublespeak."

13.   UW Art Museum, "Sculpture: A Wyoming Invitational," exhibit guide, University of Wyoming, August 2010.

14.   A. L. Carroll et al., "Impacts of Climate Change on Range Expansion by the Mountain Pine Beetle," Mountain Pine Beetle Initiative Working Paper 2006–14, Canadian Forest Service, 2006; J. Logan and J. Powell, "Ghost Forests, Global Warming, and the Mountain Pine Beetle (Coleoptera: Scolytidae)," *American Entomologist* 47 (2001): 160–73; Barbara Bentz, "Western U.S. Bark Beetles and Climate Change," US Department of Agriculture, Forest Service, Climate Change Resource Center, May 20, 2008, accessed May 22, 2014, http://www.fs.fed.us/ccrc/topics/bark-beetles.shtml.

15.   Jeremy Pelzer, "University of Wyoming Sculpture Blasts Fossil Fuels," *Casper Star-Tribune*, June 13, 2011, accessed May 22, 2014, http://trib.com/search/?l=25&skin=/&sd=desc&s=start_time&f= html&q=blasts%20fossil%20fuels; Paul Wallem, "New UW Sculpture Attacks Wyoming's Energy Industry," *Gillette News Record*, July 17, 2011.

16.   Wallem, "New UW Sculpture."

17.   Kurt Andersen, "Disputed Art Disappears from University Campus," Studio 360, accessed May 22, 2014, http://www.studio360.org/story/227066-disputed-art-disappears-from-university-campus.

18.   Laura Hancock, "Criticism of 'Carbon Sink' Art at UW Generates Heat," *Gillette News Record*, July 18, 2011.

19.   Ibid.

20.   Chris Drury, "Microcosm and Macrocosm," artist's blog, July 13, 2011, accessed May 22, 2014, http://chrisdrury.blogspot.com/2011/07/coal-themed-sculpture-annoys-lawmakers.html.

21.   Susan B. Moldenhauer, e-mail to Don C. Richards, July 14, 2011. Acquired

from http://www.uwyo.edu/newssupport/emails/ (documents released to Wyoming Public Media through the Freedom of Information Act, hereafter cited as FOIA).

22. Chad Calvert, e-mail to Christopher A. Spooner, July 13, 2011 (FOIA).

23. Randy C. Teeuwen, e-mail to William B. Blalock et al., July 13, 2011 (FOIA).

24. Marion Loomis, e-mail to Don C. Richards, July 12, 2011 (FOIA).

25. Phil Nicholas, e-mail to Don C. Richards, July 14, 2011 (FOIA).

26. Don C. Richards, e-mail to Tom Lubnau, September 1, 2011 (FOIA).

27. Tom Lubnau, e-mail to Gregg Blikre, Tom Buchanan et al., July 13, 2011 (FOIA).

28. Bruce Hinchey, e-mail to Ken Henricks et al., July 13, 2011 (FOIA).

29. University of Wyoming, School of Energy Resources, "School of Energy Resources Director, Dr. Mark A. Northam," accessed December 5, 2013, http://www.uwyo.edu/ser/about-us/mnortham.html.

30. Mark A. Northam, e-mail to Randy C. Teeuwen et al., July 13, 2011 (FOIA).

31. Ibid.

32. Two anonymous sources formerly or currently working at the University of Wyoming, interviews with the author in 2014.

33. Don C. Richards, e-mail to Tom Lubnau et al., July 13, 2011 (FOIA).

34. Ibid.

35. Chris Drury, "Winnemucca Whirlwind," artist's statement, accessed May 22, 2014, http://chrisdrury.co.uk/winnemucca-whirlwind-2.

36. Don C. Richards, e-mail to Tom Lubnau et al., July 13, 2011.

37. Bruce Finley, "Northern Front Range Forests among Prime Beetle-Kill Areas in 2010," *Denver Post*, January 22, 2011, accessed May 22, 2014, http://www.denverpost.com/popular/ci_17163793?source=pkg; Kelsey Dayton, "Wilderness Act Factors into Wyoming Beetle Fight Billings Gazette, August 8, 2011, accessed May 22, 2014, http://billingsgazette.com/news/state-and-regional/wyoming/wilderness-act-factors-into-wyoming-pine-beetle-fight/article_fc159f34-ea4e-5f09-b344-f9e0cb52a52b.html; Lily Durfee, "Saving the Western United States from Pine Beetles," *Huffington Post*, March 22, 2011, accessed May 22, 2014, http://www.huffingtonpost.com/lily-durfee/saving-the-western-united_b_839268.html.

38. Chris Drury, *Carbon Sink* artist, interview with the author, March 8, 2013.

39. Ibid.

40. Don C. Richards, e-mail to Tom Lubnau et al., July 13, 2011.

41. Drury interview.

42. Kelly Mader, e-mail to Don C. Richards, July 21, 2011 (FOIA).

43. Kermit C. Brown, e-mail to Don C. Richards, July 14, 2011 (FOIA).

44. Gregg Blikre, e-mail to Don C. Richards, July 28, 2011 (FOIA).

45. Bill Mai, e-mail to Don C. Richards, July 22, 2011 (FOIA).

46. Suzanne Goldenberg, "University Sculpture Upsets Wyoming Coal Industry," *Guardian*, July 22, 2011, accessed May 22, 2014, http://www.theguardian.com/environment/2011/jul/22/wyoming-university-coal-chris-drury.

47. Tom Lubnau, e-mail to Doc Curry, July 25, 2011 (FOIA).

48. Ibid.

49. Mark A. Northam, e-mail to Don C. Richards, August 10, 2011 (FOIA).

50. Warren Lauer, e-mail to Betty Fear et al. (UW Board of Trustees), July 27, 2011 (FOIA).

51. Don C. Richards, e-mail to Thomas Buchanan, August 29, 2011 (FOIA).

52. Deborah Sontag, "Where Oil and Politics Mix," *New York Times*, November 24, 2014, A1, 16–17.

53. Dustin Bleizeffer, "Sen. Alan Simpson Rails against Money in Politics," WyoFile, March 15, 2016, accessed March 16, 2016, http://www.wyofile.com/sen-alan-simpson-rails-against-money-in-politics.

54. "Thomas E. Lubnau II," Ballot-Pedia, accessed May 22, 2014, http://ballotpedia.org/wiki/index.php/Thomas_E._Lubnau,_II; "Thomas E. Lubnau II's Campaign Finances," Project Vote Smart, accessed May 22, 2014, http://votesmart.org/candidate/campaign-finance/52747/tom-lubnau-ii#.U36FkHYzbGl.

55. Tom Lubnau, Gregg Blikre, and Rep. Norine Kasperik, "Trying to Make Silk Purses from Sows' Ears," *Gillette News Record*, September 6, 2011, A3.

56. Ibid.

57. Ibid.

58. Jeffrey Lockwood, "Art and Energy: Coal's Reaction to 'Carbon Sink' Sculpture Reveals the Power of Art—and the Essence of Education," WyoFile, November 8, 2011, accessed May 22, 2014, http://wyofile.com/jeffrey_lockwood/art-energy-coals-reaction-to-carbon-sink-sculpture-reveals-the-power-of-art-%E2%80%94-and-the-essence-of-education.

59. Ibid.

60. Ibid.

61. John Ridley, "How Bad Is 'Uppity'?" *National Public Radio*, accessed May 22, 2014, http://www.npr.org/blogs/visibleman/2008/09/how_bad_is_uppity.html; American Experience, "People and Events: Lynching in America," Public Broadcasting Service, accessed May 22, 2014, http://www.pbs.org/wgbh/amex/till/peopleevents/e_lynch.html; United States Census Bureau, "Wyoming," US Department of Commerce, accessed May 22, 2014, http://quickfacts.census.gov/qfd/states/56000.html.

62. Gerald E. Schuman, e-mail to Francis D. Galey and Bret W. Hess, November 22, 2011 (FOIA).

63. Myron B. Allen, e-mail to Francis D. Galey and Thomas Buchanan, November 22, 2011 (FOIA).

64. Lockwood, "Art and Energy."

65. Ibid.

66. Andersen, "Disputed Art Disappears."

67. Personal conversation with the author, September 2012, Laramie, Wyoming.

68. Mark A. Northam, e-mail to Jeffrey Alan Lockwood, July 25, 2012.

69. Chris Drury interview.

70. Irina Zhorov, "Documents Show Artwork Removed Early Due to Pressure," Wyoming Public Media, September 28, 2012, accessed May 22, 2014, http://wyomingpublicmedia.org/post/documents-show-artwork-removed-early-due-pressure.

71. Diane Elaine Panozzo, e-mail to Harvey Hix et al., January 6, 2012 (FOIA).

72. Mark A. Northam, e-mail to Jeffrey Alan Lockwood, July 25, 2012.

Chapter 2

1. Tom Olliff and Jim Caslick, "Wildlife-Human Conflicts in Yellowstone," *Yellowstone Science* 11 (Winter 2003): 18–22.

2. Aesop, "The Gardener and His Dog," *Aesop's Fables*, Full Books, accessed July 15, 2014, http://www.fullbooks.com/Aesop-s-Fables3.html.

3. Bruce Hinchey, e-mail to Ken Hendricks et al., July13, 2011. Acquired from http://www.uwyo.edu/newssupport/emails (documents released to Wyoming Public Media through the Freedom of Information Act [FOIA]).

4. Paul Wallem, "New UW Sculpture Attacks Wyoming's Energy Industry," *Gillette News Record*, July 17, 2011.

5. Gary Negich, e-mail to Susan B. Moldenhauer, December 28, 2011 (FOIA).

6. Barbara Dilts, e-mail to Susan B. Moldenhauer and Ruth Arnold, April 20, 2012 (FOIA).

7. Susan B. Moldenhauer, e-mail to Thomas Buchanan, January 10, 2012 (FOIA).

8. Thomas Buchanan, e-mail to Susan B. Moldenhauer, April 13, 2012 (FOIA). Prexy's Pasture is the name given to the grassy quad in the center of campus.

9. Susan B. Moldenhauer, e-mail to Thomas Buchanan, May 16, 2012 (FOIA).

10. Don C. Richards, e-mail to Norine Kasperik, Thomas Lubnau, Sue Wallis, Gregg Blikre, John Hines, and Michael Von Flatern, May 21, 2012.

11. Larry Munn, professor of soil science, Department of Ecosystem Science and Management, interview by the author, April 22, 2013.

12. Joe Riis, e-mail to Office of the President, May 21, 2012; Don C. Richards, e-mail to Joe Riis, May 22, 2012 (FOIA).

13. James L. Scott, e-mail to Susan B. Moldenhauer, April 24, 2012; Susan B. Moldenhauer, e-mail to Jim Scott, April 25, 2012.

14. Susan B. Moldenhauer, e-mail to Chris Drury, April 20, 2012; Chris Drury, artist of *Carbon Sink*, interview with the author, March 8, 2013.

15. Mike Massie, letter to Anne Jakle, embedded in e-mail from Mike Massie to Susan B. Moldenhauer, June 29, 2012 (FOIA).

16. Dustin Bleizeffer, "Carbon Sink: University of Wyo Doesn't Have to Bend to Energy Politics," WyoFile, October 18, 2012, accessed July 15, 2014, http://wyofile.com/dustin/help-uw-grow-a-backbone.

17. Ibid. This is the same fellow, Dave Bostrom, who argued in a *Casper Star-Tribune* op-ed piece that Wyoming should not raise severance taxes on coal, oil, or gas (or the industries will go elsewhere, as if minerals were mobile) while also maintaining that the state needs a "tax environment that is more representative of the state's economy," which evidently undervalues fossil fuels. Dave Bostrom, "Diversification Is the Answer, at All Levels," *Casper Star-Tribune*, June 24, 2009, accessed July 15, 2016, https://chambermaster.blob.core.windows.net/userfiles/UserFiles/chambers/9071/CMS/Guest_Columns/2009_Diversification_is_the_issue_at_all_levels.pdf; Dave Bostrom, "Understanding Taxes and Spending Constraints," *Casper Star-Tribune*, July 19, 2009, accessed July 21, 2014, http://www.google.com/url?sa=t&rct=j&q=&esrc=s&source=web&cd=1&ved=0C-BOQFjAA&url=http%3A%2F%2Fwww.wyomingbusinessalliance.com%2Fread_file.php%3Fcontent_type%3DPDF%26file_name%3D878.pdf&ei=f23NU-e1BYKWyAS1kIKQCA&usg=AFQjCNHu2dF-SylE6iIG3OsykALIkmcI-Jw&sig2=6-HsBlwfylokM4Chmz6NAw&bvm=bv.71198958.d.aWw.

18. Jim Robbins, "Coal-Themed Sculpture Annoys Lawmakers," *New York Times*, July 21, 2011, accessed July 15, 2014, http://green.blogs.nytimes.com/2011/07/21/coal-themed-sculpture-annoys-lawmakers/?_php=true&_type=blogs&_r=0.

19. Chris Drury interview, "Carbon Sink: What Goes Around, Comes Around," University of Wyoming Television, uploaded November 16, 2011, accessed July 15, 2014, http://www.youtube.com/watch?v=tHgpIlfjyWM.

20. Mark Northam, director of the School of Energy Resources, University of Wyoming, e-mail to author, July 25, 2012.

21. Ibid.

22. E-mail from author to Susanna Goodin et al., August 8, 2012.

23. Wendy E. Bredehoft, e-mail to author, August 2, 2012; Dave Jost, e-mail to author, July 31, 2012.

24. Joel Otto, post in response to "Behind the Carbon Curtain: Art and Freedom in Wyoming," WyoFile, August 28, 2012, accessed July 15, 2014, http://wyofile.com/jeffrey_lockwood/behind-the-carbon-curtain-art-and-freedom-in-wyoming.

25. Irina Zhorov, "Documents Show Artwork Removed Early Due to Pressure," Wyoming Public Media, September 28, 2012, accessed July 15, 2014, http://wyomingpublicmedia.org/post/documents-show-artwork-removed-early-due-pressure.

26. Ibid.

27. Ibid.

28. Jeremy Fugleberg, "Emails: University of Wyoming Officials Sped Up, Touted Removal of Anti-Coal Sculpture," *Casper Star-Tribune*, October 14, 2012, accessed July 15, 2014, http://trib.com/business/energy/emails-university-of-wyoming-officials-sped-up-touted-removal-of/article_4f9332ee-d83c-5d58-a38b-19e913ba739d.html.

29. *Star-Tribune* Editorial Board, "UW's 'Carbon Sink' Fiasco Marked by Lies, Censorship," *Casper Star-Tribune*, October 22, 2012, accessed July 15, 2014, http://trib.com/opinion/editorial/uw-s-carbon-sink-fiasco-marked-by-lies-censorship/article_0b8b9b0d-7657–528a-9123–28df69ae25f4.html.

30. Ben Mitchell, art curator, e-mail to author, March 19, 2013.

31. Wade Sikorski, "Don't Let Education Depend on Resource Taxes," *Billings Gazette*, October 27, 2012, accessed July 16, 2014, http://billingsgazette.com/news/opinion/mailbag/don-t-let-education-depend-on-resource-taxes/article_d237bbac-a4fc-5c51-ac73-c7501bdcf031.html.

32. Kurt Anderson, "Disputed Art Disappears from University Campus," *Studio360* radio program, August 3, 2012, accessed July 16, 2014, http://www.studio360.org/story/227066-disputed-art-disappears-from-university-campus.

33. Tom Lubnau quoted in "Disputed Art Disappears from University Campus," *Studio360* listener comments, August 6, 2012, accessed July 16, 2014, http://www.studio360.org/story/227066-disputed-art-disappears-from-university-campus.

34. Michelle Nijhuis, "The Artwork that Infuriated Big Coal," *Slate*, October 31, 2012, accessed July 16, 2014, http://www.slate.com/articles/health_and_science/science/2012/10/carbon_sink_sculpture_at_university_of_wyoming_mining_and_energy_donors.html.

35. Dan Frosch, "Art that Irked Energy Executives Is Gone, but Wyoming Dispute Whirls On," *New York Times*, October 26, 2012, accessed July 16, 2014, http://www.nytimes.com/2012/10/27/us/controversy-lingers-over-wyoming-universitys-removal-of-carbon-sink.html?_r=1.

36. Jim Scott, UW physical plant, e-mail to author, July 20, 2012.

37. "US Artwork that Angered Energy Industry Pulled—Could It Happen Here?," *Index on Censorship*, November 16, 2012, accessed July 16, 2014, http://www.indexoncensorship.org/2012/11/energy-donor-artistic-freedom-censorship.

38. Tom Buchanan, "Buchanan on 'Carbon Sink': UW Didn't Kowtow to Powerful Interests," WyoFile op-ed, October 26, 2012, http://wyofile.com/dustin/buchanan-on-carbon-sink-uw-didnt-kowtow-to-powerful-interests; Tom Buchanan, "Buchanan: Carbon Sink Removal Didn't Fit Conspiracy Narrative," *Casper Star-Tribune* op-ed, October 26, 2012.

39. Buchanan, "Carbon Sink Removal."

40. Gary Beauvais, director, Wyoming Natural Diversity Database, interview with the author, April 10, 2013.

41. Jeremy Fugleberg, "University of Wyoming President Buchanan Hits Back on Carbon Sink Controversy," *Casper Star-Tribune*, October 26, 2012, accessed July 16, 2014, http://trib.com/news/state-and-regional/university of-wyoming-president-buchanan-hits-back-on-carbon-sink/article_2ead9a06-67b8-5091-8c57-8ebff9be8267.html.

42. Ibid.; Jeremy Fugleberg, "Fugleberg: Down the Carbon Sink," *Casper Star-Tribune* editorial, October 28, 2012, accessed July 16, 2014, http://trib.com/business/fugleberg-down-the-carbon-sink/article_47f942f7-1809-538b-93d3-f51c8c529497.html.

43. Bob Beck, "UW President Tom Buchanan Announces Retirement," Wyoming Public Media, September 6, 2012, accessed July 16, 2014, http://wyomingpublicmedia.org/post/uw-president-tom-buchanan-announces-retirement.

44. "University of Wyoming Presidential Profile," University of Wyoming, accessed July 16, 2014, http://www.uwyo.edu/presidentsearch/_files/docs/uw%20presidential%20profile%2011-15.pdf.

45. "UW Breaks Ground on Buchanan Center for Performing Arts," *UW News*, May 10, 2013, accessed July 16, 2014, http://www.uwyo.edu/uw/news/2013/05/uw-breaks-ground-on-buchanan-center-for-performing-arts.html.

46. Matt Laslo, "Wyo. Lawmakers Reject New Climate Change Report," Wyoming Public Media, May 16, 2014, accessed January 11, 2016, http://wyomingpublicmedia.org/post/wyo-lawmakers-reject-new-climate-change-report.

47. Mead Gruver, "Cheney Center at University of Wyoming Draws Protests," *Huffington Post*, September 8, 2009, accessed July 16, 2014, http://www.huffingtonpost.com/2009/09/09/cheney-center-at-universi_n_280696.html.

48. Bleizeffer, "Carbon Sink."

49. Associated Students of the University of Wyoming, "Resolution: ASUW Support for the Preservation of a Censorship Free Environment," December 4, 2012.

50. Author's notes, ASUW meeting on the campus of the University of Wyoming, January 22, 2013.

51. Ibid.

52. Joel Defebaugh, UW student, interview with the author, March 13, 2013.

53. Wyoming Department of Education, "Quick References for Counselors/Advisors," Wyoming Hathaway Scholarship Program, accessed October 7, 2014, https://edu.wyoming.gov/downloads/college-career-readiness/Quick_Reference_Guide_for_Counselors_and_Advisors.pdf; Jeremy Pelzer, "Gap Widens between University of Wyoming Costs, Hathaway Aid," *Casper Star-Tribune*, August 1, 2012, accessed October 7, 2014, http://trib.com/news/state-and-regional/gap-widens-between-university-of-wyoming-costs-hathaway-aid/article_f3e15ab2–067c-5645–9f4d-e41401ac1939.html.

54. Defebaugh, interview.

55. Ibid.

56. Michael Gary Barker, e-mail to author, November 7, 2012.

57. Alexandre Vsevolo Latchininsky, e-mail to All Senators (members of the UW faculty senate), forwarded to the author, December 13, 2012.

58. Robin Waldo Groose, e-mail to Michael Gary Barker, Warrie J. Means, and Alexandre Vsevolo Latchininsky, forwarded to the author, January 23, 2013.

59. Latchininsky, e-mail to All Senators.

60. Author's notes, UW faculty senate meeting, University of Wyoming, January 28, 2013.

61. Ibid.

62. Ibid.

Chapter 3

1. Jeffrey T. Richelson and Michael L. Evans, "Tiananmen Square, 1989: The Declassified History," National Security Archive at George Washington University, accessed August 16, 2014, http://www2.gwu.edu/~nsarchiv/NSAEBB/NSAEBB16;

Zhao Ziyang, *Prisoner of the State: The Secret Journal of Premier Zhao Ziyang* (New York: Simon and Schuster, 2010); Louisa Lim, *The People's Republic of Amnesia: Tiananmen Revisited* (New York: Oxford University Press, 2015).

2. Dustin Bleizeffer, "Carbon Sink: University of Wyo Doesn't Have to Bend to Energy Politics," WyoFile, October 18, 2012, accessed August 16, 2014, http://wyofile.com/dustin/help-uw-grow-a-backbone.

3. Associated Press, "Wyoming Legislature Passes Budget Compromise," *Gillette News Record*, February 16, 2013, accessed August 16, 2014, http://www.gillettenewsrecord.com/news/wyoming/article_77fe4f3b-beec-5ed4-b06b-9352f8fcd521.html.

4. Gregory Nickerson, "UW Trustees Wary of Enforcing Legislature's Public Art Rule," WyoFile, September 16, 2013, accessed August 16, 2014, http://wyofile.com/gregory_nickerson/uw-trustees-wary-of-enforcing-legislatures-public-art-rule.

5. Ben Mitchell, art curator, e-mail to author, March 19, 2013.

6. Nickerson, "UW Trustees Wary."

7. Ibid.

8. University of Wyoming, "Attachment C to UW Regulation 1–102, University of Wyoming Public Art Policy," Board of Trustees' Report, January 16–18, 2014, 9, accessed August 16, 2014, http://www.uwyo.edu/trustees/_files/docs/2014-board-meeting-materials/2014%20-jan%20report%20final%20with%20appex.pdf.

9. Ibid.; Sonjia G. Weinstein, *"Carbon Sink: What Goes Around Comes Around: The Art Controversy"* (MA thesis in American Studies, University of Wyoming, 2014).

10. Greenpeace, "Factsheet: Wyoming Heritage Foundation, Wyoming Business Alliance," 2009, accessed August 16, 2014, http://www.exxonsecrets.org/html/orgfactsheet.php?id=159%20Council.

11. Weinstein, *"Carbon Sink."*

12. Patrick Witty, "Behind the Scenes: Tank Man of Tiananmen," *New York Times*, June 3, 2009, accessed August 16, 2014, http://lens.blogs.nytimes.com/2009/06/03/behind-the-scenes-tank-man-of-tiananmen/?_php=true&_type=blogs&_r=0.

13. Chris Drury, interview with author, March 8, 2013.

14. Lim, *People's Republic of Amnesia.*

15. Dustin Bleizeffer, "Mead, Freudenthal and Al Simpson Stump for UW College of Engineering Project in Dallas," WyoFile, February 22, 2013, accessed August 16, 2014, http://www.wyofile.com/blog/20527.

16. Ibid.

17. Gregory Nickerson, "Governor Mead Travels to Dubai to Promote Fracking Research by Mohammed Piri," WyoFile, April 16, 2013, accessed August 16, 2014, http://wyofile.com/gregory_nickerson/gov-mead-promotes-dr-piris-fracking-research-indubai.

18. University of Wyoming, "School of Energy Resources Director, Dr. Mark A. Northam," School of Energy Resources, accessed August 16, 2014, http://www.uwyo.edu/ser/about-us/mnortham.html; Irina Zhorov, "UW's School of Energy Resources Working to Forge Research Relationship with Saudi Arabia," Wyoming Public Media, April 17, 2013, accessed August 16, 2014, http://wyomingpublicmedia.org/term/mark-northam.

19. William Gern, Vice President of Research and Economic Development, e-mails to author, April 24 and 25, 2014.

20. Ibid.

21. Ziyang, *Prisoner of the State*.

22. Diana Henriques, "The 2000 Campaign: The Republican Running Mate; Cheney Is Said to Be Receiving $20 Million Retirement Package," *New York Times*, August 12, 2000, accessed August 16, 2014, http://www.nytimes.com/2000/08/12/us/2000-campaign-republican-running-mate-cheney-said-be-receiving-20-million.html; Dick Cheney and Liz Cheney, *In My Time: A Personal and Political Memoir* (New York: Threshold Editions, 2011).

23. Gregory Nickerson, "Halliburton Joins University of Wyoming's List of Energy Donors," WyoFile, March 20, 2014, accessed August 16, 2014, http://wyofile.com/gregory_nickerson/halliburton-joins-university-of-wyomings-list-of-energy-donors.

24. Ibid.

25. Publius, "Halliburton: Be Nice to Us or Else," WyPols, March 21, 2014, accessed August 16, 2014, http://wypols.com/2014/03/21/halliburton-be-nice-to-us-or-else.

26. Ziyang, *Prisoner of the State*.

27. Leah Todd, "UW Trustees, Lawmakers Talk Engineering, Outreach," *Casper Star-Tribune*, July 16, 2014, accessed August 16, 2014, http://trib.com/news/

local/education/uw-trustees-and-lawmakers-talk-engineering-outreach/article_
cdf68e74–9533–5c5a-962e-508faf407e9e.html.

28. Leah Todd, "University of Wyoming Interim President Dick McGinity: 'I misspoke,'" *Casper Star-Tribune*, December 14, 2013, accessed August 16, 2014, http://trib.com/news/local/education/university-of-wyoming-interim-president-dick-mcginity-i-misspoke/article_ba45b86e-628a-57a6-b999-5ce076421561.html.

29. Ibid.

30. Nadia Hill, "Legislature Relationship a Pressing Issue for UW Board of Trustees," *Laramie Boomerang* and *Rocket-Miner*, January 22, 2014, 3, accessed August 16, 2014, http://now.dirxion.com/Rocket_Miner/library/Rocket_Miner_01_22_2014.pdf.

31. Ibid.

32. Leah Todd, "Look Back: University of Wyoming's Sternberg Comes and Goes in 2013," *Casper Star-Tribune*, December 22, 2013, accessed August 16, 2014, http://trib.com/news/local/education/look-back-university-of-wyoming-s-sternberg-comes-and-goes/article_28dc736e-affe-500e-b351-7e4176eb3432.html.

33. University of Wyoming, "UW Names 24th President: Current Oklahoma State Provost Robert Sternberg Will Assume UW Post July 1," *UW News*, February 26, 2013, accessed August 16, 2014, http://www.uwyo.edu/uw/news/2013/02/uw-names-24th-president-current-oklahoma-state-provost-robert-sternberg-will-assume-uw-post-july-1.html.

34. As told to the author by Susanna Goodin, professor of philosophy, in an interview with the author, May 8, 2014.

35. Susan Anderson, "University of Wyoming President Sternberg on a Mission to Educate Leaders," *Casper Star-Tribune*, August 4, 2013, accessed August 16, 2014, http://trib.com/news/state-and-regional/university-of-wyoming-president-sternberg-on-a-mission-to-educate/article_2e257bbf-3611-51a0-824f-22518a39d581.html.

36. Laura Hancock, "Big Changes in Leadership at UW," *Casper Star-Tribune*, August 26, 2013, accessed August 16, 2014, http://trib.com/news/state-and-regional/big-changes-in-leadership-at-uw/article_df84ac96-1692-57be-a9d6-de94248d87e6.html.

37. Ry Rivard, "Cleaning House," *Inside Higher Ed*, November 18, 2013, accessed August 16, 2014, https://www.insidehighered.com/news/2013/11/18/how-new-president-supposed-clean-house; Gregory Nickerson, "Students and Faculty Question Spate of Resignations at University of Wyoming under Sternberg,"

WyoFile, November 5, 2013, accessed August 16, 2014, http://wyofile.com/gregory_nickerson/students-and-faculty-question-spate-of-resignations-at-university-of-wyoming-under-sternberg.

38. Gregory Nickerson, "Email Shows Trustee Pushed for Wyoming Law School Taskforce," WyoFile, December 17, 2013, accessed August 16, 2014, http://wyofile.com/gregory_nickerson/email-shows-trustee-pushed-wyoming-law-school-taskforce; Leah Todd, "University of Wyoming Law School Dean Resigns as Task Force Preps Review," *Casper Star-Tribune*, November 1, 2013, accessed August 16, 2014, http://trib.com/news/local/education/university-of-wyoming-law-school-dean-resigns-as-task-force/article_cca10ec1-a62c-5dbf-b949-2c431a209e58.html.

39. Nickerson, "Email Shows Trustee Pushed."

40. Ibid.

41. "Palmerlee Elected President of the UW Board of Trustees," *UW News*, May 8, 2014, accessed August 16, 2014, http://www.uwyo.edu/uw/news/2014/05/palmerlee-elected-president-of-uw-board-of-trustees.html.

42. Trevor Brown, "Sternberg's Departure Leaves UW with Hefty Bill," *Wyoming Tribune Eagle*, November 23, 2013, accessed August 16, 2014, http://www.wyomingnews.com/articles/2013/11/24/news/01top_11-24-13.txt#.U_LDOWMfKJU.

43. Leah Todd, "University of Wyoming Pres. Bob Sternberg Resigns Post after Weeks of Turmoil," *Casper Star-Tribune*, November 14, 2013, accessed August 16, 2014, http://trib.com/news/local/education/university-of-wyoming-pres-bob-sternberg-resigns-post-after-weeks/article_c1a8291e-862f-5ed6-9298-14e41ce17752.html.

44. Gregory Nickerson, "Trustees Discuss Making Dick McGinity University of Wyoming President," WyoFile, January 15, 2014, accessed August 16, 2014, http://www.wyofile.com/blog/trustees-discuss-making-dick-mcginity-university-wyoming-president.

45. UW Management and Marketing, "Richard McGinity, Bill Daniels Chair of Business Ethics," accessed August 16, 2014, http://www.uwyo.edu/mgtmkt/faculty-staff/faculty-pages/mcginity.html.

46. Canadian Oil Sands Trust, "Annual Information Form, 2008," accessed August 16, 2014, http://www.cdnoilsands.com/files/FinancialReports/AIF-final%20execution%20copy%20MARCH%2020.pdf; "Petro-Canada Bids $113M US for Canada Southern Petroleum," *CBC News*, May 11, 2006, accessed August 16, 2014, http://www.cbc.ca/news/business/petro-canada-bids-113m-us-for-canada-southern-

petroleum-1.569579; James Stevenson, "Canada Southern Petroleum Rejects Petro Canada's Offer," Hard Assets, May 25, 2006, accessed August 16, 2014, http://www.resourceinvestor.com/2006/05/25/canada-southern-petroleum-rejects-petro-canadas-of; "Canadian Oil Sands Comes Out on Top in Bidding War for Canadian Southern," NGI's Daily Gas Price Index, August 25, 2006, accessed August 16, 2014, http://www.naturalgasintel.com/articles/72733-canadian-oil-sands-comes-out-on-top-in-bidding-war-for-canadian-southern.

47. Todd, "Dick McGinity: 'I misspoke.'"

48. Ibid.

49. Jerry Paxton, Wyoming State Representative, interview with the author, April 26, 2013.

50. Kerry Drake, "Why Did UW Board Rush to Put a New President in Office?," WyoFile, January 21, 2014, accessed August 16, 2014, http://wyofile.com/kerry-drake/uw-board-rush-new-presidente.

51. Jonathan D. Spence, The Search for Modern China (New York: Norton, 1999).

52. Gregory Nickerson, "UW Pres Candidate Laurie Nichols: Salary, Energy Key Issues," WyoFile, December 11, 2015, accessed December 12, 2015, http://www.wyofile.com/uw-pres-candidate-laurie-nichols-salary-energy-key-issues.

53. "UW Names Kate Miller Provost/Vice President for Academic Affairs," University of Wyoming, accessed June 20, 2016, http://www.uwyo.edu/uw/news/2016/06/uw-names-kate-miller-provostvice-president-for-academic-affairs-html.

54. "Tiananmen Square Protests."

55. Amnesty International, "Changing the Soup But Not the Medicine: Abolishing Reeducation through Labor in China," Amnesty International, accessed July 15, 2016, https://www.amnesty.org/en/documents/asa17/042/2013/en.

56. Joan Barron, "Wyoming Senate Advances Energy Curriculum Bill; Ousts Two Other School Bills," Casper Star-Tribune, January 22, 2013, accessed August 20, 2014, http://trib.com/news/state-and-regional/govt-and-politics/wyoming-senate-advances-energy-curriculum-bill-ousts-two-other-school/article_e5df9427-1eb2-51b4-b533-0123f606d91a.htm.

57. Kyle Roerink, "Energy Company Eyes $75k Consulting Fee for Wyoming School Program," Casper Star-Tribune, January 17, 2013, accessed August 20, 2014, http://trib.com/news/state-and-regional/govt-and-politics/energy-company-eyes-k-

consulting-fee-for-wyoming-school-program/article_a22926e4-33d9-5ced-9466-6bf5dfea0b7b.html.

58. Ibid.

59. School of Energy Resources, "Energy Literacy Education," University of Wyoming, accessed August 20, 2014, http://www.uwyo.edu/ser/energy-literacy.

60. "2013 Annual Report of the University of Wyoming School of Energy Resources," University of Wyoming, Laramie, accessed August 20, 2014, http://www.uwyo.edu/ser//_files/docs/annualreports/ser_annual_report_2103.pdf.

61. Ibid.; "ExxonMobil Enhances K–12 Energy Education in Wyoming," *UW News*, July 9, 2013, accessed August 20, 2014, http: www.uwyo.edu/uw/news/2013/07/exxonmobil-enhances-k-12-energy-education-in-wyoming.html.

62. Wyoming Afterschool Alliance, "Statewide Energy and Natural Resource Education Initiative Report," December 9, 2013, accessed August 20, 2014, http://wyafterschoolalliance.org/wp-content/uploads/2013/08/Wyoming-ENR-Report-Web.pdf.

63. Jeffrey Lockwood, "Art and Energy: Coal's Reaction to 'Carbon Sink' Sculpture Reveals the Power of Art—and the Essence of Education," WyoFile, November 8, 2011, accessed August 20, 2014, http://wyofile.com/jeffrey_lockwood/art-energy-coals-reaction-to-carbon-sink-sculpture-reveals-the-power-of-art-and-the-essence-of-education.

64. Ibid.

65. Publius, "Wyoming Lawmakers Say No to Science—That Will Show Those Fancy Thinkers in DC," WyPols, March 5, 2014, accessed August 20, 2014, http://wypols.com/2014/03/05/wyoming-lawmakers-say-no-to-science-that-will-show-those-fancy-thinkers-in-dc.

66. Ron Micheli, e-mail to Jim Verley (provided to the author by Verley), February 20, 2014.

67. Aerin Curtis, "Science Standards Find Rough Ride in Wyoming," *Laramie Boomerang*, March 23, 2014, B5.

68. Ibid.

69. Kerry Drake, "Education Board Punts Science Standards Back to Panel," WyoFile, April 12, 2014, accessed August 20, 2014, http://wyofile.com/kerrydrake/education-board-punts-science-standards-back-panel.

70. Leah Todd, "State Board Sends Science Standards Back to Education Department," *Laramie Boomerang*, April 12, 2014, A5.

71. Publius, "Ron Micheli's View on Not Teaching Science in Wyoming: 'If that's putting our head in the sand, then so be it!'" WyPols, April 12, 2014, accessed August 20, 2014, http://wypols.com/2014/04/12/rep-michelis-view-on-not-teaching-science-in-wyoming-if-thats-putting-our-head-in-the-sand-then-so-be-it.

72. Jim Verley, Wyoming Department of Education, interview with the author, March 28, 2014.

73. National Center for Science Education, "Climate Science Students Bill of Rights," accessed August 20, 2014, http://ncse.com/taking-action/climate-bill-rights.

74. James C. M. Ahern et al., "Why the Critics of the Next Generation Science Standards Are Wrong," letter to the Wyoming Board of Education, accessed August 20, 2014, http://www.nsta.org/docs/ngss/PositionPaperGivenToWyoming BoardOfEducation.pdf.

75. Leah Todd, "UW Stays Neutral on Science Standards," *Casper Star-Tribune*, July 17, 2014, accessed August 20, 2014, http://trib.com/news/local/education/ uw-stays-neutral-on-science-standards/article_08eb7cb4–16f3–589f-9a7e-08a7b-fa441d1.html.

76. Nick Balatsos, "Complaints about Global Warming, Race Stall Cody School Board," *Casper Star-Tribune*, May 20, 2015, accessed May 26, 2015, http://trib.com/ news/local/education/complaints-about-global-warming-race-stall-cody-school-board/article_e08beaef-f0b5-53c4-8e67-5b949a59316b.html.

77. Rob Gifford, *China Road: A Journey into the Future of a Rising Power* (New York: Random House, 2008).

78. Tsao Tsing-yuan, "The Birth of the Goddess of Democracy," in *Popular Protest and Political Culture in Modern China*, ed. Jeffrey N. Wasserstrom and Elizabeth J. Perry (Boulder: Westview Press, 1994).

79. "$6 Million McMurry Gift Supports Gateway Center," *UW News*, October 10, 2012, accessed August 20, 2014, http://www.uwyo.edu/uw/news/2012/ 10/6-million-mcmurry-gift-supports-gateway-center.html.

80. Ibid.

81. Ibid.

82. "Exhibits Put Marian H. Rochelle Gateway Center 'Over the Top,'" *UW News*, January 16, 2014, accessed August 20, 2014, http://www.uwyo.edu/uw/news/2014/01/exhibits-put-marian-h.-rochelle-gateway-center-over-the-top.html.

Chapter 4

1. Geoffrey Thyne, interviews with the author, March 6 and September 9, 2013. All material and quotations attributed to Thyne in this chapter are derived from these two interviews.

2. Thyne, March 6, 2013.

3. Thyne, September 9, 2013.

4. US Environmental Protection Agency, "Evaluation of Impacts to Underground Sources of Drinking Water by Hydraulic Fracturing of Coalbed Methane Reservoirs," Office of Water, Office of Ground Water and Drinking Water (4606M), EPA 816-R-04–003, June 2004.

5. Thyne, March 6, 2013.

6. Ibid.

7. Peter Heller, "The Fight over Fracking in Colorado's North Fork Valley," *Bloomberg Businessweek*, accessed December 5, 2013, http://www.bloomberg.com/news/articles/2012-07-12/the-fight-over-fracking-in-colorados-north-fork-valley.

8. Thyne, March 6, 2013.

9. Mark Jaffe, "Colorado Study Finds Fracking Risks for Nearby Residents," *Denver Post*, March 19, 2012, accessed December 5, 2013, http://www.denverpost.com/ci_20206688.

10. Thyne, March 6, 2013.

11. University of Wyoming, "Enhanced Oil Recovery Institute," accessed December 5, 2013, http://www.uwyo.edu/eori.

12. Micaela Myers, "A Perfect Match," *UWyo Magazine*, 16, no. 1 (September 2014): 42.

13. Harold Bergman, former director of the School and Institute of Environment and Natural Resources, University of Wyoming, interview with the author, October 14, 2013.

14. Myers, "A Perfect Match."

15. "Industry Collaboration," *UWyo Magazine*, 16, no. 2 (January 2015): 40.

16. Gregory Nickerson, "Wyoming Mining Association Conference Paints Picture of Challenges and Opportunities," WyoFile, June 29, 2013, http://wyofile. com/gregory_nickerson/wyoming-mining-association-conference/#sthash. oPb8QSRo.dpuf; Jessica Lowell, "Freudenthal Joins UW Faculty as Distinguished Visiting Professor," University of Wyoming, December 17, 2010, http://www.uwyo. edu/uw/news/2010/12/freudenthal-joins-uw-faculty-as-distinguished-visiting-professor.html; "Shocker! Exiting Gov. Dave to Teach at UW," *Wyoming Politico*, September 18, 2010, accessed December 5, 2013, http://wyomingpolitico.blogspot. com/2010/12/shocker-exiting-gov-dave-to-teach-at-uw.html.

17. Nickerson, "Wyoming Mining Association Conference."

18. "Enhanced Oil Recovery Commission," State of Wyoming, accessed December 5, 2013, http://eorc.wy.gov.

19. David Mohrbacher, director of the University of Wyoming's Enhanced Oil Recovery Institute, interview with the author, April 11, 2013.

20. "About the Enhanced Oil Recovery Institute," University of Wyoming, accessed December 5, 2013, http://www.uwyo.edu/eori/about/index.html.

21. Thyne interview, March 6, 2013.

22. Mohrbacher interview.

23. Ibid.

24. Achilles Research, "Breitburn Energy: Why Not Buy This Expansion Hungry Oil and Gas Play at a 10.3% Unit Yield?," Seeking Alpha, accessed December 5, 2013, http://seekingalpha.com/article/1746272-breitburn-energy-why-not-buy-this-expansion-hungry-oil-and-gas-play-at-a-10–3-unit-yield; "Acquisitions," Merit Energy, accessed December 5, 2013, http://www.meritenergy.com/acquisitions.

25. Micaela Myers, "Untapped Oil," *UWyo Magazine* 15, no. 37 (2014); "Anadarko Petroleum Corp. (APC)," Stock Analysis on Net, accessed April 30, 2014, http://www.stock-analysis-on.net/NYSE/Company/Anadarko-Petroleum-Corp/Financial-Statement/Income-Statement.

26. "About the EORI."

27. "Enhanced Oil Recovery Commission."

28. Mohrbacher interview.

29. Ibid.

30. Shauna Stephenson, "Water Worries," *Wyoming Tribune-Eagle*, May 4, 2011, accessed December 5, 2013, http://www.wyomingnews.com/news/water-worries/article_f51efc67-7951-5fae-84a3-50e509d549c2.html.

31. Ibid.; emphasis added.

32. Ibid.

33. Thyne interview, March 6, 2013.

34. Stephenson, "Water Worries."

35. Noble Energy, "Operating and Financial Data—2011 Annual Report," accessed December 5, 2013, http://www.nobleenergyinc.com/annualreport/nei11/operating-financial-data.html.

36. Geoffrey Thyne, e-mail to Don Richards (UW director for governmental and community affairs), David Mohrbacher, and Mark Northam, June 10, 2011.

37. Thyne interview, March 6, 2013.

38. Shauna Stephenson, newspaper reporter for the *Wyoming Tribune Eagle*, interview with the author, March 12, 2013.

39. Thyne interview, March 6, 2013.

40. Ibid.

41. Ibid.; Jefferson Dodge, "Fracking and Academic Freedom," *Boulder Weekly*, August 16, 2012, accessed December 5, 2013, http://www.boulderweekly.com/article-9467-fracking-and-academic-freedom.html.

42. Thyne interview, March 6, 2013.

43. Mohrbacher interview.

44. Irina Zhorov, "UW's School of Energy Resources Working to Forge Research Relationship with Saudi Arabia," Wyoming Public Media Statewide Network, accessed December 5, 2013, http://wyomingpublicmedia.org/post/uw-s-school-energy-resources-working-forge-research-relationship-saudi-arabia.

45. Thyne interview, September 9, 2013; anonymous conference attendee, interview with the author.

46. Mark Northam, e-mail to author, July 25, 2012.

47. "Arch Coal Gives $1.5 Million to UW," *UW News*, accessed December 5, 2013, http://www.uwyo.edu/uw/news/2009/04/arch-coal-gives-1.5-million-to-uw.html.

48. "Arch Coal Inc., Revenue and Financial Data," Hoovers, accessed December 5, 2013, http://www.hoovers.com/company-information/cs/revenue-financial.Arch_Coal_Inc.57f780e43189807e.html.

49. "UW Board of Trustees Gains Three New Members," *UW News*, accessed December 5, 2013, http://www.uwyo.edu/uw/news/2013/03/uw-board-of-trustees-gains-three-new-members-another-reappointed.html.

50. "Technical Advisory Board Members," University of Wyoming, accessed December 5, 2013, http://www.uwyo.edu/eori/technical-advisory-board/tab_members/index.html.

51. Thyne interview, September 9, 2013.

52. Jeffrey Lockwood, "Conflicts of Interest: Can We Trust UW Trustees?" WyoFile, November 12, 2013, accessed December 5, 2013, http://wyofile.com/jeffrey_lockwood/conflicts-of-interest-can-we-trust-uw-trustees.

53. Ibid.

54. "History," True Companies, accessed December 5, 2013, http://www.truecos.com/history.

55. "University of Wyoming Trustees' Agenda, September 12–13, 2013," accessed January 8, 2014, http://www.uwyo.edu/trustees/_files/docs/2013-board-meeting-materials/sept_2013_agenda_ %20final%20sept%209.pdf; "Cowboy Ethics," UW Institutional Marketing, accessed January 8, 2014, http://www.uwyo.edu/anniversaries/cowboy-ethics.

56. Jeremy Pelzer, "Wyoming Lawmaker Lobbies for CBM, Pulls Bill to Promote It," *Billings Gazette*, February 18, 2013, accessed December 5, 2013, http://billingsgazette.com/news/state-and-regional/wyoming/wyoming-lawmaker-lobbies-for-cbm-pulls-bill-to-promote-it/article_6187c1cb-3639-506a-a0ca-0d3f1789837a.html.

57. Greg Nickerson, "$115 Million Pledged to Make UW Engineering Top Tier," WyoFile, January 22, 2013, accessed December 5, 2013, http://wyofile.com/gregory_nickerson/115-million-pledged-to-make-uw-engineering-top-tier.

58. "Wyoming Governor's Energy, Engineering, STEM Integration Task Force, 2012," University of Wyoming, accessed December 5, 2013, http://www.uwyo.edu/acadaffairs/plans/gov_task_on_engineering_dec_12.pdf.

59. "Brief Report on Dean Robert Ettema's 5-Year Review," University of Wyoming, accessed December 5, 2013, https://www.uwyo.edu/aadocs/eng_dean/ettema_brief_report.pdf (password protected).

60. "CEAS Welcomes Dean Khaled A. M. Gasem," *UW News*, accessed December 5, 2013, http://www.uwyo.edu/ceas/news/2013/130910. Today, the college is led by a chemical engineer with extensive experience in private industry. "College of Engineering and Applied Science, Dean's Office," University of Wyoming, accessed June 2, 2015, http://www.uwyo.edu/ccas/dean/index.html.

61. "Dave True," UW Board of Trustees, accessed December 5, 2013, http://www.uwyo.edu/trustees/members-of-the-board-of-trustees/dave-true-information.html.

Chapter 5

1. Shauna Stephenson, "Water Worries," *Wyoming Tribune Eagle*, May 4, 2011, accessed December 5, 2013, http://www.wyomingnews.com/news/water-worries/article_f51efc67-7951-5fae-84a3-50e509d549c2.html.

2. Jefferson Dodge, "Fracking and Academic Freedom," *Boulder Weekly*, August 16, 2012, accessed December 5, 2013, http://www.boulderweekly.com/article-9467-fracking-and-academic-freedom.html.

3. Geoffrey Thyne, interview with the author, March 6, 2013.

4. Ibid.

5. Rob Wile, "The Entire Oil and Gas Industry Is Watching a Tiny Town in Wyoming," *Business Insider*, accessed December 9, 2013, http://www.businessinsider.com/oil-gas-industry-fracking-pavillion-wyoming-2012–10; Abrahm Lustgarten, "EPA Abandons Fracking Study in Pavillion, Wyoming Following Similar Closed Investigations," *Huffington Post*, accessed December 9, 2013, http://www.huffingtonpost.com/2013/07/03/epa-fracking-study-pavillion-wyoming_n_3542365.html; Dominic C. DiGiulio, Richard T. Wilkin, Carlyle Miller, and Gregory Oberley, "Investigation of Ground Water Contamination near Pavillion, Wyoming," US Environmental Protection Agency, Office of Research and Development, Ada, Oklahoma (December 2011), accessed March 15, 2016, https://yosemite.epa.gov/OA/eab_web_docket.nsf/Filings%20By%20Appeal%20Number/31D599B4E8A2EFC185257F4000521505/$File/Attachment%202...4.pdf.

6. In the midst of this mess in Pavillion, the supervisor of the Wyoming Oil and Gas Conservation Commission opined, "I really believe greed is driving a lot of this," not corporate greed but, rather, the avarice of the local townsfolk who were "just looking to be compensated"—evidently a most appalling expectation by those who have suffered damages; he resigned shortly thereafter. Mead Gruer, "Top Wyo.

Oil-Gas Regulator Quits after Remarks," Yahoo Finance, June 15, 2012, accessed July 15, 2016, http://www.businessweek.com/ap/2012–06–15/top-wyo-dot-oil-gas-regulator-quits-after-remarks and http://finance.yahoo.com/news/top-wyo-oil-gas-regulator-quits-remarks-145702385--finance.html. Encana Corporation, "Why Encana Refutes U.S. EPA Pavillion Groundwater Report," Encana website, accessed December 9, 2013, http://www.encana.com/news-stories/news-releases/details.html?release=632327; Mark Drajem, "Fracking Pollution Probe in Wyoming Cast in Doubt by EPA," Bloomberg, accessed December 9, 2013, http://www.bloomberg.com/news/articles/2013-06-20/wyoming-replaces-u-s-to-study-water-woes-tied-to-fracking-1-.

7. Acton and Mickelson and Wyoming Department of Environmental Quality, "Pavillion, Wyoming Area Domestic Water Wells," draft final report and palatability study, December 14, 2015, accessed March 31, 2016, http://deq.wyoming.gov/media/attachments/Water%20Quality/Pavillion%20Investigation/Draft%20Report/01_Pavillion%20WY%20Area%20Domestic%20Water%20Wells%20Draft%20Final%20Report.pdf.

8. D. C. DiGiulio and R. B. Jackson, "Impact to Underground Sources of Drinking Water and Domestic Wells from Production Well Stimulation and Completion Practices in the Pavillion, Wyoming, Field," *Environmental Science and Technology* (2016) (DOI: 10.1021/acs.est.5b04970), http://pubs.acs.org/doi/abs/10.1021%2Facs.est.5b04970, accessed December 15, 2015; Elizabeth Shogren, "Fracking Linked to Groundwater Contamination in Pavillion, Wyoming," *High Country News*, March 30, 2016, accessed March 31, 2016, https://www.hcn.org/articles/new-research-links-fracking-contamination-groundwater-pavillion-wyoming.

9. Abrahm Lustgarten, "EPA's Abandoned Wyoming Fracking Study One Retreat among Many," State Impact, National Public Radio, July 3, 2013, accessed December 9, 2013, http://stateimpact.npr.org/texas/2013/07/ 03/epas-abandoned-wyoming-fracking-study-one-retreat-of-many.

10. Mark Drajem, "EPA Official Links Fracking and Drinking Water Issues in Dimock, Pa.," *Washington Post*, July 29, 2013, accessed December 9, 2013, https://www.washingtonpost.com/politics/epa-official-links-fracking-and-drinking-water-issues-in-dimock-pa/2013/07/29/7d8b34b2-f8a1-11e2-afc1-c850c6ee5af8_story.html.

11. Don Hopey, "Court Reveals How Shale Drillers, Pittsburgh-Area Family Agreed," *Pittsburgh Post-Gazette*, August 12, 2013, accessed December 9, 2013, http://www.post-gazette.com/washington/2013/08/12/Court-reveals-how-shale-drillers-Pittsburgh-area-family-agreed/stories/201308120178; Suzanne Goldenberg, "Children Given Lifelong Ban on Talking about Fracking," *Guardian*, August 5,

2013, accessed December 9, 2013, http://www.theguardian.com/environment/2013/aug/05/children-ban-talking-about-fracking.

12. Walter Brasch, "Fracking: Pennsylvania Gags Physicians," Truth Out, March 18, 2012, accessed December 9, 2013, http://www.truth-out.org/news/item/7323:fracking-pennsylvania-gags-physicians; Alicia Gallegos, "Doctors Fight 'Gag Orders' over Fracking Chemicals," *American Medical News* (publication of the AMA), August 27, 2012, accessed December 9, 2013, http://www.amednews.com/article/20120827/government/308279957/1.

13. Geoffrey Thyne, interview with the author, September 9, 2013.

14. Ramit Plushnick-Masti, "EPA's Water Contamination Investigation Halted in Texas after Range Resources Protest," *Huffington Post*, January 16, 2013, accessed December 9, 2013, http://www.huffingtonpost.com/2013/01/16/epa-water-contamination-investigation-fracking_n_2484568.html; Mike Soraghan, "Barnett Shale: Homeowners Renew Complaints about Water Near Range Wells," EnergyWire, September 18, 2013, accessed December 9, 2013, http://www.eenews.net/energywire/stories/1059987422.

15. Plushnick-Masti, "EPA's Water Contamination."

16. Thyne interview, March 6, 2013.

17. It didn't help that there was personal friction based on Thyne having suggested to Northam that there were problems in EORI and Northam having relayed these concerns back to Mohrbacher. But when Thyne tried to appeal his firing to the employment practices office, he was told, "There are people on this campus who like what Dave's [Mohrbacher] done and don't like what you've done. Drop it." Thyne interview, September 9, 2013.

18. Dodge, "Fracking and Academic Freedom."

19. Ibid.

20. Bill Mai and Don Richards, "Wyoming State Government Revenue Forecast, Fiscal Year 2014–Fiscal Year 2018," Consensus Revenue Estimating Group, October 2013, accessed December 9, 2013, http://eadiv.state.wy.us/creg/GreenCREG_Oct13.pdf; University of Wyoming Office of Academic Affairs, "University Plan 4," accessed December 9, 2013, http://www.uwyo.edu/acadaffairs/plans/14-20/up4_position_paper_2.pdf.

21. Mohrbacher interview. Mohrbacher left EORI in 2014 and was replaced by Ron Hurless, who served as energy and telecommunications advisor to Governor Dave Freudenthal and chairman of the Wyoming Public Service Commission.

"EORI Staff," University of Wyoming, accessed November 4, 2014, http://www. uwyo.edu/eori/staff; "Rob Hurless, Deputy Director," University of Wyoming School of Energy Resources, accessed November 4, 2014, http://www.uwyo.edu/ser/ about-us/rhurless.html.

22. University of Wyoming, "Laboratory Research in Enhanced Oil Recovery," accessed December 9, 2013, http://www.uwyo.edu/eori/areas-of-focus/research. html.

23. Thyne interview, March 6, 2013.

24. Justin Pidot, "Forbidden Data: Wyoming Just Criminalized Citizen Science," *Slate*, May 11, 2015, accessed May 11, 2015, http://www.slate.com/articles/health_ and_science/science/2015/05/wyoming_law_against_data_collection protecting_ ranchers_by_ignoring_the.html.

25. Angus M. Thuermer Jr., "No Punitive Damages against Western Water- sheds," WyoFile, February 19, 2016, accessed February 23, 2016, http://www. wyofile.com/no-punitive-damages-against-western-watersheds/?utm_source= newsletter&utm_medium=email&utm_campaign=weeklynewsletter.

26. Matthew Copeland, "Judge Hears Arguments in Landmark Data Trespass Case," WyoFile, January 26, 2016, accessed January 26, 2016, http://www.wyofile. com/landmark-data-trespass-case-heard.

27. Pidot, "Forbidden Data."

28. Gregory Nickerson, "Lawsuit Challenges Constitutionality of Data Trespass Laws," WyoFile, October 20, 2015, accessed October 20, 2015, http://www.wyofile. com/blog/lawsuit-challenges-constitutionality-of-data-trespass-laws/?utm_ source=newsletter&utm_medium=email&utm_campaign=weeklynewsletter. Although the Wyoming legislature stripped out the most egregiously unconstitu- tional parts of the law by limiting its scope to private lands, the amended statute may still violate the First Amendment by singling out people because of the infor- mation they're seeking. Ben Neary, "Coalition: Revision of State Data Collection Laws Not Enough," *Laramie Boomerang*, March 10, A9.

29. Nickerson, "Lawsuit Challenges Constitutionality."

30. Michael Behar, "Whose Fault?" *Mother Jones* (March–April 2013): 39–64.

31. Marcia McNutt, "Integrity—Not Just a Federal Issue," *Science* 347 (March 27, 2015): 1397.

32. Mireya Navarro, "Institute's Gas Drilling Report Leads to Claims of Bias and Concerns for a University's Image," *New York Times*, June 11, 2012, accessed

December 9, 2013, http://www.nytimes.com/2012/06/12/nyregion/university-at-buffalo-faces-scrutiny-over-gas-drilling-report.html?_r=1&; Kate Fried, "Where's Timothy Considine?," Food and Water Watch, accessed December 9, 2013, http://www.foodandwaterwatch.org/blogs/wheres-timothy-considine.

33. Joseph W. Belluck, State University of New York Trustee and member of the Research and Economic Development Committee, comments during a public meeting, transcription provided by Jim Holstun, September 12, 2012.

34. Jim Efstathiou, "SUNY Closes Industry-Backed Fracking Institute," Bloomberg, accessed December 9, 2013, http://www.bloomberg.com/news/articles/2012-11-19/suny-closes-industry-backed-fracking-institute.

35. Dustin Bleizeffer, "University of Wyoming Professor Draws Scrutiny for Energy Industry-Funded Analyses," Casper Star-Tribune, July 24, 2010, accessed December 9, 2013, http://trib.com/news/state-and-regional/university-of-wyoming-professor-draws-scrutiny-for-energy-industry-funded/article_ec03f5e9-feed-5869-9832-ad02723b0d30.html.

36. Thyne interview, March 6, 2013.

37. Jeremy Fugleberg, "The Niobrara Play Stutters," Casper Star-Tribune, May 24, 2012, accessed December 9, 2013, http://trib.com/business/energy/the-niobrara-play-stutters/article_f0884abc-fd4d-5bd6-a731-b30a8626ed1d.html. Northeastern Colorado has managed to become the sweet spot for the Niobrara Shale, at least for now. Trevor Brown, "Laramie County Still Waiting on Oil Boom," Wyoming Tribune Eagle, December 1, 2013, accessed December 9, 2013, http://www.wyomingnews.com/articles/2013/12/01/news/19local_12_01_13.txt.

38. Larry Munn and Ginger Paige, interview with the author, April 22, 2013.

39. Paige interview.

40. Munn interview.

41. Myron Allen, University of Wyoming provost, e-mails to author, April 22 and 25, 2013; Susan Weidel, University of Wyoming's Office of General Counsel, interview with the author, May 15, 2013.

42. Dustin Bleizeffer, editor in chief, WyoFile, e-mail to author, October 23, 2013.

43. Dustin Bleizeffer, "Aftermath of a Drilling Boom: Wyoming Stuck with Abandoned Gas Wells," WyoFile, May 21, 2013, accessed January 8, 2013, https://

wyomingoutdoorcouncil.org/2013/05/22/wyofile-aftermath-of-a-drilling-boom-wyoming-stuck-with-abandoned-gas-wells.

44. Ibid.

45. Robert W. Howarth, Renee Santoro, and Anthony Ingraffea, "Methane and Greenhouse-Gas Footprint of Natural Gas from Shale Formations," *Climate Change* (2011) (DOI 10.1007/s10584-011-0061-5); Ingraffea, "Gangplank to Warm Future"; "Does the Natural Gas Industry Need a New Messenger?" *CBC News*, November 29, 2011, accessed December 9, 2013, http://www.cbc.ca/news/canada/new-brunswick/does-the-natural-gas-industry-need-a-new-messenger-1.1002634; Horn, "Smeared but Still Fighting.

46. Tom Shepstone, "There Ought to Be a (Natural Gas) Law—Part I," *Energy in Depth*, April 25, 2012, accessed December 9, 2013, http://energyindepth.org/marcellus/there-ought-to-be-a-natural-gas-law-part-i.

47. Joe Massaro, "Professor Ingraffea: The Next Monster under the Bed," *Energy in Depth*, accessed December 9, 2013, http://energyindepth.org/marcellus/professor-ingraffea-the-next-monster-under-the-bed.

48. Robert B. Jackson et al., "Increased Stray Gas Abundance in a Subset of Drinking Water Wells near Marcellus Shale Gas Extraction," *Proceedings of the National Academy of Sciences* (2013) (DOI: 10.1073/pnas.1221635110); Dave Lucas, "Duke Study Links Hydrofracking to Water Contamination," WAMC Northeast Public Radio, June 28, 2013, accessed December 9, 2013, http://wamc.org/post/duke-study-links-hydrofracking-water-contamination.

49. Chris Tucker, "Another Duke Rebuke?" *Energy in Depth*, July 9, 2012, accessed December 9, 2013, http://energyindepth.org/marcellus/another-duke-rebuke-2.

50. Jeremy Miller, "Bakken to School," *High Country News*, January 21, 2013, 16–18; Stephanie Joyce, "Amid Boom, Regulators Struggle with Staffing," Wyoming Public Media Statewide Network, May 16, 2014, accessed May 20, 2014, http://wyomingpublicmedia.org/post/amid-boom-regulators-struggle-staffing.

51. Miller, "Bakken to School"; Joshua Zaffos, "An Industry-Funded Education?," *High Country News*, January 21, 2013, 20–22.

52. Miller, "Bakken to School."

53. Ibid.; Zaffos, "Industry-Funded Education?," 22.

54. William Gern, University of Wyoming vice president of research and

economic development, interview with the author, June 6, 2013; Irina Zhorov, "For UW's School of Energy Resources Transparency Is the Key," Open Spaces program, KUWR, Wyoming Public Media Statewide Network, January 5, 2013, accessed December 9, 2013, http://wyomingpublicmedia.org/post/uw-s-school-energy-resources-transparency-about-funding-key.

55. "Roles and Responsibilities of the University of Wyoming's Board of Trustees," University of Wyoming's Trustees, accessed December 9, 2013, http://www.uwyo.edu/trustees.

56. However, the institution seems somewhat confused about how to apply the business metaphor, given that the president referred to the provost as the "chief executive officer." Laura Hancock, "Big Changes in Leadership at UW," *Casper Star-Tribune*, August 26, 2013, accessed December 9, 2013, http://billingsgazette.com/news/state-and-regional/wyoming/big-changes-in-leadership-at-uw/article_c1948d03-8e46-54f6-ad75-349224e2d803.html.

57. Bruce E. Pitman, interviewed by Susan Arbetter, transcribed by Jim Holstun, "Interview with UB Dean Bruce Pitman," *Capital Pressroom*, July 8, 2012.

58. Nancy Zimpher, interviewed by Susan Arbetter, transcribed by Jim Holstun, "Interview with SUNY Chancellor Nancy Zimpher," *Capital Pressroom*, July 8, 2012.

59. Eliot Marshall, "University of Texas Revamps Conflict of Interest Rules after Critical Review," *Science* 338 (December 2012): 14.

60. David Matthews, "Fossil Fuel Ties with Universities Highlighted by Report," [London] *Times Higher Education*, October 21, 2013, accessed December 9, 2013, http://www.timeshighereducation.co.uk/news/fossil-fuel-ties-with-universities-highlighted-by-report/2008360.article.

61. American Association of University Professors, "Statement on Corporate Funding of Academic Research," AAUP, accessed December 9, 2013, http://www.aaup.org/report/statement-corporate-funding-academic-research (member only content).

62. Shauna Stephenson, interview with the author, March 12, 2013.

63. Thyne interview, September 9, 2013.

64. Ibid.

Chapter 6

1. "Medicine Bow," Carbon County, accessed July 15, 2016, http://www.

wyomingcarboncounty.com/index.php/places-to-visit/medicine-bow; "About Us," DKRW Advanced Fuels, accessed December 15, 2015, http://www.dkrwaf.com/about-us.html http://www.dkrwadvancedfuels.com/About-Us-38.html.

2. "US Census Bureau State and County QuickFacts: Carbon County, Wyoming," United States Department of Commerce, accessed May 7, 2013, http://quickfacts.census.gov/qfd/states/56/56007.html.

3. Terry Weickum, Carbon County commissioner, interview with the author, March 14, 2013.

4. Pamela King, "AFL-CIO Sees Little Progress in Addressing 'Workplace Fatality Crisis' in Oil and Gas," WyoFile, May 13, 2014, accessed May 13, 2014, http://wyofile.com/ee_daily/afl-cio-sees-little-progress-addressing-workplace-fatality-crisis-oil-gas.

5. Dustin Bleizeffer, "Wyoming Should Recognize Workers' Memorial Day," WyoFile, April 25, 2013, accessed May 7, 2013, http://www.wyofile.com/blog/wyoming-should-recognize-workers-memorial-day; Cally Carswell, "Sinclair Flare Up," High Country News, April 23, 2010, accessed May 7, 2013, http://www.hcn.org/issues/42.7/flare-up/print_view; "History of Sinclair," Town of Sinclair, Wyoming, accessed May 7, 2013, http://www.sinclairwyoming.com.

6. David Throgmorton, director of Carbon County Higher Education Center, interview with the author, March 14, 2013.

7. Allen Best, "Locals Say DKRW's Coal-to-Gasoline Plant Needs More Scrutiny," WyoFile, March 31, 2013, accessed May 7, 2013, http://www.wyofile.com/specialreport/locals-say-dkrws-coal-to-gasoline-plant-needs-more-scrutiny.

8. Letter from Board of Carbon County Commissioners to Board of Cooperative Higher Education Services, May 1, 2012.

9. Throgmorton interview.

10. Leo Chapman, "Letter: Commissioner Chapman Condemns Statement Made about Higher Ed Director," *Rawlins Daily Times*, accessed May 7, 2013, http://www.rawlinstimes.com/opinion/letters_to_editor/article_4f52a685-8bf6-55c4-9010-300f0175b364.html.

11. Weickum interview.

12. Jerry Paxton, Carbon County commissioner, interview with the author, April 26, 2013.

13. David Throgmorton, "Letter to the Editor; DKRW Plant Isn't Passing Sniff Test," *Casper Star-Tribune*, April 1, 2012, accessed May 7, 2013, http://trib.com/

opinion/columns/dkrw-plant-isn-t-passing-sniff-test/article_0929ade1-7aa8-5338-884f-30d4fd2c3bb2.html.

14. Weickum interview.

15. Paxton interview.

16. Leo Chapman, Carbon County commissioner, interview with the author, April 25, 2012.

17. Throgmorton interview.

18. Letter from Board of Carbon County Commissioners, 2012.

19. Christopher Hayes, *Twilight of the Elites: America after Meritocracy* (New York: Crown, 2012), 72–74.

20. Jason Leopold, "Former Army Sec, Enron VP, Thomas White Wants Govt Funding for New Energy Project," Common Dreams, accessed May 7, 2013, http://www.commondreams.org/views05/0608–28.htm.

21. "Speaker's Biography: Robert Kelly," Milken Institute, accessed May 7, 2013, http://www.milkeninstitute.org/events/gcprogram.taf?function=bio&Event ID=GC07&SPID=2654; "The CIA for Everyman," *Forbes*, April 17, 2000, accessed May 7, 2013, http://www.forbes.com/forbes/2000/0417/6509404a_print.html; Jason Leopold and Jessica Berthold, "Enron Unit Chiefs' Compensation Raises Fresh Questions," Dow Jones Newswire, accessed May 7, 2013, http://faculty.msb.edu/bodurthj/teaching/ENRON/Enron%20Unit%20Chiefs'%20Compensation%20 Raises%20Fresh%20Questions.htm.

22. "H. David Ramm," UH Energy Advisory Board, University of Houston, accessed May 7, 2013, http://www.uh.edu/uh-energy/advisory-board/david-ramm/index.php; "David Ramm, Chairman," Bright Source Limitless, accessed May 7, 2013, http://www.brightsourceenergy.com/david-ramm.

23. Richard A. Oppel Jr. and Thom Shanker, "Army Secretary Steps Down; Had Clashed with Rumsfeld," *New York Times*, April 26, 2003, accessed May 7, 2013, http://www.nytimes.com/2003/04/26/us/army-secretary-steps-down-had-clashed-with-rumsfeld.html?ref=thomasewhite; Patty Reinert, "Army Secretary Walks Tightrope in Enron Scandal," *Houston Chronicle*, April 8, 2002, accessed May 7, 2013, https://business.highbeam.com/5874/article-1G1-120499510/army-secretary-walks-tightrope-enron-scandal; Robert L. Borsage, "White Must Go," *Nation*, February 21, 2002, accessed May 7, 2013, http://www.thenation.com/article/white-must-go#; Jason Leopold, "Bush Crook Tom White Played Key Role in Enron

Coverup," *Salon*, August 29, 2002, accessed May 7, 2013, http://archive.democrats. com/preview.cfm?term=enron.

24. Letter from Board of Carbon County Commissioners to the Board of Cooperative Higher Education Services, May 1, 2012.

25. Weickum interview.

26. Mark Northam, former researcher for ExxonMobil, expert in the field of coal conversion, and director of the University of Wyoming's School of Energy Resources, estimates that the technology to turn coal into liquids is "probably fifty years out"—and he's supposed to be a cheerleader for the industry; Matthew L. Wald, "Why Decades Can Pass between Idea and 'Eureka!'" *New York Times*, April 13, 2012, accessed November 6, 2012, http://www.nytimes.com/2012/04/11/business/energy-environment/for-energy-innovation-a-long-development-period.html.

27. Throgmorton, "Letter to the Editor."

28. Dustin Bleizeffer, "Long-Delayed DKRW Coal Conversion Plant Still Lacks Complete Financing," WyoFile, March 31, 2013, accessed May 7, 2013, http://www. wyofile.com/specialreport/long-delayed-dkrw-coal-conversion-plant-still-lacks-complete-financing. There have been other attempts at building CTL plants in Indiana, Tennessee, and West Virginia, but these projects have stalled: Howard Greninger, "Coal Liquefaction Plant Eyes Newport," *Terre Haute Tribune-Star*, September 16, 2010, accessed May 8, 2013, http://tribstar.com/news/x1561141982/ Coal-liquefaction-plant-eyes-Newport; Ed Marcum, "Coal Liquefaction Plant Proposed for Tennessee: More Info Sought on Firm Proposing Coal Plant," *Knoxville News*, May 27, 2011, accessed May 8, 2013, http://www.americanfuelscoalition. com/2011/05/27/ctl-for-tennessee.

29. To be the first, DKRW will need to beat Wyoming's ultrawealthy McMurry companies, who made it big in the oil and gas business and were planning to build a gas-to-gasoline conversion plant on the shores of Lake DeSmet, a treasured recreational site in northern Wyoming, with the help of millions of dollars in public funding. Jeremy Fugleberg, "Wyoming Legislators Support Plans to Convert Natural Gas, Coal to Gasoline," *Casper Star-Tribune*, June 22, 2011, accessed May 8, 2013, http://trib.com/news/state-and-regional/wyoming-legislators-support-plans-to-convert-natural-gas-coal-to/article_e71507a7-6d62-5412-a8e1-360fb37ded25.html.

30. C. Lowell Miller, Mark Ackiewicz, and Daniel C. Cicero, *Coal-to-Liquids Technology: Clean Liquid Fuels from Coal* (Washington, DC: US Department of Energy, 2008).

31. Nicholas Ducote and H. Sterling Burnett, "Turning Coal into Liquid Fuel," National Center for Policy Analysis, May 1, 2009, accessed September 12, 2013, http://www.ncpa.org/pub/ba656; "AAAS Policy Brief: Coal-to-Liquid Technology," AAAS, accessed September 12, 2013, http://www.aaas.org/spp/cstc/briefs/coaltoliquid.

32. Jeremy Fugleberg, "There's an Enormous Potential Here," *Casper Star-Tribune*, March 8, 2012; US Department of Energy, "Notice of Intent to Prepare an Environmental Impact Statement," *Federal Register*, vol. 74, no. 227 (November 27, 2009); Wyoming Division of Air Quality, approval of permit CT-5873 to construct Medicine Bow IGL Plant, Wyoming Department of Environmental Quality, March 4, 2009; David Throgmorton, "Trade You the Tetons for an Educated Citizen," *Rawlins Daily Times*, February 4, 2012; Medicine Bow Fuel and Power, LLC, presentation to Wyoming Infrastructure Authority, Jackson, reported by Jason Lillegraven, in a letter provided to the author, January 31, 2012; Bleizeffer, "Long-Delayed."

33. Liz Wood, "Industrial Siting Council Approves DKRW Amendment," *Saratoga Sun*, December 25, 2013, 7.

34. Throgmorton, "Letter."

35. Mary Throne, attorney, interview with the author, May 16, 2013.

36. Throgmorton, "Letter."

37. Benjamin Storrow, "DKRW Seeks Financing from Federal Program that Funded Solyndra," *Casper Star-Tribune*, February 24, 2014, December 15, 2015, http://trib.com/business/energy/dkrw-seeks-financing-from-federal-program-that-funded-solyndra/article_f36c797a-0585-59f6-848d-6a786b847b75.html.

38. Bleizeffer, "Long-Delayed."

39. Ibid.

40. Ibid.

41. Throgmorton interview.

42. Bleizeffer, "Long-Delayed."

43. David Throgmorton, "Trade You the Tetons for an Educated Citizen," *Rawlins Daily Times*, December 23, 2011.

44. Medicine Bow Fuel and Power presentation; "Coal-to-Liquids Project Carbon County," Wyoming industrial siting permit application, prepared by CH2MHill, September 2007; Throgmorton, "Letter."

45. Best, "Locals Say."

46. Jason Lillegraven, letter to the administrator of the Wyoming Industrial Siting Division, Department of Environmental Quality, March 24, 2013.

47. Wyoming Industrial Siting Council, order granting permit to Medicine Bow Fuel and Power, LLC, for construction of Coal-to-Liquids Project, Industrial Siting Division, Wyoming Department of Environmental Quality, January 16, 2008.

48. Jason Lillegraven, letter to the program principle of the Industrial Siting Division, Wyoming Department of Environmental Quality, January 9, 2013.

49. Throne interview.

50. Best, "Locals Say."

51. Medicine Bow Fuel and Power, LLC, 2007, "Presentation"; Liz Wood, "Is There Enough Coal in the Hanna Basin for DKRW?," *Saratoga Sun*, April 11, 2012; US Bureau of Land Management, Rawlins Field Office, January 1999, "Final Carbon Basin Coal Project Environmental Impact Statement, Carbon County, Wyoming," FEIS-98–42, TRC Mariah Associates, Inc.; Lillegraven, letter to program principle; Jason A. Lillegraven, "DKRW: A Sound Wyo Investment?" *Casper Star-Tribune*, February 12, 2012, accessed July 15, 2016, http://trib.com/opinion/columns/dkrw-a-sound-wyo-investment/article_004e196f-42df-5a81-89e9-554ac21feb69.html.

52. Best, "Locals Say"; Lillegraven, "Sound Wyo Investment?"; Liz Wood, "Enough Water for DKRW?" *Saratoga Sun*, March 14, 2012.

53. Lillegraven, letter to program principle.

54. Ibid.

55. Ibid.

56. From 1990 to 2009, Wyoming paid about $51 billion in federal taxes and received about $70 billion in federal spending. This means that the federal government returned $1.37 for every $1.00 that Wyoming sent to Washington. Only Alaska receives more federal aid per capita than Wyoming. Gregory Nickerson, "Wyoming: Where Independent People Rely on Federal Funds," WyoFile, May 14, 2013, accessed May 14, 2013, http://www.gillettenewsrecord.com/news/article_e9b925fc-8518-5326-a4db-bf5c01d67933.html.

57. Miller, Ackiewicz, and Cicero, *Coal-to-Liquids Technology.*

58. Ibid, 6.

59. Throgmorton interview.

Chapter 7

1. David Throgmorton, "Who's Driving?," *Rawlins Daily Times*, January 14, 2012.

2. Terry Weickum, Carbon County commissioner, interview with the author, March 14, 2013.

3. Leo Chapman, Carbon County commissioner, interview with the author, April 25, 2012.

4. Jerry Paxton, Carbon County commissioner, interview with the author.

5. Dustin Bleizeffer, "Long-Delayed DKRW Coal Conversion Plant Still Lacks Complete Financing," WyoFile, March 31, 2013, accessed May 7, 2013, http://wyofile.com/2013/03/long-delayed-dkrw-coal-conversion-plant-still-lacks-complete-financing.

6. Jeroen Veldman, "Politics of the Corporation," *British Journal of Management* 24 (2013): S18–S30, http://onlinelibrary.wiley.com/doi/10.1111/1467-8551.12024/epdf.

7. Various scholars have tried to make a case for the moral agency of corporations, but these efforts appear to have largely failed such that corporations remain as instruments of maximizing profits with either no or only vague and unsubstantial ethical duties to society. Ibid.; Wesley Cragg and Dirk Matten, "Ethics, Corporations, and Governance," *Business Ethics* 102 (2011): 1–4; John R. Danley, *The Role of the Modern Corporation in a Free Society* (Notre Dame, IN: University of Notre Dame Press, 1994).

8. Christopher Hayes, *Twilight of the Elites: America after Meritocracy* (New York: Crown, 2012), 74.

9. David Throgmorton, "A Big Gulp of Air," *Rawlins Daily Times*, December 24, 2012.

10. Dustin Bleizeffer, "Wyoming Should Recognize Workers' Memorial Day," WyoFile, April 25, 2013, accessed May 7, 2013, http://www.wyofile.com/blog/wyoming-should-recognize-workers-memorial-day.

11. Quoted in Drake, "Wyoming Should Recognize."

12. Jim Snyder, "Republicans Critical of Solyndra Sought U.S. Coal-Projects Aid," *Business Week*, October 31, 2011, accessed January 7, 2014, http://www.bloomberg.com/news/articles/2011-10-28/republicans-critical-of-solyndra-sought-u-s-coal-projects-aid; Benjamin Storrow, "Another Solyndra? Wyoming Delegation

Feels Differently about DKRW Advanced Fuels," *Casper Star-Tribune*, March 30, 2014, accessed March 31, 2014, http://trib.com/business/energy/another-solyndra-wyoming-delegation-feels-differently-about-dkrw-advanced-fuels/article_a5c87d21-4ab9-5e82-99bb-66a60a2f5937.html. The unflattering assessment has been further validated with reports from Arch Coal that DKRW has lost $62 million since 2007, prompting the coal company to cut its losses and write off its parasitic partner. Benjamin Storrow, "Arch Calls DKRW Plant a Write-Off," *Casper Star-Tribune*, April 23, 2014, A3–4.

13. Adam Weinstein, "Battle of the Beltway," *Mother Jones* (March/April 2013); Joe Romm, "Is the Energy Department Still Looking to Give Coal-to-Liquid Plant a Loan Guarantee?" Climate Progress, April 2, 2014, accessed April 3, 2014, http://thinkprogress.org/climate/2014/04/02/3345481/loan-guarantee-coal-to-liquid; Throgmorton, "Who's Driving?"

14. Eric Lipton, "Energy Firms in Secretive Alliance with Attorneys General," *New York Times*, December 6, 2014, accessed January 5, 2015, http:/www.nytimes.com/2014/12/07/us/politics/energy-firms-in-secretive-alliance-with-attorneys-general.html?_r=0.

15. David Throgmorton, "Trade You the Tetons for an Educated Citizen," *Rawlins Daily Times*, February 4, 2012.

16. David Throgmorton, "Letter: DKRW Plant Isn't Passing Sniff Test," *Casper Star-Tribune*, April 1, 2012, accessed May 7, 2013, http://trib.com/opinion/columns/dkrw-plant-isn-t-passing-sniff-test/article_0929ade1-7aa8-5338-884f-30d4fd-2c3bb2.html. Throgmorton was referring to a study conducted jointly by the Center for Public Integrity, Global Integrity, and Public Radio International, which ranked Wyoming as the third-worst state in the nation for having laws to prevent corruption or to promote openness and accountability according to Jeremy Pelzer, "Study Ranks Wyoming's Corruption Risk as High," *Casper Star-Tribune*, March 21, 2012, accessed November 8, 2013, http://trib.com/news/state-and-regional/govt-and-politics/study-ranks-wyoming-s-corruption-risk-as-high/article_309a1a52-86ed-5efe-8a81-12318382eff3.html. A 2015 report by the Center for Public Integrity showed no improvement, as Wyoming ranked forty-ninth in terms of public integrity and received a failing grade: Yue Qiu, Chris Zubak-Skees, and Erik Lincoln, "How Does Your State Rank for Integrity?," the Center for Public Integrity, November 9, 2015, accessed November 13, 2015, http://www.publicintegrity.org/2015/11/09/18822/how-does-your-state-rank-integrity.

17. Allen Best, "Locals Say DKRW's Coal-to-Gasoline Plant Needs More Scrutiny," WyoFile, March 31, 2013, accessed May 7, 2013, http://www.wyofile.com/specialreport/locals-say-dkrws-coal-to-gasoline-plant-needs-more-scrutiny.

18. Ibid.

19. Ibid.

20. Mary Throne, attorney and state representative, interview with the author, May 16, 2013.

21. Jason Lillegraven, personal communication, November 25, 2012.

22. David Throgmorton, director of the Carbon County Higher Education Center, interview with the author, March 14, 2013.

23. Weickum interview.

24. Chapman interview.

25. Weickum interview.

26. Paxton interview.

27. Barbara J. Bentz et al., "Climate Change and Bark Beetles of the Western United States and Canada: Direct and Indirect Effects," *Bioscience* 60 (2012): 602–13.

28. "United States Department of Commerce, US Census Bureau State and County QuickFacts: Carbon County, Wyoming," accessed May 7, 2013, http:// quickfacts.census.gov/qfd/states/56/56007.html; "QuickFacts: Wyoming," http:// quickfacts.census.gov/qfd/states/56000.html.

29. Jill Morrison, community organizer for Powder River Basin Resource Council, interview with the author, May 2, 2013.

30. Bob LeResche, vice chair of the board for Powder River Basin Resource Council, interview with the author, May 2, 2013.

31. Weickum interview.

32. Ibid.

33. Paxton interview.

34. Weickum interview.

35. Gilbert Archuleta, chair of the board of the Carbon County Higher Education Services, interview with the author, April 25, 2013.

36. Letter from Board of Cooperative Higher Education Services to the Board of Carbon County Commissioners, May 30, 2012.

37. Letter from Board of Carbon County Commissioners to the Board of Cooperative Higher Education Services, May 1, 2012.

38. Letter from Board of Cooperative Higher Education Services.

39. Ibid. On the fallout, see Jeremy Fugleberg, "Rawlins Center Director Takes Fire for DKRW Project Opinions," *Casper Star-Tribune*, June 1, 2012, accessed May 8, 2013, http://trib.com/news/state-and-regional/rawlins-center-director-takes-fire-for-dkrw-project-opinions/article_39ec05a7–8258–58f2–8adb-26e873631bba.html.

40. Fugleberg, "Rawlins Center Director."

41. Weickum interview.

42. Leo Chapman, "Letter: Commissioner Chapman Condemns Statement Made about Higher Ed Director," *Rawlins Daily Times*, June 4, 2012, accessed May 8, 2013, http://www.rawlinstimes.com/opinion/letters_to_editor/article_4f52a685-8bf6-55c4-9010-300f0175b364.html.

43. Weickum interview.

44. Chapman interview.

45. Bleizeffer, "Long-Delayed."

46. Ibid.

47. Liz Wood, "Industrial Siting Council Approves DKRW Amendment," *Saratoga Sun*, December 25, 2013, 7.

48. David Throgmorton, "Throgmorton: Can't We Just Put DKRW Behind Us?" *Casper Star-Tribune* guest editorial, December 28, 2014, accessed July 15, 2016, http://trib.com/opinion/columns/throgmorton-can-t-we-just-put-dkrw-behind-us/article_71285182-757d-5cc4-bf04-465e08688e49.html.

49. Ibid.

50. Transcription of presentation given by William Gathmann, DKRW senior vice president for finance, on January 5, 2016, at the Community Center of Medicine Bow, Wyoming.

51. Ibid.

52. Liz Wood, "DKRW Terminates Sinopec Contract," *Saratoga Sun*, March 12, 2014, 24.

53. Best, "Locals Say"; Kate Snyder, "County Opposes DKRW Delay," *Rawlins Daily Times*, March 21, 2013, accessed May 8, 2013, http://www.rawlinstimes.com/news/article_047aa7e2–91d6–11e2-a9e8–0019bb2963f4.html.

54. Paxton interview.

55. Weickum interview.

56. Ibid.

57. Ibid.

58. Throgmorton interview.

59. Ibid.

60. Ibid.

Chapter 8

1. Michael Smith, "Three Crowns Golf Club Transitions from Oil Refinery to Golf Course: An Environmental Disaster Sparks Change and Growth," Golf Course Superintendent Association of America, accessed August, 27, 2013, http://www.gcsaa.org/_common/templates/GcsaaTwoColumnLayout.aspx?id=6444&LangType =1033; "Three Crowns Golf Club Hits the Wyoming Golf Scene," accessed August 27, 2013, http://www.cybergolf.com/golf_news/three_crowns_golf_club_hits_the_wyoming_golf_scene; Rita and Bob, "Golf Three Crowns Golf Club," *MyTripJournal*, August 21, 2007, accessed August 27, 2013, http://www.mytripjournal.com/travel-477226-golf-club-standard-oil-bob-crowns-tees-walk.

2. Joanne Davidson, "Record Turnout Hails True Family, Citizens of the West," *Denver Post*, January 25, 2004, accessed May 8, 2013, http://search.proquest.com/docview/410773174; Jeremy Fugleberg, "Wyoming Legislators Support Plans to Convert Natural Gas, Coal to Gasoline," *Casper Star-Tribune*, June 22, 2011, accessed May 8, 2013, http://trib.com/news/state-and-regional/wyoming-legislators-support-plans-to-convert-natural-gas-coal-to/article_e71507a7-6d62-5412-a8e1-360fb37ded25.html; Dan Neal, former editor of the *Casper Star-Tribune*, interview with the author, April 5, 2013.

3. Press release, Ucross Foundation, January 9, 2006.

4. Becky Bohrer, "Art Exhibit Attempts to Chronicle 'New Gold Rush,'" Associated Press Worldstream, *Environmental News Network*, February 7, 2006, accessed August 15, 2013, http://www.enn.com/wildlife/article/3629.

5. Dustin Bleizeffer, "Nicolaysen Blocks Methane Exhibit," *Casper Star-Tribune*, February 8, 2006, accessed August 15, 2013, http://trib.com/news/local/nicolaysen-blocks-methane-exhibit/article_0fd7d185-f008-5b61-8652-2be98bc-dc2e2.html.

6. Ted Wood, interview with the author, April 9, 2013.

7. Ibid.; Ted Wood, "Bios of Former Fellows," University of Colorado School of

Journalism and Mass Communication's Center for Environmental Journalism, accessed August 16, 2013, http://www.colorado.edu/journalism/cej/scripps_fellowships/formerfellowsList.html.

8. "President John F. Kennedy: Remarks at Amherst College, October 26, 1963," About the NEA, National Endowment for the Arts, accessed August 15, 2013, http://www.arts.gov/about/Kennedy.html.

9. Association of Art Museum Directors, "Managing the Relationship between Art Museums and Corporate Sponsors," May 2007 report, accessed August 15, 2013, https://aamd.org/sites/default/files/document/Corporate%20Sponsors_clean%2006-2007.pdf.

10. Wyoming State Historical Society, "The Powder River Basin: A Natural History," WyoHistory, accessed August 15, 2013, http://www.wyohistory.org/encyclopedia/powder-river-basin-natural-history.

11. Dustin Bleizeffer," Cheyenne Lecture Will Focus on Powder River Basin Coal Leasing Program," August 16, 2013, WyoFile Energy Report, accessed August 27, 2013, http://www.wyofile.com/blog/24498.

12. Ibid.; "Powder River Basin," *Wikipedia*, acccssed August 15, 2013, http://en.wikipedia.org/wiki/Powder_River_Basin.

13. Ruckelshaus Institute of Environment and Natural Resources (2005), "Water Production from Coalbed Methane Development in Wyoming: A Summary of Quantity, Quality and Management Options," University of Wyoming, accessed January 20, 2014, http://www.uwyo.edu/haub/ruckelshaus-institute/_files/docs/publications/2005-cbm-water-final-report.pdf.

14. Powder River Basin Resource Council, "CBM Overview," PowderRiver Basin.org, accessed August 15, 2013, http://www.powderriverbasin.org/cbm-overview.

15. Associated Press, "Noise from Coal Bed Compressor Draws Complaints from Rural Residents," *Billings Gazette*, April 23, 2001, accessed August 28, 2013, http://billingsgazette.com/news/state-and-regional/wyoming/noise-from-coal-bed-compressor-draws-complaints-from-rural-residents/article_4358d94a-84f8-56e1-a2ae-f2c9a18f4bc8.html.

16. Ibid.

17. Sharon Soule, legal instruments examiner, BLM Buffalo Field Office, interview with the author, August 2, 2013.

18. US Department of the Interior, "Split Estate Mineral Ownership," Bureau of

Land Management, Wyoming, accessed August 28, 2013, http://www.blm.gov/wy/st/en/programs/mineral_resources/split-estate.print.html.

19. 30 USC §§ 181 et seq.

20. Katharine Collins, "Open for Business: Wyoming Throws Away Its Water to Get Out the Gas," *High Country News*, September 25, 2000, accessed August 15, 2013, http://www.hcn.org/issues/186/6053; Dustin Bleizeffer, "State of Wyoming Seeks Buyers for Abandoned CBM Wells," *Casper Star-Tribune*, September 1, 2010, accessed August 15, 2013, http://trib.com/news/state-and-regional/state-of-wyoming-seeks-buyers-for-abandoned-cbm-wells/article_a99db0de-f08d-5d54-8fe9-ab26672c6a31.html.

21. Jill Morrison and Bob LeResche, Powder River Basin Resource Council community organizer and board vice chair, interview with the author, May 2, 2013; Gregory Nickerson, "Wyoming Mining Association Conference Paints Picture of Challenges and Opportunities," WyoFile, June 29, 2013, accessed August 29, 2013, http://wyofile.com/gregory_nickerson/wyoming-mining-association-conference/#sthash.d0XQEjPj.dpuf.

22. Morrison and LeResche interview.

23. "Coal Bed Methane Development: Past to Present," Buffalo Field Office, US Department of the Interior, Bureau of Land Management, accessed August 15, 2013, http://www.blm.gov/wy/st/en/field_offices/Buffalo/cbm.print.htm.

24. Bleizeffer, "Nicolaysen Blocks Methane Exhibit"; US Energy Information Administration, "Top 100 U.S. Oil and Gas Fields by 2009 Proved Reserves," accessed August 15, 2013, http://www.eia.gov/oil_gas/rpd/topfields.pdf.

25. Jeremy Fugleberg, "Wyoming Well Blowout Rattles Residents Company Hopes to Cap It Today," *Casper Star-Tribune*, April 26, 2012, accessed August 15, 2013, http://trib.com/news/state-and-regional/wyoming-well-blowout-rattles-residents-company-hopes-to-cap-it/article_e8fc2e2c-6816–59eb-aec2–69e0776a3dd2.html; Associated Press, "Year after Wyoming Blowout No Fines for Chesapeake," *Billings Gazette*, April 11, 2013, accessed August 15, 2013, http://trib.com/news/state-and-regional/wyoming-well-blowout-rattles-residents-company-hopes-to-cap-it/article_e8fc2e2c-6816-59eb-aec2-69e0776a3dd2.html.

26. Some would contend that the Buffalo Bill Historical Center in Cody or the National Museum of Wildlife Art in Jackson are better known, but this would just further Casper's sense of being Wyoming's "second city."

27. Sharon Dynak, Ucross Foundation president, interview with the author, May 21, 2013; Wyoming Oil and Gas Conservation Commission, "Coal Bed Methane

Wells," Wyoming Oil and Gas Conservation Commission, accessed October 1, 2013, http://wogcc.state.wy.us/coalbedMenu.cfm?Skip=%27Y%27&oops=ID2980.

28. Morrison interview.

29. Dynak interview.

30. Tina Lam, "Detroit-Area Municipalities Find Pension Venture Coming Up Dry," *Detroit Free Press*, July 10, 2003, accessed August 15, 2013, https://www.highbeam.com/doc/1G1-105096002.html; Ronald Yee, "Director's Report," *Wayne County Employee Retirement System Newsletter*, September 2003, accessed August 15, 2013, http://wcers.org/Messenger/September,2003.pdf.

31. Morrison and Dynak interviews.

32. Bohrer, "Art Exhibit."

33. Dynak interview.

34. Dustin Bleizeffer, "Aftermath of a Drilling Boom: Wyoming Stuck with Abandoned Gas Wells," WyoFile, May 21, 2013, accessed August 16, 2013, https://wyomingoutdoorcouncil.org/2013/05/22/wyofile-aftermath-of-a-drilling-boom-wyoming-stuck-with-abandoned-gas-wells; Dustin Bleizeffer, "Wyoming's Multi-Million Dollar Effort to Clean Up Abandoned Wells Fails to Launch," WyoFile, September 26, 2013, accessed October 1, 2013, http://wyofile.com/dustin/wyomings-multi-million-dollar-effort-to-clean-up-abandoned-wells-fails-to-launch.

35. Given the scale of the problem, Wyoming's governor proposed using the conservation tax paid by producers to accelerate the cleanup of what could be more than three thousand wells at a cost exceeding $25 million: Dustin Bleizeffer, "Gov. Mead Wants additional $3M from Industry Account to Plug Orphaned Wells," WyoFile, December 11, 2013, accessed December 17, 2013, http://wyofile.com/dustin/gov-mead-wants-additional-3m-industry-account-plug-orphaned-wells. Recent reports have revealed cases such as that of Pure Petroleum, which went bankrupt in 2001, leaving behind reclamation bonds of $118,045 to cover reclamation costs exceeding $3 million: Irina Zhorov, "Coalbed Methane Bust Leaves Thousands of Orphaned Gas Wells in Wyoming," *High Country News*, January 1, 2014, accessed July 15, 2016, https://www.hcn.org/issues/45.22/the-coalbed-methane-bust-has-left-orphaned-gas-wells-across-wyoming.

36. Elizabeth Shogren, "Coal Company Bankruptcies Jeopardize Reclamation," *High Country News*, January 25, 2016, 5; Dylan Brown, "Mine Cleanup Concerns Spike as Industry Sputters," Greenwire, March 1, 2016, accessed July 15, 2016, http://www.eenews.net/stories/1060033248.

37. Dustin Bleizeffer, "State Strikes Deal to Secure 18.5% of Arch's Bond

Obligation," WyoFile, February 12, 2016, accessed February 16, 2016, http://www.wyofile.com/blog/state-strikes-deal-to-secure-18–5-of-archs-bond-obligation; Dylan Brown, "Despite 'Systemic Problems,' Wyo. Defends Alpha Deal," WyoFile (reprinted from *Environment and Energy News*), February 16, 2016, accessed February 22, 2016, http://www.wyofile.com/50502-2.

38.   Bleizeffer, "State Strikes Deal"; Benjamin Storrow, "Arch Coal Bankruptcy Ripples across American Coal Sector," *Billings Gazette*, January 12, 2016, accessed January 18, 2016, http://billingsgazette.com/news/state-and-regional/wyoming/arch-coal-bankruptcy-ripples-across-american-coal-sector/article_bcae6a10-8b00-5886-997f-cb43f1269e34.html.

39.   Benjamin Hulac and Dylan Brown, "Arch Coal Paid Execs $8M in Bonuses on Eve of Bankruptcy," WyoFile, March 22, 2016, accessed March 23, 2016, http://www.wyofile.com/arch-coal-paid-execs-8m-in-bonuses-on-eve-of-bankruptcy.

40.   Dustin Bleizeffer, "Feds Challenge Peabody's Mine Reclamation Bonding in 3 States," WyoFile, February 17, 2016, accessed February 22, 2016, http://www.wyofile.com/blog/feds-question-peabodys-mine-reclamation-bonding-in-3-states.

41.   Bob LeResche, "The New Gold Rush: Images of Coalbed Methane," exhibit guide, Ucross Foundation and the Powder River Basin Resource Council (2006).

42.   Ann Chambers Noble, *Hurry McMurry* (Casper, WY: VLM Publishing, 2010), 2.

43.   Neal interview.

44.   Ibid.

45.   Tom Doyle, Natrona County treasurer, provided revenue data, July 12, 2013.

46.   Ben Mitchell, interview with the author, February 13 and March 3, 2013.

47.   Ibid.

48.   Bruce Richardson, interview with the author, February 12, 2013.

49.   Anonymous source close to the Nicolaysen Art Museum, interview with the author.

50.   Dynak interview.

51.   Mitchell interview.

52.   Ben Mitchell wasn't sure of the politician's name; Morrison and LeResche had no doubt as to his identity.

53.   Jennings's Democratic opponent in the 2012 elections said of him, "It

certainly seems like he's in it for his own personal and financial gain," in reference to Jennings's work as a federal lobbyist for an energy company. Jeremy Pelzer, "State Senate Fight Brewing in Casper," *Casper Star-Tribune*, June 2, 2012, accessed October 1, 2013, http://trib.com/news/state-and-regional/govt-and-politics/state-senate-fight-brewing-in-casper/article_2d30e04e-ad84–5839-b61b-a5f0dbd6f19b.html http://trib.com/news/state-and-regional/govt-and-politics/state-senate-fight-brewing-in-casper/article_2d30e04e-ad84-5839-b61b-a5f0dbd6f19b.html.

54. Neal interview; Edith Cook, "Creativity," Edith Cook online, accessed September 4, 2013, http://www.edithcook.com/ resources/CreativityOct29.pdf.

55. Alexandra Fuller, "Recovering from Wyoming's Energy Bender," *New York Times*, April 20, 2008, accessed November 8, 2013, http://www.nytimes.com/2008/04/20/opinion/20fuller.html?pagewanted=print&_r=0.

56. Mitchell interview.

57. Ibid.

58. Vickie Goodwin, interview with the author, November 10, 2014. Cathy Killean, *To Save a Mountain* (Casper, WY: Bessemer Bend, 1998).

59. Ibid.

60. Ibid.

61. Ibid.

62. Holly Turner, "A Banner Year: Annual Report 2006–2007," Nicolaysen Art Museum and Discovery Center, accessed September 12, 2013, http://www.thenic.org/documents/2006_2007.pdf.

63. Adam Voge, "Once Center of Scandal, 'Teapot Dome' Oil Field Prepped for Sale," *Casper Star-Tribune*, March 4, 2013, accessed August 15, 2013, http://trib.com/business/energy/once-center-of-scandal-teapot-dome-oil-field-prepped-for/article_5d3f7c75-bbc1-5de5-8762-6971630b0213.html.

Chapter 9

1. Ben Mitchell, interviews with the author, February 13 and March 3, 2013.

2. Anonymous source close to the Nicolaysen Art Museum, interview with the author.

3. Dale Bohren, ed., "John Wold Biography," Made in Wyoming, accessed August 15, 2013, http://www.madeinwyoming.net/profiles/extras/woldbio.pdf.

4. "Global Warming Forum to Be Held in Casper," *Casper Star-Tribune*, November 17, 2008, accessed August 15, 2013, http://trib.com/news/local/article_ 664fab8e-a878–58b6-a4e4–2a096638953a.htmlhttp://trib.com/news/local/ global-warming-forum-to-be-held in-casper/article_664fab8e-a878-58b6-a4e4-2a096638953a.html.

5. Rena Delbridge, "H. A. 'Dave' True," Made in Wyoming, accessed August 15, 2013, http://madeinwyoming.net/profiles/true.php; "History," True Oil LLC, http://www.truecos.com/history.htm; US Tubular Steel Products, "Diemer True Honored with Chief Roughneck Award at IPAA Annual Meeting," Independent Petroleum Association of America, November 13, 2018, accessed August 15, 2013, http://www.ipaa.org/2008/11/13/diemer-true-honored-with-chief-roughneck-award-at-ipaa-annual-meeting; Joanne Davidson Seen, "Record Turnout Hails True Family, Citizens of the West," *Denver Post*, January 25, 2004, L09.

6. Delbridge, "H.A. 'Dave' True"; IPAA, "Diemer True, IPAA Treasurer," Independent Petroleum Association of America, accessed August 15, 2013, http://www. ipaa.org/about-ipaa/board-of-directors/diemer-true; "UW Board of Trustees Gains Three New Members; Another Reappointed," *UW News*, March 7, 2013, accessed August 15, 2013, http://www.uwyo.edu/uw/news/2013/03/uw-board-of-trustees-gains-three-new-members-another-reappointed.html.

7. An exact value for the True Companies is difficult to ascertain, but the patriarch of the family had an estate valued at $120 million, according to *Estate of True III v. Commissioner of Internal Revenue*, FindLaw, decided December 2, 2004, accessed December 9, 2013, http://caselaw.findlaw.com/us-10th-circuit/1059549. html.

8. Anonymous source close to the Nicolaysen Art Museum, interview by the author.

9. Ibid.

10. Ibid.

11. Repeated requests for an interview with Mick McMurry through the McMurry Foundation failed to yield a response, and the University of Wyoming Foundation, with close connections to the McMurrys, was unwilling to facilitate communications. We will never know Mick McMurry's side of the story because he committed suicide in March 2015. "Officials Rule McMurry's Death a Suicide," *Casper Star-Tribune*, March 11, 2015, accessed March 19, 2015, http://trib.com/ news/local/casper/officials-rule-mcmurry-s-death-a-suicide/article_3b5c303f-eba0-52ce-a0f7-88eb611935f4.html.

12. The story of the McMurry family is chronicled in the hagiography by Ann Chambers Noble, *Hurry McMurry* (Casper, WY: VLM Publishing, 2010).

13. Ann Chambers Noble, "The Jonah Field and Pinedale Anticline: A Natural Gas Success Story," Wyoming State Historical Society, accessed August 15, 2013, http://www.wyohistory.org/essays/jonah-field-and-pinedale-anticline-natural-gas-success-story; Noble, *Hurry McMurry*, 115; Angus M. Theurmer Jr., "Grouse Count Plummets in NPL Breeding Complex," WyoFile, May 5, 2015, accessed May 5, 2015, http://www.wyofile.com/specialreport/grouse-count-plummets-npl-breeding-complex-sage-grouse.

14. Noble, *Hurry McMurry*, 121.

15. "Annual Information Form," Encana, February 19, 2003, accessed August 15, 2013, http://www.encana.com/pdf/investors/financial/2002/p002884.pdf.

16. Justin Dullum, "Wyoming Energy Family Opens De Novo Bank," *Bay Ledger*, December 31, 2006, accessed August 15, 2013, http://www.blnz.com/news/2008/04/23/Wyoming_energy_family_opens_novo_8328.html. Quite remarkably, the McMurrys apparently considered their creating the bank to be an act of philanthropy. Robert Gagliardi, "Arena Auditorium Court to Be Named after Cheyenne Businessman," WyoSports, accessed May 14, 2014, http://www.wyosports.net/university_of_wyoming/mens_basketball/arena-auditorium-court-to-be-named-after-cheyenne-businessman/article_3a6933e6-86b3-11e3-a1df-0019bb2963f4.html.

17. University of Wyoming Athletics, "$5 Million Gift Names 'Jonah Field' at War Memorial Stadium: State of Wyoming Match Brings Total to $10 Million," Wyoming Official Athletics, May 6, 2005, accessed August 15, 2013, http://www.gowyo.com/sports/m-footbl/spec-rel/050605aad.html.

18. The floor of the newly renovated basketball arena is called the Maury Brown Court, after the owner of a liquor store and oil and gas drilling business. It seems that donors and flooring go together in Wyoming.

19. Sally Ann Shurmur, "McMurrys of Casper Help Others Pay It Forward," *Casper Star-Tribune*, April 14, 2013, accessed August 15, 2013, http://trib.com/news/local/casper/mcmurrys-of-casper-help-others-pay-it-forward/article_053209ab-7b01-56fa-8cd1-2b3963ca3d78.html.

20. Anonymous interview; Shurmur, "McMurrys of Casper."

21. Mitchell interview, February 13, 2013.

22. Anonymous interview.

23. Dustin Bleizeffer, "Nicolaysen Blocks Methane Exhibit," *Casper Star-Tribune*, February 8, 2006, accessed August 15, 2013, http://trib.com/news/local/nicolaysen-blocks-methane-exhibit/article_0fd7d185-f008-5b61-8652-2be98bc-dc2e2.html.

24. Wyoming Business Alliance, "Steering Committee," accessed September 4, 2013, http://wyomingbusinessalliance.com/pages/SteeringCommittee. "Kit Jennings," Influence Explorer, accessed October 1, 2013, http://influenceexplorer.com/politician/id/ 1a3423c87f1c49dbab62c6fa612ccbc6?cycle=2004.

25. Bleizeffer, "Nicolayson Blocks Methane Exhibit."

26. Mitchell interview, February 13, 2013.

27. Anonymous source close to the McMurry businesses, interview with the author.

28. Ted Wood, interview with the author, April 9, 2013.

29. *The New Gold Rush: Images of Coalbed Methane*, exhibit guide, Ucross Foundation and the Powder River Basin Resource Council (2006); Wood interview.

30. Bleizeffer, "Nicolaysen Blocks Methane Exhibit."

31. Ibid.

32. Ibid.

33. Mitchell interview, February 13, 2013.

34. Ibid.

35. Ibid.

36. Ibid.

37. Ibid.

38. Mitchell interview, March 3, 2013.

39. Jane Ifland, letter to the editor, *Casper Star-Tribune*, February 27, 2006. Ifland ran as a Democrat for the Wyoming House of Representatives in 2008; she was soundly defeated.

40. Allison Cole, letter to the editor, *Casper Star-Tribune*, February 16, 2006.

41. Associated Press, "Year after Wyoming Blowout No Fines for Chesapeake," *Billings Gazette*, April 10, 2013, accessed November 10, 2014, http://billingsgazette.com/news/state-and-regional/wyoming/year-after-wyoming-blowout-no-fines-for-chesapeake/article_63a7190f-4119-502b-85f2-38f635dceaa0.html.

42. Sharon Dynak, Ucross Foundation president, interview with the author, May 21, 2013.

43. Mitchell interview, March 3, 2013.

44. Marta Amundson, interviews with the author, April 12 and 17, 2013.

45. Ibid.

46. Wood interview; Associated Press, "Smithsonian Allegedly Altered Warming Exhibit," Climate Change on NBC News, May 21, 2007, accessed August 16, 2013, http://www.nbcnews.com/id/18789206/ns/us_news-environment/t/smith sonian-allegedly-altered-warming-exhibit/#.Ug1r7G1C7BY; Ingrid Sischy, "The Smithsonian's Big Chill," *Vanity Fair*, December 1, 2003, accessed August 16, 2013, http://connection.ebscohost.com/c/articles/11564959/smithsonians-big-chill.

47. Mel Evans, *Artwash: Big Oil and the Arts* (London: Pluto Press, 2015).

48. Dynak interview.

49. Ibid.

50. Jill Morrison, Powder River Basin Resource Council community organizer, interview with the author, May 2, 2013.

51. Ibid.; Bob LeResche, Powder River Basin Resource Council board vice chair, interview with the author, May 2, 2013.

52. Wood interview.

53. Mitchell interview, March 3, 2013.

54. Ibid.

Chapter 10

1. "List of Smoking Bans in the United States," *Wikipedia*, accessed March 4, 2014, http://en.wikipedia.org/wiki/List_of_smoking_bans_in_the_United_States#.C2.A0Wyoming.

2. Noah Brenner, "Safeguarding Green River Valley's Reputation," *Upstream*, March 22, 2013, accessed March 4, 2014, http://www.picarro.com/sites/default/files/Safeguarding%20Green%20River%20Valley%27s%20Reputation.pdf.

3. Bureau of Land Management, "Pinedale Anticline Project Office," US Department of the Interior, accessed March 4, 2014, http://www.wy.blm.gov/jio-papo/papo/index.htm.

4. Ibid.; Brenner, "Safeguarding."

5. Naomi Oreskes and Erik M. Conway, *Merchants of Doubt: How a Handful of Scientists Obscured the Truth on Issues from Tobacco Smoke to Global Warming* (New York: Bloomsbury, 2010).

6. Alan C. Miller, Tom Hamburger, and Julie Cart, "White House Puts the West on Fast Track for Oil, Gas Drilling," *Los Angeles Times*, August 25, 2004, accessed March 4, 2014, http://articles.latimes.com/2004/aug/25/nation/na-bog25/5.

7. John Heilprin, "Feds Cite Lapses in Oil, Gas Drilling," Highbeam Research, July 20, 2005, accessed March 4, 2014, http://www.highbeam.com/doc/1P1–111 245932.html.

8. Miller, Hamburger, and Cart, "White House."

9. Ann Chambers Noble, "The Jonah Field and Pinedale Anticline: A Natural-Gas Success Story," WyoHistory, accessed March 4, 2014, http://www.wyohistory. org/essays/jonah-field-and-pinedale-anticline-natural-gas-success-story; "Pinedale Anticline Fact Sheet," Theodore Roosevelt Conservation Partnership, accessed March 4, 2014, http://www.trcp.org/assets/pdf/pinedale-anticline-fact-sheet.pdf.

10. R[onald] Perry Walker, interview with the author, November 5, 2013; Wyoming Statute §39-14-205, 2013 Wyoming Statutes, Title 39, Taxation and Revenue; chapter 14, Mine Product Taxes; Exemptions, accessed March 4, 2014, http://law. justia.com/codes/wyoming/2013/title-39/chapter-14/article-2/section-39-14-205.

11. Dustin Bleizeffer, "Emission Questions Loom Large over Oil and Gas Industry," WyoFile, March 5, 2013, accessed March 4, 2014, http://wyofile.com/dustin/emission-questions-loom-large-over-oil-and-gas-industry; Brenner, "Safeguarding."

12. Robert Field, interview with the author, September 19, 2013.

13. Brenner, "Safeguarding."

14. "Summary of the Issues: Air Pollution," Citizens League for Environmental Action Now, accessed March 4, 2014, http://www.cleanhouston.org/air/index.htm; Wyoming Department of Environmental Quality, Air Quality Division, letter to operators: "Interim Policy on Demonstration of Compliance with WAQSR Chapter 6, Section 2(c)(ii) for Sources in Sublette County," WYDEQ Operator Permit Archive, Cheyenne, WY, July 21, 2008.

15. Angus M. Thuermer Jr. and Dustin Bleizeffer, "Study Finds Toxins, Cancer-Causing Air Pollution at Oil, Gas Wells," WyoFile, October 30, 2014, accessed

November 4, 2014, http://wyofile.com/angus_thuermer/study-finds-toxins-cancer-causing-air-pollution-oil-gas-wells.

16. Ronald Perry Walker interview, November 5, 2013; Walker, "By the Rasping in Our Lungs, Something Awful Comes this Way," unpublished paper on the history of the ozone case in the Upper Green River Valley of Wyoming, available from the author.

17. Walker interview, November 21, 2013; Ruckelshaus Institute, "Summary Report of Hydraulic Fracturing: A Wyoming Energy Forum," University of Wyoming, January 17, 2012, accessed March 4, 2014, http://www.uwyo.edu/haub/ruckelshaus-institute/_files/docs/publications/2011-hydraulic-fracturing-forum-summary-report.pdf.

18. Walker interview, November 21, 2013.

19. Dave Alberswerth and Dave Slater, "New Information Documents Bush Administration's Land-Management Shift: Secret Policy Changes Made Oil and Gas Development the Dominant Use of Federal Lands," Wilderness Society Common Dreams, May 26, 2004, accessed March 4, 2014, http://www.commondreams.org/news2004/0526-11.htm.

20. Dave Slater, "BLM Issued Record Number of Drilling Permits in 2004, but Most Went Undrilled," Wilderness Society Common Dreams, December 16, 2004, accessed March 4, 2014, http://www.commondreams.org/news2004/1216-06.htm.

21. Miller, Hamburger, and Cart, "White House."

22. Ibid.; Robert Gehrke, "Oil Industry Providing Workers for BLM Office," *Salt Lake Tribune*, July 9, 2005, accessed March 4, 2014, http://www.sltrib.com/ci_2848243.

23. Brenner, "Safeguarding"; Walker, "By the Rasping."

24. US Department of the Interior, Bureau of Land Management, Pinedale Anticline Draft Supplemental EIS, chapter 3, section 3.11 Air Quality, subsection 3.11.2. Washington: Government Printing Office, 2006; Walker, "By the Rasping."

25. Blaine Harden, "Federal Wildlife Monitors Oversee a Boom in Drilling," *Washington Post*, February 22, 2006, accessed March 4, 2014, http://www.washingtonpost.com/wp-dyn/content/article/2006/02/21/AR2006022101793.html; Miller, Hamburger, and Cart, "White House."

26. "Pinedale Anticline Fact Sheet."

27. Alberswerth and Slater, "New Information."

28. Letter from BLM State Director Robert A. Bennett to Regional Administrator of US EPA Robert Roberts, April 21, 2008.

29. Wyoming DEQ, letter to operators; Walker, "By the Rasping."

30. Robert Field, interview with the author, September 27, 2013; Walker interview, November 5, 2013; Dustin Bleizeffer, "Ozone Spikes Aren't Mother Nature's Fault," WyoFile, April 15, 2011, accessed March 4, 2014, http://wyofile.com/dustin/curse-the-weather; Dustin Bleizeffer, "Wyoming Escapes Ozone Season, but Not Ozone Problem," WyoFile, April 20, 2012, accessed March 4, 2014, http://wyofile.com/dustin/wyoming-escapes-ozone-season-but-not-the-ozone-problem; Kirk Johnson, "In Pinedale, Wyo., Residents Adjust to Air Pollution," New York Times, March 9, 2011, accessed March 4, 2014, http://www.nytimes.com/2011/03/10/us/10smog.html?_r=1&.

31. Joy Ufford, "EPA Moves on CURED Ozone Request," Sublette Examiner, December 26, 2011,

32. Angus M. Thuermer Jr. and Dustin Bleizeffer, "Study Finds Toxins, Cancer-Causing Air Pollution at Oil, Gas Wells," WyoFile, October 30, 2014, accessed November 11, 2014, http://wyofile.com/angus_thuermer/study-finds-toxins-cancer-causing-air-pollution-oil-gas-wells/#sthash.sssYEm35.dpuf. This report also reveals that air samples from another gas well nearby in Wyoming had 660 times the EPA's acutely dangerous level for hydrogen sulfide, 7,000 times the Occupational Safety and Health Administration's acceptable risk level for hexane, and above the EPA's "most hazardous cancer level" for formaldehyde.

33. Bleizeffer, "Emission Questions"; Bleizeffer, "Wyoming Escapes."

34. Walker, "By the Rasping."

35. Brenner, "Safeguarding."

36. Bleizeffer, "Wyoming Escapes."

37. Bleizeffer, "Emission Questions"; Bleizeffer, "Wyoming Escapes."

38. Bleizeffer, "Emission Questions."

39. Howard Pankratz, "Encana to Sell Its Jonah Field Properties in Wyoming for $1.8 Billion," Denver Post, March 31, 2014, accessed November 11, 2014, http://www.denverpost.com/business/ci_25458146/encana-sell-its-jonah-field-properties-wyoming-1.

40. Benjamin Storrow, "Wyoming Tightens Gas Field Emissions Rules to Curb Pinedale-Area Ozone Levels, Casper Star-Tribune, November 8, 2013, accessed March 4, 2014, http://trib.com/business/energy/wyoming-tightens-gas-field-

emission-rules-to-curb-pinedale-area/article_3e5b29ee-1cd8-5d03-ae3b-7af-15ad63c2d.htm.

41. Angus M. Thuermer Jr., "Tempest Buffets New Air Quality Rules for Sublette County," WyoFile, December 2, 2014, accessed December 2, 2014, http://wyofile.com/angus_thuermer/tempest-buffets-new-air-quality-rules-sublette-county.

42. There is some indication that drilling activity has decreased substantially due to overproduction of natural gas at a national level through widespread exploration, fracking, and development. As such, the Wyoming DEQ and gas industries are less worried about meeting air quality requirements not because of improved mitigation but thanks to declining production. Harold Bergman, former director of the School and Institute of Environment and Natural Resources, University of Wyoming, interview with the author, October 14, 2013.

43. Benjamin Storrow, "Wyoming DEQ Releases Revised Rule to Curb Pinedale Ozone Levels," *Billings Gazette*, November 4, 2014, accessed November 11, 2014, http://billingsgazette.com/news/state-and-regional/wyoming/wyoming-deq-releases-revised-rule-to-curb-pinedale-ozone-levels/article_16e9e842-7075-5f08-af2f-b12337 f109d1.html.

44. Eric Lipton, "Hard-Nosed Advice from Veteran Lobbyist: 'Win Ugly or Lose Pretty,'" *New York Times*, October 31, 2014, A19.

45. Walker interview, November 5, 2013.

46. Ronald P[erry] Walker, "Natural Gas Flare Emission Monitoring Using a Miniature Fiber Optic Spectrometer," *Coalbed Natural Gas Conference: I-Research, Monitoring and Applications, Wyoming Geological Survey Public Information Circular* 43 (2005), 120–23; Walker, "By the Rasping"; Encana public relations, internal communications copied to Ronald P[erry] Walker, July 15, 2011.

47. The Wyoming Supreme Court recently directed a district court to reconsider whether the contents of fracking fluid constituted a trade secret and required that the Wyoming Oil and Gas Conservation Commission explain why they denied environmental groups the relevant information. Benjamin Storrow, "Wyoming Supreme Court Reverses District Court Decision on Fracking Fluids," *Casper Star-Tribune*, March 12, 2014, accessed March 20, 2014, http://trib.com/business/energy/wyoming-supreme-court-reverses-district-court-decision-on-fracking-fluids/article_7d15a01f-df71-5786-99fb-f4685d0c7279.html. However, even when companies supposedly reveal the contents of their fracking fluids, they often omit chemicals as being trade secrets. Mike Soraghan, "Two-Thirds of Frack Disclosures Omit 'Secrets,'" Energy Wire, September 26, 2012, accessed March 24, 2014, http://www.eenews.net/energywire/stories/1059970474.

48. Walker interview, November 21, 2013.

49. Walker interview, November 5, 2013; Intelligence Press, "BLM Targeted for Focusing on Drilling Permits While Wyoming Wildlife Suffers Sharp Declines," NGI's Daily Gas Price Index, February 27, 2006, accessed March 4, 2014, http://www.naturalgasintel.com/articles/71130-blm-targeted-for-focusing-on-drilling-permits-while-wy-wildlife-suffers-sharp-declines.

50. Angus M. Thuermer Jr., "Grouse Count plummets in NPL Breeding Complex," WyoFile, May 5, 2015, accessed May 5, 2015, http://www.wyofile.com/grouse-count-plummets-npl-breeding-complex-sage-grouse/?utm_source=news letter&utm_medium=email&utm_campaign =weeklynewsletter.

51. Bleizeffer, "Ozone Spikes."

52. Walker interview, November 5, 2013.

53. Bureau of Land Management, "Pinedale Anticline Working Group," US Department of the Interior, accessed March 6, 2014, http://www.blm.gov/wy/st/en/field_offices/Pinedale/pawg.html.

54. Walker interview, November 21, 2013; Brenner, "Safeguarding."

55. Perry Walker, "Mixed Messages," Casper Star-Tribune, September 4, 2005, accessed March 6, 2014, http://trib.com/editorial/forum/mixed-messages/article_ d40b0b05-4361-5588-8767-3533e158de7e.html.

56. Walker interview, November 5, 2013.

57. Ibid.

58. Joe Baird, "Neighbor's Plight Is Utah's Cautionary Tale," Salt Lake Tribune, July 31, 2005, accessed March 6, 2014, http://archive.sltrib.com/article. php?id=2903061&itype=NGPSID.

59. Johnson, "In Pinedale, Wyo."

60. Walker interview, November 21, 2013.

61. "Pinedale Anticline Fact Sheet."

62. Laura Hancock, "Pinedale Ozone Task Force Submits Mitigation Recommendations," Casper Star-Tribune, September 21, 2012, accessed March 6, 2014, http://trib.com/news/state-and-regional/pinedale-ozone-task-force-submits-mitigation-recommendations/article_04ae778b-9804-51b4-9334-59bf8be79bcd.html.

63. Chad Baldwin, "Collaborative Problem Solving in the Gas Fields: A Diverse

Team Knuckles Down on a Daunting Natural Resource Issue," *Western Confluence* 1 (2014): 30.

64. Julia Stuble, "Energy Companies Raise Ante to SEIS," Pinedale Roundup, May 3, 2007, accessed March 6, 2014, http://www.sublette.com/roundup/v104n18/v104n18s3.htm; R. Perry Walker interview, November 5, 2013.

65. Walker interview, November 5, 2013.

66. R[onald] Perry Walker, e-mail to author, February 10, 2014.

67. Walker interview, November 5, 2013.

68. Whitney Royster, "Some Fear Comments Ignored," *Casper Star-Tribune*, March 27, 2005, accessed March 6, 2014, http://trib.com/news/state-and-regional/some-fear-comments-ignored/article_6587e354-2e81-5e68-aa42-87b59023a993.html.

69. Walker interview, November 5, 2013.

70. R[onald] Perry Walker, e-mail to author, December 10, 2013.

71. Walker, "By the Rasping."

72. Citizen scientists have recently made inroads with respect to collecting environmental data that meets the standards of federal agencies and peer-reviewed journals, although it's not yet clear whether even this level of rigor will be sufficient to elicit changes in policy. Thuermer and Bleizeffer, "Study Finds Toxins."

Chapter 11

1. Robert Field, interview with the author, September 19, 2013.

2. R[onald] Perry Walker, interview with the author, November 5, 2013.

3. Ibid.

4. Ibid.

5. Dustin Bleizeffer, "Methane Report Meets with Some Skepticism," *Casper Star-Tribune*, January 13, 2006, accessed March 7, 2013, http://trib.com/news/state-and-regional/methane-report-meets-with-some-skepticism/article_cbca043d-a9a5-5dae-9d58-556e3306235b.html; Associated Press, "Study Faults Wyoming for Lack of Coalbed Rules," Billings Gazette, January 13, 2006, accessed March 25, 2014, http://billingsgazette.com/news/state-and-regional/wyoming/study-faults-wyoming-for-lack-of-coalbed-rules/article_b06d7e90–3acb-5259-bfa6-b1e0dfb3284f.html;

Ruckelshaus Institute of Environment and Natural Resources, *Water Production from Coalbed Methane Development in Wyoming: A Summary of Quantity, Quality and Management Options*, University of Wyoming, Laramie, Wyoming, December 2005, accessed March 7, 2014, http://www.uwyo.edu/haub/ruckelshaus-institute/_files/docs/publications/2005-cbm-water-final-report.pdf.

6. Robert Field, interview with the author, September 26, 2013.

7. Noah Brenner, "Safeguarding Green River Valley's Reputation," Upstream, March 22, 2013, accessed March 4, 2014, http://www.picarro.com/sites/default/files/Safeguarding%20Green%20River%20Valley%27s%20Reputation.pdf; Dustin Bleizeffer, "Wyoming DEQ Blocks University Research on Ozone," WyoFile, December 20, 2012, accessed March 7, 2013, http://wyofile.com/dustin/wyoming-deq-blocks-university-research-on-ozone.

8. Connor Southard, "UW Air Quality Research Goes Global," WyoFile, July 9, 2013, accessed March 7, 2014, http://wyofile.com/connor-wroe-southard/uw-air-quality-research-goes-global.

9. Ibid.

10. Dustin Bleizeffer, "Emission Questions Loom Large over Oil and Gas Industry," WyoFile, March 5, 2013, accessed March 4, 2014, http://wyofile.com/dustin/emission-questions-loom-large-over-oil-and-gas-industry; Walker interview.

11. Field interview, September 19, 2013.

12. Ibid.

13. Phil White, "Scientists: Global Warming Seriously Affects Wyoming," *Casper Star-Tribune*, September 23, 2008, accessed March 7, 2014, http://trib.com/news/state-and-regional/scientists-global-warming-seriously-affects-wyoming/article_1fc44f36-a006-58d3-a72b-1ce869fccdbf.html.

14. US Department of Health and Human Services, "Appendix C: Comparison of the 2006–2007 and the 2007–2008 Model-Based Estimates," Office of Applied Statistics, accessed March 7, 2014, http://oas.samhsa.gov/2k8state/AppC.htm#TabC-9; Samuel Warren, "In Pictures: How Dangerous Is Your State for Drunken Driving?," *Forbes*, November 20, 2008, accessed March7, 2014, http://www.forbes.com/2008/11/20/driving-drunk-highway-forbeslife-cx_sw_1120drunk_slide_1.html; Noelle Straub, "Report: Wyo Has Alcohol Problem," *Casper Star-Tribune*, April 18, 2006, accessed March 7, 2014, http://trib.com/news/state-and-regional/report-wyo-has-alcohol-problem/article_aa0a8a87-79c1-5e01-a1ea-506a1db2ba1d.html.

15. Steve Gray, e-mail to author, January 24, 2014.

16. Pilita Clark, "Pacific Trade Winds Stall Global Warming, Study Says," *Financial Times*, February 10, 2014, accessed December 15, 2015, http://www.ft.com/cms/s/0/37930724–917a-11e3-adde-00144feab7de.html#axzz2tnKsrQL6.

17. Dustin Bleizeffer, "Most Wyomingites Question Global Warming, Poll Shows," *Casper Star-Tribune*, September 27, 2008, accessed March 10, 2014, http://trib.com/news/state-and-regional/most-wyomingites-question-global-warming-poll-shows/article_d08e1c07-a8e1–51fe-a16c-7fe91397f0b5.html.

18. Steve Gray, interview with the author, February 6, 2013.

19. Ibid.

20. Greg Kerr, "Water Research Program: Office of Water Programs," University of Wyoming, accessed March 10, 2014, http://www.uwyo.edu/owp.

21. Wyoming Water Development Commission, "Philosophy," State of Wyoming, accessed March 10, 2014, http://wwdc.state.wy.us/about/mission_statement.html.

22. Greg Kerr, interview with the author, April 18, 2013.

23. Christy Hemken, "Disappearing Glaciers: Precip Not Temp," Wyoming Livestock Roundup, accessed March 10, 2014, http://www.wylr.net/component/content/article/188-water/weather/1841-disappearing-glaciers-precip-not-temp; Wyoming State Climate Office, "State Climate Atlas: Temperature," University of Wyoming, accessed March 10, 2014, http://www.wrds.uwyo.edu/sco/climateatlas/temperature.html. For definitive evidence of increasing temperatures in the western United States over the last fifty years, see High Plains Regional Climate Center, *Climate Change on the Prairie: A Basic Guide to Climate Change in the High Plains Region* (Lincoln: University of Nebraska Press, 2013).

24. Kerr interview.

25. Ibid.

26. Gray interview.

27. Eugene Watson, letter to the editor, *Laramie Boomerang*, February 4, 2014, A4: "The AIDS industry and media want you to think there are only a handful of scientists who doubt the HIV-AIDS theory. Here's the reality." Alberta Reappraising AIDS Society, accessed April 23, 2014, http://aras.ab.ca/rethinkers.php.

28. Gray interview.

29. Ibid.

30. Secretary of State, "Composition of Wyoming's State Legislature," State of

Wyoming, accessed March 10, 2014, http://soswy.state.wy.us/information/docs/LegComposition.pdf.

31.   Jerry Paxton, Carbon County commissioner, interview with the author, April 26, 2013.

32.   Carl Haub, "How Many People Have Ever Lived on Earth?," Population Reference Bureau, October 2011, accessed March 10 2014, http://www.prb.org/Publications/Articles/2002/HowManyPeopleHaveEverLivedonEarth.aspx.

33.   Brad Johnson, "Heartland Grows New Crop of Anti-Climate Governor Candidates," Climate Progress, October 12, 2010, accessed March 10, 2014, http://thinkprogress.org/climate/2010/10/12/174811/anti-climate-gov-heartland.

34.   Dustin Bleizeffer, "Wyoming Reaches Coal Mining Milestone as Earth Breaches 400 ppm," WyoFile, May 7, 2013, accessed March 10, 2014, http://wyofile.com/dustin/22122.

35.   Dustin Bleizeffer, "Gov Mead Vows 'Bulldogged Determination' to Promote Coal," WyoFile, January 14, 2015, accessed January 20, 2015, http://www.wyofile.com/blog/gov-mead-vows-bulldogged-determination-promote-coal.

36.   Ibid.

37.   Dustin Bleizeffer, "Earth's Climate Is Changing Faster than Wyoming Politics," WyoFile, accessed March 10, 2014, http://wyofile.com/dustin/17804.

38.   "Cynthia Lummis on Energy and Oil," On the Issues, accessed March 10, 2014, http://www.ontheissues.org/house/Cynthia_Lummis_Energy_+_Oil.htm.

39.   Bleizeffer, "Earth Climate."

40.   Letter from Senator John Barrasso and Senator David Vitter to Charles Bolden, administrator of NASA, March 31, 2010, accessed March 10, 2014, http://www.barrasso.senate.gov/public/_files/3_31_10_barrasso_NASA_letter.pdf; John Lancaster, "Rising from the Right: Barrasso's Climb in Senate Follows Increasingly Conservative Course," WyoFile, May 31, 2011, accessed March 10, 2014, http://wyofile.com/john_lancaster/barrasso-profile.

41.   Matt Laslo, "Wyo. Lawmakers Reject New Climate Change Report," Wyoming Public Media, May 16, 2014, accessed May 21, 2014, http://wyomingpublicmedia.org/post/wyo-lawmakers-reject-new-climate-change-report.

42.   Lancaster, "Rising from the Right."

43.   Laslo, "Wyo. Lawmakers."

44.   Steve McVicker and Daniel Stone, "Senator's Clean-Coal Bonanza," *Daily*

Beast, November 2, 2011, accessed March 10, 2014, http://www.thedailybeast.com/articles/2011/11/02/sen-mike-enzi-seeks-to-boost-clean-coal-industry-that-employs-his-son.html.

45. Rone Tempest, "'Stimulus' for Two Elk: Big Checks but No New Jobs," Wyo-File, September 27, 2011, accessed March 27, 2014, http://wyofile.com/rtempest/doe-stimulus-goes-to-millionaire-senators-son.

46. Lancaster, "Rising from the Right

47. Gray interview.

48. Ibid.

49. Dev Niyogi et al., "2012/2013 Annual Summary," *State Climatologist* 31, no. 1 (2013): 1–188, accessed March 10, 2014, https://www.stateclimate.org/sites/default/files/upload/pdf/publications/2013AASCAnnualReport.pd.

50. Mike Purcell, ex-director of the Water Development Commission, e-mail to author, April 17, 2013.

51. Kerr interview.

52. White, "Scientists"; Wyoming State Climate Office, "Drought," Water Resources Data System, accessed March 27, 2014, http://www.wrds.uwyo.edu/sco/drought/drought.html.

53. Gregory Nickerson, "University of Wyoming Battles Faculty Turnover," WyoFile, November 11, 2014, accessed November 12, 2014, http://wyofile.com/gregory_nickerson/university-wyoming-battles-faculty-turnover-university-of-wyoming-faculty.

54. Chris Nicholson, interview with the author, March 12, 2013.

55. Ibid.

56. Robert Field, interview with the author, September 26, 2013.

57. Southard, "UW Air Quality Research."

58. R. A. Field, J. Soltis, M. C. McCarthy, S. Murphy, and D. C. Montague, "Influence of Oil and Gas Field Operations on Spatial and Temporal Distributions of Atmospheric Non-Methane Hydrocarbons and Their Effect on Ozone Formation in Winter," *Atmospheric Chemistry and Physics* 14 (2014): 24943–84.

59. Harold Bergman, former director of the School and Institute of Environment and Natural Resources, University of Wyoming, interview with the author, October 14, 2013.

60. Nicholson interview.

61. Stephen Gray, Christina Alvord, and Jacqueline Shinker, "Climate, Drought and Wyoming's Water Resources," *Water News* (Winter 2007), accessed March 10, 2014, http://wwdc.state.wy.us/newsletter/2007-1.pdf.

62. Marcia McNutt, "Integrity—Not Just a Federal Issue," *Science* 347 (March 27, 2015): 1397.

63. Water Resources Data System, "Water and Climate Data for the State of Wyoming," University of Wyoming, accessed March 10, 2014, http://www.wrds. uwyo.edu.

64. Field interview, September 26, 2013.

65. Michael Behar, "Whose Fault?" *Mother Jones* (March/April 2013): 39–64.

66. Heather Douglas, "Opinion: Canadian Science under Attack," *Scientist*, April 2, 2013, accessed March 10, 2014, http://www.the-scientist.com/?articles. view/articleNo/34958/title/Opinion—Canadian-Science-Under-Attack.

67. Nicholson interview.

68. Field interview, September 26, 2013.

69. Ibid.

Chapter 12

1. Mark Bowen, *Censoring Science: Inside the Political Attack on Dr. James Hansen and the Truth of Global Warming* (New York: Dutton, 2007), 238.

2. Peter Rowe, "Philip Morris Couldn't Snuff Out Victor DeNoble," *San Diego Union-Tribune*, January 25, 2012, accessed October 15, 2014, http://www.utsan diego.com/news/2012/jan/25/philip-morris-couldnt-snuff-out-victor-denoble/2/ ?#article-copy.

3. Ibid.

4. Chris Mooney, *The Republican War on Science* (New York: Basic, 2006).

5. Hugh Jim Bissell, "The Decline of Democracy and the Rise of Corporatocracy: Causes and Outcomes," *Daily Kos*, June 17, 2011, accessed October 20, 2014, http://www.dailykos.com/story/2011/06/17/986222/-The-Decline-of-Democracy-and-the-Rise-of-the-Corporatocracy-Causes-and-Outcomes#.

6. Emily Holleman, "The Right's Myth about Obama's Cabinet," *Salon*,

December 7, 2009, accessed October 20, 2014, http://www.salon.com/2009/12/07/
obama_cabinet_4.

7. Laura Hancock, "Mark Gordon Will Seek Another Term as State Treasurer," *Casper Star-Tribune*, March 25, 2014, accessed July 15, 2016, http://trib.com/
news/state-and-regional/govt-and-politics/mark-gordon-will-seek-another-term-as-
state-treasurer/article_1592b52c-672f-5f9f-ad4a-00baef4e05bc.html; "Senator Eli
Bebout," State of Wyoming Legislator Information, accessed October 20, 2014,
http://legisweb.state.wy.us/LegislatorSummary/LegDetail.aspx?LegID=1123.

8. "Linda J. Fisher," DuPont Senior Leadership, accessed October 20, 2014,
http://www.dupont.com/corporate-functions/our-company/leadership/executive-
leadership/articles/fisher.html; Rob Kerth and Shelley Vinyard, "Wasting Our
Waterways 2012: Toxic Industrial Pollution and the Unfulfilled Promise of the
Clean Water Act," Environment America Research and Policy Center, May 2012,
accessed November 28, 2014, http://www.environmentamerica.org/sites/environ
ment/files/reports/Wasting%20Our%20Waterways%20vUS.pdf.

9. Thomas B. Edsall, "The Trouble with That Revolving Door," *New York
Times*, December 18, 2011, accessed October 20, 2014, http://campaignstops.blogs.
nytimes.com/2011/12/18/the-trouble-with-that-revolving-door/?_php=true
&_type=blogs&_r=0.

10. Stephanie Joyce and Willow Belden, "Wyoming Public Media's 2014 Forum
on Coal," Wyoming Public Media, February 28, 2014, accessed December 15, 2015,
ttp://wyomingpublicmedia.org/post/wyoming-public-medias-2014-forum-coal-
open-spaces; Gregory Nickerson, "Wyoming Mining Association Conference Paints
Picture of Challenges and Opportunities," WyoFile, June 29, 2013, accessed
October 15, 2014, http://wyofile.com/gregory_nickerson/wyoming-mining-association-
conference/#sthash.oPb8QSRo.dpuf.

11. "Does Money Buy Elections?" Americans for Campaign Reform, accessed
October 20, 2014, https://www.scribd.com/document/2383850/Does-Money-Buy-
Elections.

12. "*Citizens United v. the Federal Election Commission*," *Wikipedia*, accessed
October 20, 2014, http://en.wikipedia.org/wiki/Citizens_United_v._Federal_
Election_Commission#Majority_opinion.

13. Julian Petley, *Censorship: A Beginner's Guide* (Oxford: Oneworld, 2009);
Naomi Oreskes and Erik M. Conway, *Merchants of Doubt: How a Handful of Scientists
Obscured the Truth on Issues from Tobacco Smoke to Global Warming* (New York:
Bloomsbury, 2011); Lawrence Soley, *Censorship Inc.: The Corporate Threat to Free*

Speech in the United States (New York: Monthly Review Press, 2002); Mooney, *Republican War on Science.*

14. Oreskes and Conway, *Merchants of Doubt.*

15. Ibid.

16. James Hogan, *Climate Cover-Up: The Crusade to Deny Global Warming* (Nashville: Greystone, 2009).

17. Oreskes and Conway, *Merchants of Doubt.*

18. Mooney, *Republican War on Science.*

19. Soley, *Censorship Inc.*, 92–93.

20. Oreskes and Conway, *Merchants of Doubt.*

21. Mooney, *Republican War on Science.*

22. Ibid., 60.

23. Oreskes and Conway, *Merchants of Doubt.*

24. Hogan, *Climate Cover-Up.*

25. Bowen, *Censoring Science.*

26. Ibid, 104–5.

27. Ibid.

28. Hogan, *Climate Cover-Up.*

29. Ibid., 171–74.

30. Ibid.

31. Suzanne Goldenberg, "US Presidential Debates' Great Unmentionable: Climate Change," *Guardian*, October 23, 2013, accessed October 20, 2014, http://www.theguardian.com/environment/2012/oct/23/us-president-debates-climate-change.

32. Dustin Bleizeffer, "Burning Money, Fouling the Air: Citizens Ask the State to Curb Flaring," WyoFile, June 18, 2013, accessed October 20, 2014, http://wyofile.com/dustin/burning-money-fouling-the-air-citizens-ask-the-state-to-curb-flaring/#sthash.ww6U2Y10.dpuf.

33. Kerry Drake, "State Needs Public Alternative to Private Site for Legislature," WyoFile (opinion), January 12, 2016, accessed January 12, 2016, http://www.wyofile.com/column/state-needs-public-alternative-to-private-site-for-legislature/?utm_source=newsletter&utm_medium=email&utm_campaign=weeklynewsletter.

34. Bowen, *Censoring Science*, 303–5.

35. Soley, *Censorship Inc.*

36. Nickerson, "Wyoming Mining Association Conference."

37. Harold Bergman, former director of the School and Institute of Environment and Natural Resources, University of Wyoming, interview with the author, October 14, 2013.

38. Raymond S. Bradley, *Global Warming and Political Intimidation: How Politicians Cracked Down on Scientists as the Earth Heated Up* (Amherst: University of Massachusetts Press, 2011), 153.

39. Ibid.

40. Ibid.

41. "Michael E. Mann," *Wikipedia*, accessed October 20, 2014, http://en.wikipedia.org/wiki/Michael_E._Mann.

42. David Matthews, "Fossil Fuel Ties with Universities Highlighted by Report," *Times Higher Education*, October 21, 2013, accessed October 20, 2014, http://www.timeshighereducation.co.uk/news/fossil-fuel-ties-with-universities-highlighted-by-report/2008360.article.

43. Mel Evans, *Artwash: Big Oil and the Arts* (London: Pluto Press, 2015).

44. Bradley, *Global Warming*, 154–56.

Chapter 13

1. Michael J. Sandel, *What Money Can't Buy: The Moral Limits of Markets* (New York: Farrar, Straus and Giroux, 2012), 5.

2. Naomi Oreskes and Erik M. Conway, *Merchants of Doubt: How a Handful of Scientists Obscured the Truth on Issues from Tobacco Smoke to Global Warming* (New York: Bloomsbury, 2011), 249.

3. Sandel, *What Money Can't Buy*, 6.

4. Abigail Haworth, "Surrogate Mothers: Womb for Rent," *Marie Claire*, July 29, 2007, accessed November 28, 2014, http://www.marieclaire.com/world-reports/news/surrogate-mothers-india.

5. Ibid.

6. Ibid.

7. Eric Zuesse, "United States Is Now the Most Unequal of All Advanced Economies," *Huffington Post*, December 8, 2013, accessed October 20, 2014, http://www.huffingtonpost.com/eric-zuesse/us-is-now-the-most-unequa_b_4408647.html; Tom Kertscher, "Bernie Sanders, in Madison, Claims Top 0.1% of Americans Have Almost as Much Wealth as Bottom 90%," Politifact Wisconsin, July 29, 2016, accessed July 15, 2016, http://www.politifact.com/wisconsin/statements/2015/jul/29/bernie-s/bernie-sanders-madison-claims-top-01-americans-hav.

8. Sue Curry Jansen, *Censorship: The Knot That Binds Power and Knowledge* (New York: Oxford University Press, 1991), 138.

9. Oreskes and Conway, *Merchants of Doubt*, 254.

10. Sandel, *What Money Can't Buy*, 78.

11. Mark Dowie, "Pinto Madness," *Mother Jones*, September/October 1977, accessed October 20, 2014, http://www.motherjones.com/politics/1977/09/pinto-madness.

12. Sandel, *What Money Can't Buy*, 72–75.

13. William Wordsworth, "The World Is Too Much with Us," Poetry Foundation, accessed October 20, 2014, http://www.poetryfoundation.org/poem/174833.

14. Alison Fitzgerald, "Koch, Exxon Mobil among Corporations Helping Write State Laws," *Bloomberg*, July 20, 2011, accessed October 20, 2014, http://www.bloomberg.com/news/articles/2011-07-21/koch-exxon-mobil-among-corporations-helping-write-state-laws.

15. *Wyoming Tribune Eagle* editorial board, "Legislative Meddling Hurting UW," WyoFile, September 18, 2014, accessed October 20, 2014, http://wyofile.com/wyofile/wyoming-tribune-eagle-opinion-legislative-meddling-hurting-uw.

16. Ibid.

17. "Board of Directors," Cimarex, accessed June 2, 2015, https://www.cimarex.com/about-cimarex/board-of-directors.

18. Alyssa Carducci, "More than 400 Prominent Democrats Sign Letter Supporting Coal," *Heartlander*, December 16, 2013, accessed June 2, 2015, http://news.heartland.org/newspaper-article/2013/12/16/more-400-prominent-democrats-sign-letter-supporting-coal.

19. Malcolm Gladwell, *The Tipping Point: How Little Things Can Make a Big Difference* (New York: Back Bay Books, 2002).

20. First Amendment Center, "State of the First Amendment: 2013," accessed

June 2, 2015, http://www.firstamendmentcenter.org/madison/wp-content/
uploads/2013/07/SOFA-2013-final-report.pdf.

21. John Esterbrook, "Support for First Amendment Slipping," *CBS News*,
August 30, 2002, accessed June 2, 2015, http://www.cbsnews.com/news/
support-for-1st-amendment-slipping.

22. First Amendment Center, "State of First Amendment."

23. "George S. Patton's Speech to the Third Army," *Wikipedia*, accessed
June 2, 2015, http://en.wikipedia.org/wiki/George_S._Patton%27s_speech_
to_the_Third_Army.

24. "Maryanne Williamson quotes," Thinkexist.com, accessed July 15, 2016,
http://thinkexist.com/quotation/our-deepest-fear-is-not-that-we-are-inadequate/
397505.html.

Epilogue

1. Matt Mead, "Leading the Charge: Wyoming's Action Plan for Energy, Environment and Economy," Cheyenne, Wyoming.

2. Trevor Brown, "Mead Includes 11 New Initiatives in Energy Policy," *Laramie Boomerang*, March 15, 2016, A1.

3. Mead, "Leading the Charge," 51.

4. Matt Mead, "Gov. Mead: Wyoming Will Keep Fighting for Coal," WyoFile
guest column, January 16, 2016, accessed January 19, 2016, http://www.wyofile.
com/column/gov-mead-wyoming-will-keep-fighting-for-coal.

5. Brown, "Mead Includes New Initiatives."

6. Mead, "Leading the Charge," 47.

7. Ibid., 49.

8. "Collapse" (2012) and "Ghosts of the Gulf" (2014), Brandon Ballengée,
accessed March 21, 2016, brandonballengee.com/collapse and http://brandon
ballengee.com/ghosts-of-the-gulf.

9. Dustin Bleizeffer, "Black Thursday: Layoffs Hit 500 Wyoming Coal Miners,"
WyoFile, April 5, 2016, accessed April 5, 2016, http://www.wyofile.com/blog/black-
thursday-layoffs-hit-500-wyoming-coal-miners; Kerry Drake, "Put Coal Miners
Ahead of Company Executives," WyoFile, April 5, 2016, accessed April 5, 2016,
http://www.wyofile.com/column/put-coal-miners-ahead-company-executives.

10. David Louis, "Wyoming Losing Energy Sector Jobs," *Laramie Boomerang*, March 19, 2016, A8.

11. Hunter Woodall, "More People Are Leaving Wyoming Than Entering It," *Casper Star-Tribune*, December 19, 2015, accessed March 21, 2016, http://trib.com/business/energy/more-people-are-leaving-wyoming-than-entering-it/article_34e893af-7dc3–53d0-ad63–2cbc567e22d1.html.

12. Elizabeth Shogren, "Coal Company Bankruptcies Jeopardize Reclamation," *High Country News*, January 25, 2016.

13. Mead, "Wyoming Will Keep Fighting."